# The Ancient Quarrel between Philosophy and Poetry

From its beginnings, philosophy's language, concepts, and imaginative growth have been heavily influenced by poetry and poets. Drawing on the work of a wide range of thinkers throughout the history of Western philosophy, Raymond Barfield explores the pervasiveness of poetry's impact on philosophy and, conversely, how philosophy has sometimes resisted or denied poetry's influence. Although some thinkers, such as Giambattista Vico and Friedrich Nietzsche, praised the wisdom of poets and saw poetry and philosophy as mutually beneficial pursuits, others resented, diminished, or eliminated the importance of poetry in philosophy. Beginning with the famous passage in Plato's *Republic* in which Socrates exiles the poets from the city, this book traces the history of the ancient quarrel between philosophy and poetry through the works of thinkers in the Western tradition ranging from Plato to the contemporary thinker Mikhail Bakhtin. This new perspective provides an illuminating way of reading philosophy that can be extended and applied to other philosophers.

Raymond Barfield is associate professor in the Schools of Divinity, Nursing, and Medicine at Duke University.

# The Ancient Quarrel between Philosophy and Poetry

RAYMOND BARFIELD

*Duke University*

CAMBRIDGE
UNIVERSITY PRESS

CAMBRIDGE UNIVERSITY PRESS
Cambridge, New York, Melbourne, Madrid, Cape Town,
Singapore, São Paulo, Delhi, Mexico City

Cambridge University Press
32 Avenue of the Americas, New York NY 10013-2473, USA

Published in the United States of America by Cambridge University Press, New York

www.cambridge.org
Information on this title: www.cambridge.org/9781107677845

© Raymond Barfield 2011

First published 2011
First paperback edition 2013

*A catalogue record for this publication is available from the British Library*

*Library of Congress Cataloguing in Publication Data*
Barfield, Raymond, 1964–
The ancient quarrel between philosophy and poetry / Raymond Barfield.
p.   cm.
Includes bibliographical references and index.
ISBN 978-1-107-00032-2 (hardback)
1. Philosophy.   2. Poetry.   I. Title.
B66.B37 2011
100–dc22        2010030607

ISBN 978-1-107-00032-2 Hardback
ISBN 978-1-107-67784-5 Paperback

*For Karen, Micah, and Alexandra*
*And in memory of John Stone, physician and poet*

Poems are but evidence of Poetry.
Ben Mazer, *Poems*

# Contents

# Acknowledgments

I have been supported in so many ways by so many people in the course of writing this book, and for this support I am deeply grateful. Every part of this book has been influenced by my friend Donald Philip Verene, a philosopher who taught me to read with attention to the real problems of philosophy and to listen for the influence of the poets among the philosophers as they find ways to say their ideas. Likewise, my life as a physician was opened up to the possibilities of philosophy and poetry over many years because of the example set by the physician and poet John Stone, and I cannot overstate the importance he had on my own development, my curiosity about the world, and my own efforts to speak and to serve. I am deeply grateful to Larry Lacy, Jim Jobes, and Timothy Jackson, who are among my most important teachers. My work at the intersection of poetry and philosophy has been, and continues to be, influenced by the poets Philip Nikolayev, Katia Kapovich, and Ben Mazer. Openness to the influence of such people depends in part on habits that start very early, and these habits have been shaped by my oldest friend and sparring partner, Scott Bader-Saye, whose gifts as a writer, theologian, and scholar have long set the mark I hope to hit.

I could not have found the time to write this book without the opportunities that were opened up for me at Duke University by Greg Jones, Stanley Hauerwas, Rich Payne, Joe St. Geme, and Dan Wechsler. Nor could I have completed this without the support and the vigilant attention to detail of Brian Belyea, Jessica Sun, Cassandra Moran, Nichol Harris, Jennifer Newlin, Sheila Perry, Anne Fitzgerald, Carl Weisner, Cheryl Thaxton, Sharron Docherty, Debra Brandon, Margarita Bidegain, and Kavin Rowe, all of whom, in one way or another, guided me through my first two years at Duke. I am grateful to Sam Wells and Tony Galanos for showing the kind of insight that can be gained in a great symposium. In my time at Duke I have encountered so many fine people, and so many fine minds, that my own work has benefited simply by being in proximity to people who care so deeply about what they give to the rest of us in the course of their scholarship and service.

In the process of bringing this book to completion, several people have been especially gracious and generous with their help, including Beatrice Rehl, Emily Spangler, and Brian MacDonald at Cambridge University Press; Judith Heyhoe, who was enormously helpful in my own efforts to rethink and revise; and Jed Poston, who spent many hours helping me with the endless details of getting the manuscript in final form. I am likewise grateful to Victoria van Loan for her comments on early portions of this manuscript and to Chip Clay for sharing his experience and insight into this process drawn from his many productive years at Red Bird and Grackle.

The biggest influence and support in my work and life is by far my family. To my mother and father, Pearl and Ray, and to my sister Carole, I am forever grateful. And to my wife Karen and my children Micah and Alexandra, I have no words to express all that you have brought into my life, but I will continue to search for them with joy.

# Introduction

Western philosophy, from early in its history, has characterized itself in part by distinguishing how its statements and methods were different from those of the poets and, having made this distinction, what role the work of poetry was to have in philosophy. This book examines some of the philosophical writers who have participated in this effort. At the beginning of this story, Plato defined the relationship between poetry and philosophy as a quarrel, indeed, as an ancient quarrel. One theme in this book is that the so-called ancient quarrel between poetry and philosophy is itself neither poetry nor philosophy. Rather, it is an image portraying the interaction of poetry and philosophy as important for the pursuit of insight into the truth of things human and divine, a truth less accessible both to poets devoid of philosophy and to philosophers devoid of poetry. The domain of the quarrel is one that longs for a certain fullness of thought that goes beyond the exigencies of inquiry confined to the boundaries of either poetry or philosophy. Whether reluctantly or not, the philosophers addressed here acknowledge the importance of poetry to philosophy by acknowledging the peculiarity and value of the poets' insights, by using the tools of the poets in their own work, or by struggling to put the poets in their proper place.

Plato fretted over the poets' claims to wisdom and, in particular, their claims to sometimes be speaking for the gods. He likewise fretted over the way in which the poets and poetry controlled the Greek mind and culture. His answer was to do battle with the poets using the philosophical question, testing the claims of the poets, and so freeing Greek consciousness from the control and power of poetry. His solution was to exile the poets from the Republic, or at least to severely restrict their activity while he replaced their work with something new. But there comes a point when the exile of the poets leaves the freed consciousness mute: human consciousness, as many thinkers in this history assert, lives most fully among the poetical limits of life – portents, history, stories, the gods – and to these the philosophers repeatedly, and sometimes grudgingly, return. Just as philosophy can become a technical profession devoid of wonder, so poetry without philosophy can become a linguistic sideshow, fascinating in the way a contortionist is fascinating for being able to stretch so as to gaze directly at her own back. The philosophers started the quarrel, and so their voice is heard most vehemently at the beginning when they are defining their own endeavor against the work of the poets. The poets will have their say in time.

Aristotle said that both poetry and philosophy are grounded in wonder: both explore, both transform our vision of the world. It is precisely the similarities between poetry and philosophy that lend energy to the quarrelsome relationship between the two. But many of the thinkers in this book also argue that, however important it is to distinguish poetry and philosophy, both are diminished in the absence of the other, especially in regard to the human effort to uncover the truth of things about the world, about ourselves, and about the divine. Regarding the last truth, the question how we might approach and explore the divine is an especially common theme in the course of the quarrel.

I pursue the history of this quarrel against the background assumption that the human search for truth about the world, ourselves, and the divine is worthwhile. I do not, however, argue that our grasp of truth is ever infallible. In other words, as I consider the history of the quarrel between poetry and philosophy, I am also maintaining the position that we can remain realists in regard to truth while acknowledging our capacity for error: this humility is crucial for both poetry and philosophy (and for the sort of writing that occurs through what Mikhail Bakhtin calls "novelistic consciousness"), but it in no way reduces itself to relativism. Accompanying this modest posture is the further background assumption that while the domain of speculative inquiry such as this is neither warranted nor testable in the usual sense of the word, it is nonetheless the means available to us to ask certain kinds of questions and to pursue answers to those questions meaningfully even in the face of well-justified doubt that the questions can ever be fully answered. From the very beginning in the work of Plato, this is the kind of effort that relies on surprising clues, hints that to the skeptical eye might seem merely accidental. Sometimes they will be merely accidental, of course, but that is a risk we take, for sometimes they are not. One must be willing at the outset to accept help from any quarter, as Socrates does, never limiting who can sit at the table, but allowing no participant to go unquestioned. Even the voices of fools and madmen have played their part in the history of this topic.

That said, in some ways this book is straightforwardly epistemic in its concerns. At many points in the story, poetry seems to offer a peculiar and important kind of starting point for discovery that registers in the mythopoeic mind most completely, but which continues in various forms to be an artifact of growing human consciousness in a way that no other artifact is. For example, sometimes the poets seem to take themselves as speaking in the voice of a god. Far from simply dismissing such claims, many of the philosophers in this history acknowledge at the very least that something important may be going on among these poets and, indeed, that the gods or God may be making use of these human voices in ways that are of interest to the philosopher. It may be that some things must be believed to be seen, and for things that fall into this category, the odd condition for their being known does not, a priori, count against their reality. Speculative inquiry demands a wide range of tools simply because the questions that are asked are often of the following sort: What is the importance of the possibility of transcendent reality to philosophical and poetic inquiry? Might the activities of poetry and philosophy be sustained by the longing for something transcendent, eternal, divine? Where would one look for clues if the answer is yes? Questions about humanity's relationship to the divine are pervasive in the quarrel.

In the course of telling a story, one is necessarily selective in details and episodes. That is certainly true of this story, which comprises thinkers from the ancient, medieval, early modern, and modern worlds. The roughly two dozen thinkers addressed in this book, some more deeply than others, provide a range of opportunities for attending to the ways in which the quarrel manifests itself and to the lessons that can be learned from these various manifestations. This is also an example of one illuminating way of reading philosophy that can be applied to many other thinkers: no doubt most readers could quickly write a long list of philosophers beyond those considered here who might profitably be studied in this way. Some of the thinkers I chose to address because they are foundational for understanding this approach to thinking about the tasks of philosophy and philosophy's relation to poetry – Plato and Aristotle, for example. Others were chosen because, though they have many interesting things to say related to this subject, they do not always appear on short lists of philosophers who show some new aspect of the quarrel between philosophy and poetry – Aquinas and Kant come to mind. While the thinkers who were chosen do form a coherent and interconnected story, I can see enormous room for developing a much more thorough account of the quarrel in the history of philosophical thought, though as Aristotle said of the attempt to rehearse the whole history of form leading up to that of Greek tragedy, "it would probably be a long piece of work to go through the details."[1]

The story as I offer it here begins with Plato, whose portrayal of Socrates reveals deep concerns about the claims of the poets, the influence of the poets over the Greek mind, and the ways in which such unfounded claims coupled to considerable influence interfere with the search for true wisdom. At the hands of Socrates, the poets are questioned, sometimes ridiculed, and ultimately excluded from the Republic. Plato himself began as a poet, and it was under the influence of Socrates that he turned to philosophy. But he knew the power and potential danger of the poets from the inside. Nevertheless, he was quick to seize upon the tools of the poets and put them at the service of philosophy, or at least at the service of portraying an image of what philosophy is.

Plato's student Aristotle approaches the poets in a very different way. He never directly addresses his teacher's position on poetry. His approach is rather to ask what is valuable in the work of the poets and how the poets can best do their work. Thus, for example, he makes use of tragic poetry as a cauldron in which important human characteristics and vulnerabilities are usefully portrayed, a portrayal that is of great service in ethical inquiry. Indeed, even the tragic poetry that shows how humanity ought not to be, how people should not choose, is useful in forming the virtuous citizen. His answer to the poets is not to exclude them but to produce a manual that shows how great poetry ought to be written. That manual is still of astonishing use.

Plato and Aristotle provide the backdrop for the remainder of the book, so great their influence has been. The next thinkers in the history are Plotinus and Augustine. Plotinus was a Neo-Platonist who had tremendous impact on poets such as Dante, Goethe, and Coleridge. His incorporation of Platonic ideas into his own philosophy turns on his use of metaphor to help the seeker make the leap from the world of images to the world of the forms, and this movement from metaphor and image to the inward "seeing" of eternal forms is a common

---

[1] Aristotle, *Poetics*, in *The Complete Works of Aristotle*, ed. Jonathan Barnes (Cambridge: Cambridge University Press, 1988), 1449a30.

theme in the quarrel between poetry and philosophy. But perhaps the most important reason for including Plotinus in this discussion is the influence he had on Augustine. As with many of the philosophers in this history, Augustine was also a poet. When he read Plotinus after his conversion to Christianity, he claims to have experienced there the very voice that appears in the Gospel of John, and so he brings together Platonic thought and Christian thought in a way that changed theology. In the course of his life and thought, though, Augustine became concerned about the potentially dangerous aspects of poetry, and indeed, far from denying that "the gods" might be speaking through the poets, he considers the possibility that the poets do indeed speak for spirits, namely, the demonic. It is from this perspective that he uses philosophy to correct the errors of the poets.

Boethius and Dionysius likewise build upon a Platonic foundation but with very different results. Boethius is facing execution as he writes, and so his circumstance provides considerable urgency to his search for the truth of things. At the beginning he, like so many others, is lured by the poetic Muses to a false and harmful understanding of life, virtue, and God. However, Lady Philosophy soon shows up in his prison cell and, dispatching the Muses, takes over his education herself. In instructing Boethius, Lady Philosophy uses poetry as a way of soothing him as he undergoes the harsh but necessary remedies she has to give him in order for him to be whole. Dionysius, like Plotinus, makes fascinating use of metaphor in presenting ideas and produces a poetry that, when tempered by philosophy, becomes hymnody. Along the way, the Forms of Plato that became ideas in the Divine Mind in Plotinus become, in the work of Dionysius, angels. Augustine, Boethius, and Dionysius along with Aristotle all have profound effect on the work of the next thinker, Thomas Aquinas.

Aquinas was trained as a poet. He acknowledges that in ancient times the divine may well have spoken through the theological poets predating Plato and Aristotle and referenced in Aristotle's *Metaphysics*. As a trained poet, however, he has a very different view of poetry in his time. Far from being "out of their minds" or "beside themselves," as Socrates said they were when they express their poetic utterances, Aquinas says the poets know exactly what they are doing and, indeed, that the quality of their poems depends on the extent to which they know what they are doing. From his perspective on imagination, language, and poetry grows a Thomistic poetics in which expression of the divine voice is nowhere to be found. The expression of the divine, inviting similar questions raised by poets claiming to speak for God, is found elsewhere in Aquinas, namely, among the prophets.

Giambatista Vico covers much of the same ground as Augustine did in *City of God*. But he makes a crucial move that allows him to develop a new vision of "poetic wisdom": he argues that there are two histories in the world – that of the Hebrew people and that of the Gentiles. The former is sacred history. Vico turns his attention to Gentile history, which unfolds, he says, under the influence of an immanent providence. He then traces the course of human culture and ideas from the first people who spoke in poetry, and from whom language grew, through the arrival of the philosophers, who, through irony and the critical question, transformed our relationship to human institutions and to the divine. Arriving at the central insights in his great work, *The New Science*, required twenty years of labor, he claims. Despite the strange and difficult form of the work, it influenced many writers who came after him, in particular James Joyce in his writing of *Finnegans Wake*.

In the work of Immanuel Kant, poetry takes center stage in the last of his three critiques, *The Critique of Judgment*. No longer does the divine speak through the poets. But the poets do have a surprising oracular function. The gift of the poet is genius. But the poets cannot give an account of their own genius. They do not know whence it comes or how it works. It is part of their nature, and so it is part of nature. But the very fact that the work of the poets arises from genius as a part of nature allows the work of the poets to carry a weight that other writing does not, for it is nature speaking. In poetry and in aesthetic judgment generally, Kant says that we access insight about the supersensible world that we cannot reach through critical reason, the topic of his first critique. Though such a conclusion opens up the realm of human experience in fascinating ways, it was not enough for Kant's students and critics Hamann and Herder. Hamann, like Vico, viewed poetry as the mother tongue of the human race, from which grew all human knowledge. For Hamann, most of the philosophical problems that occupied Kant his entire life were nothing more than the results of a misuse of language and a failure to recognize the language of the poets and the prophets as God's gift to us, as the currency of God's speech to us, complemented by God's revelations through nature. Herder, again like Vico, was repelled by the efforts of philosophers such as Kant to isolate human faculties one from another, and he considers our ability to speak to God and each other to be the fundamental human activity. Like Hamann and Vico, he thinks that the very language we use to explore the highest philosophy is inextricably rooted in poetry, calling the poet the creator of a people who gives us a world to contemplate.

Hegel calls poetry the most universal and widespread teacher of the human race and says that the realm of poetry includes human ideas, deeds, actions, fates, and the divine rule of the universe. At first glance, there does not seem to be much left to occupy the realm of philosophy uniquely, and indeed, given this list, the content of the realm of poetry is the content of the realm of philosophy. But there is an important difference between poetry and philosophy that emerges at the heart of his work. Hegel is "the philosopher of consciousness" As such, he follows a pattern that appears throughout the quarrel, namely, that of finding two moments in the experience of the seeker: encounter with the content of the poetic (ideas, fates, the divine), and consciousness of this content that results from philosophical questioning. These are the two moments, and the movement between the two involves conflict and expands consciousness. The process of philosophical advance is an invasion of consciousness in the realm of the mythopoeic, and Hegel charts this battle in his great work, *The Phenomenology of Spirit.*

Kierkegaard, the great critic of Hegel, says of himself, "I'm a poet – alas, just a poet." When he speaks of philosophy he is generally referring to the Hegelians and their "system." He opposes the totalizing approach of such a system and says that we are out not to get some answer right but, rather, to get a life right – and the stakes are eternal. He therefore approaches his work through pseudonyms, individual characters who are themselves struggling with some idea and piece of reality. In the course of his work, the quarrel that emerges is not between poetry and philosophy but between poetry and religion, with the former, because it is so glorious, being a threat to those who would follow the way of poetry and miss the greater glory found in true faith. As to what lies between these poles of true religion and poetry, he says that it is all silly talk.

Dilthey understands the pull of metaphysics that so attracted Kant and Hegel, as well as the pull of religion that so attracted Kierkegaard and Luther. But he claims that such things can no longer be held as tenable. Nonetheless, he still feels the longing that led people to be attracted to these things. He calls this pull "the metaphysical mood." Even though, according to Dilthey, metaphysics is silenced, this mood that creates a sense of wonder at the stars, a sense of the meaningfulness of things, will never leave. This impulse is distilled and transferred into the realm of poetry, which is best suited of all human endeavors to deliver the vividness of our experience of the meaning of life, though it remains with philosophy to see that this is so.

Nietzsche and Heidegger both continue the struggle with metaphysics, each in his own way. Nietzsche's portrayal of the quarrel is quite different from any that preceded his work, and he laments the loss of Greek tragic poetry, which was destroyed by the influence of Socrates. There is nothing to be done about this rupture in tragic poetry – it is accomplished once and for all. But there is a way forward, he says, and it will come not through philosophy but rather through art. Now that the solution of the Greek tragedians is no longer tenable, he takes it upon himself to find a new solution, one he calls "the gay science," a joyful and intoxicating embrace of the world as it is and of our place in the world as people who belong. Heidegger is one of the most important interpreters of Nietzsche in the twentieth century, and he says that his own way forward is made possible because of the "consummation of metaphysics" wrought by Nietzsche, allowing us to move beyond it. Humans have forgotten how to question Being, and this is a central crisis for Heidegger, as such questioning is the highest task of philosophy. Without such questioning, we cannot be fully human. The hints that philosophy requires to set it on this way are found in poetry. The clues come from the poets who are the mortals tracing the "fugitive gods." If we are going to find our way back to the most important questions in philosophy, and the most important tasks in humanity, we begin by listening to the poets whose work is a kind of light illuminating the truth of being.

The last thinker addressed is Mikhail Bakhtin, who, in his work on novelistic consciousness in the art of Dostoevsky, shows a new way that the quarrel is portrayed in a form of literature that grew out of the Socratic dialogues, namely, the novel. It is an idealized history that actually conceives of poetry as arising within a single language, voicing the gods or erupting in the privileged naming of things by Adam. Nonetheless, there is a tendency in poetry to speak with a single voice. Throughout this history, philosophy has interrupted such monologic utterances with a question, or critique, or doubt, or even ridicule. When this happens, there are two voices encountering each other. The novel – especially in the hands of Dostoevsky – is a place where such encounters are portrayed without reducing either consciousness to the other. It is the arena in which many languages and ideas meet.

And so this story ends with a literary form that arose from its starting point, the Socratic dialogues. But it begins with the invention of the "ancient" quarrel. The journey from the invention of the quarrel to its current form encompasses the history of Western philosophy and literature. Again, there are many other thinkers who could justifiably be included in this book, and the length of the book could easily be doubled or tripled. The steps along the way are therefore necessarily selective but also, I hope, suggestive. The pilgrimage starts at the temple of Apollo in Delphi.

# 1

# Socrates, Plato, and the Invention
# of the Ancient Quarrel

The quarrel between poetry and philosophy finds its first footing where most of Western philosophy originates, in the work of Plato, and it still reverberates from the assaults of Socrates on the poets when he exiled them from the Republic and claimed that the supreme music was no longer poetry but rather philosophy.[1] There is a nearly journalistic thrill that comes from noting one further fact: the starting point of wisdom for that titanic human being, Socrates, instigator of the philosophical question, source of a new kind of human self-consciousness and critique, founder of true dialectical challenge to the status quo, and chief propagator of the assault on poetry, is accomplished at the temple of Apollo, god of poetry, when the oracle forgoes favoring of the poets and sophists and pronounces Socrates the wisest of men. Even more worthy of journalistic note is his own admission that the sum of his wisdom is that he knows that he does not know, that he is merely a seeker of wisdom. This admission is the very heart of what is most attractive about his engagement in the quarrel between poetry and philosophy, a quarrel and struggle that has a rich history and that constitutes one of the finest examples of humanity exploring the world through every means available to it, including attention to prophecy, oracular utterance, systematic questioning, and even truth uncovered through the instability of madness. Perhaps the poets do speak for the gods, and they may indeed cocoon in their utterances the deepest truths of the world, human and divine. Indeed, Socrates would rejoice if this turned out to be true. But before embracing this entirely, he says, just because he is not yet wise, a few questions are in order. The poets speak. Socrates questions. The

[1] Eric A. Havelock, *Preface to Plato* (Cambridge, Mass.: Harvard University Press, 1963), 305.

problems arise when the speaking of the poets forms a peoples' world view of humanity and the divine, and the questioning becomes a challenge to this given world view.

On the temple of Apollo were inscribed the words "Know thyself." From before the archaic period (700–480 B.C.) these words meant "know your place, know that you are not a god." Socrates introduced a radically new understanding of the words. In order for the journey toward knowledge of things human and divine to begin, the starting place is self-knowledge, understanding who the knower is. And the starting place for self-knowledge is to know at least that you do not know. This seems absurd to the people whom Socrates encounters. We know all sorts of things – which acts are just, which things are beautiful, how best to venerate the gods. We must know these things because we use this knowledge all the time. Just read Homer and Hesiod. It is all right there. But, Socrates asks, do we really know these things? He is anxious to find the true knowers so that he too can know. But as things stand, when he asks about himself, "Do I know this?" he becomes aware of his own lack of knowledge, and through the power of questioning, he becomes aware that others apparently do not know these things either. Socrates introduces a power of awareness, of self-consciousness, and it becomes the central power of philosophy.

With the power of questioning and the goal of true knowledge, it is possible now to mine the whole world, human and divine, already staked out by the poets, but now it will be mined in a very different way. Armed with self-knowledge and awareness of his own ignorance, the philosopher can start on the road toward true knowledge of intelligible reality and test ideas rather than merely accept them as received wisdom. On the doorsteps of the temple of poetry, the oracle discovers and reveals Socrates, the lover of wisdom, a philosopher. Socrates, in turn, identifies his own power as residing in the organon of judgment, the power of reason that is the instrument of the lover of wisdom.[2] But what does it mean to be a lover of wisdom? In book 5 of the *Republic*, Socrates tells us more about what the philosopher is.

The philosopher encounters particulars in the world and loves these – a beautiful body, for example, or a just act. The poets do as much. What distinguishes the philosopher is dissatisfaction with the particular and

---

[2] Plato, *The Republic*, trans. Paul Shorey, in *The Collected Dialogues*, ed. Edith Hamilton and Huntington Cairns (Princeton: Princeton University Press, 1963), 583d, hereafter cited in text as *Rep*.

a longing to know more. Yes, this body is beautiful, but what exactly is beauty? Yes, this act seems to be just, but how can I know this unless I first know what justice is? The lover of wisdom, like any lover, is unsatisfied with merely a portion or part and wants all of wisdom. Like the lovers of spectacles who travel to all the Dionysian festivals, the philosopher loves the spectacle of truth, which is a matter of knowledge, not opinion (*Rep.*, 478c). Unsatisfied with the particulars of beautiful bodies or individual just acts, the lover of wisdom longs for what transcends the particulars – beauty and justice as such. Because it is only the philosopher who goes beyond particulars to seek what is most real, it is impossible, Socrates tells us, for anyone except the philosopher to savor "the delight that the contemplation of true being and reality brings" (*Rep.*, 582c). Speaking the truth of things had been the purview of the theological poets and their rhapsodes. The keepers of the poets' words were not pleased when Socrates added that the organon of judgment makes use of words and discussion and that, indeed, "words and discussion are the instrument mainly of the philosopher" (*Rep.*, 582d). The quarrel is born.

These are the rumblings that will become a full and complex attack on poetry. The sword wielded in the attack is humble in form. It is merely this – the power to question with the aim of moving beyond the particulars of the world in order to get to what is most real. Such questioning includes any power, such as irony, that pries open what seems to be given, assumed, or taken as the truth of things, and as such it uncovers the entire domain of the poet as opinion rather than knowledge. This deflation of the poets' claims to knowledge takes work to defend. Socrates' first serious discussion of the poets in the *Republic* lays the ground for expelling them from the city.

The starting point is pedagogical. Socrates points out that children are malleable and have a relative lack of mental form. Because they are pliable, we must take care about what stories they hear. Stories will shape their souls (*Rep.*, 377c). But they do not have the power of discrimination and cannot tell a true story from a false story. And so we must ensure that they hear only true tales. How do we know what a true tale is? One approach is to identify false tales and to ask what it is about the tales that makes them false. Socrates explains that humans, and especially young children, can be harmed by untruths uttered by the poets, the tellers of false tales. Who exactly are the tellers of false tales? They are, above all, the poets Homer and Hesiod (*Rep.*, 377d). Socrates uses many examples from these poets to bolster his claim. He points out, for example, that Hesiod tells a tale of mistreatment and revenge among the gods when

Uranus and Cronus conflict. This makes great theater but terrible theology. We cannot show the gods fighting among themselves and seeking retaliation or petty revenge. Indeed, even if such tales were true, we still ought not to tell them to children (*Rep.*, 378a). Neither the stories of the poets and mythmakers nor even the actions of the gods themselves constitute the criteria we use to shape children, for the gods' actions must also be judged as good or evil. But because we can *reason* our way to the conclusion that, because a god is good, a god cannot be a cause of evil, we can at the outset exclude some poetic statements from Homer such as "two urns stand on the floor of the palace of Zeus and are filled with dooms he allots, one of blessings, the other gifts that are evil." Nor may the poets show the gods to be mutable or deceiving (*Rep.*, 381c). They may not, however beautiful the poetry, discuss the afterlife in terms of terror, lamentation, hate, or decay – such vocabulary might undermine the courage of the city's guardians (*Rep.*, 387c). The gods cannot be shown as laughing, for this indicates loss of control (*Rep.*, 389). Step by step, Socrates moves toward evaluative considerations about the city, virtue, and theology not through the poem as such but through that faculty which is able to test, question, and censor the poem. It is not surprising that poetry serves as the starting place for such inquiry. The poets, after all, dominated Greek society up to the archaic age. But because of the power of poetry over Greek culture and the minds of Athenian citizens, though philosophy might call the effort to test the tales a quarrel, it is in fact all-out war.

What if the poets enthrall and delight us to no end? It does not matter. The proper first response to such a poet might be veneration and the bestowal of fine gifts, but after this he must be sent on to another city, for his grand poetry does not conform to the ends and aims of the city, ends and aims arrived at through reason rather than through attention to the authority of Homer or Hesiod (*Rep.*, 398a). In the first part of the *Republic*, Socrates is critical of the poets but still tentative about whether to admit tragedy and comedy of a sort into the city. The discussion of the poets returns at the end of book 10. Now he wants the poets gone. Socrates learned something important in the interim between the two discussions. What happened?

Book 10 opens with an affirmation made by Socrates and his dialogue partners that their early judgment against poetry was correct: "And truly we were entirely right in our organization of the state, and especially I think in the matter of poetry" (*Rep.*, 595a). After sorting out the meaning of justice, the organization of the Republic, and the education of each group in the city, Socrates returns to the judgment against poetry as a point that is *especially* right. This priority and its emphasis are surprising, but they underscore how powerful and potentially dangerous poetry is in Socrates' view.

The problem is with imitation, the very stuff of art. Homer is the first teacher, and his art is imitation. Why is imitation dangerous? Socrates is pursuing truth. Imitation is removed from the truth (*Rep.*, 597e). More than that, imitation not only is removed from truth but can actually distract from truth. Simply put, the most real is the form, say the form of tree, the tree that *is in itself*, as opposed to some particular tree here or there. So a gardener plants a particular tree – one remove from the most real form of the tree. Then an artist paints a picture of the gardener's tree – two removes from the most real form of the tree. The gardener's tree can be viewed from the front and the back and so forth, so the artist does not paint a picture of the actual tree, but rather of only one appearance of the tree – this is far indeed from what is most real. The problem is that, executed masterfully, this portrait of one appearance of a particular instantiation of a form might trick children and fools into believing that it is a real tree. This is the danger: when an artist depicts a small part of a particular thing, we may be fooled into believing that what we are seeing is sufficient for full comprehension, that we are beholding reality rather than some small detail. Furthermore, because imitators do not have to concern themselves with the whole truth but only with this or that angle, they can appear to be masters of many things while the one laboring to get at the truth of things seems incompetent, with starts and stops and second guessing (*Rep.*, 598b). Indeed, the philosopher can look like a fool, unable to see the truth of even the simplest thing.

The material of the painter is the world as it is seen. This is just an illustration used to get to a far deeper concern with imitation. For Socrates, the poets are the ones who make truly dangerous use of imitation because they have as their material all that pertains to the virtues and vices of humans, and all things divine. The real danger of the poets is that they lay claim to *wisdom*, but they give only an imitation of this most important kind of truth. What is more, they do so in the medium of language, which is the instrument of the philosopher. The argument is this: Homer spoke of medicine but did not heal; he spoke of government but did not govern; he spoke of wars but did not lead. Genuine knowledge of any of these things would have led him to actually engage in them rather than to compose a poem about them. Nonetheless, he is venerated for his wisdom, and the fools among us have been fooled indeed. When you imitate, you do not question. And for those who do not question and who stop short of what is most real, most true, the mind becomes the ground on which unchallenged ideas hold sway, affecting the way we see the world and so, for us, affecting the *truth* of the world. Insofar as we are satisfied with the wisdom of the mimetic poet Homer, we do not recognize our own ignorance, or entertain the possibility of Homer's, and we do not forge on toward the truth.

Now the real target has come into view. Socrates says, "The poet himself knowing nothing but how to imitate, lays on with words and phrases the colors of the several arts in such fashion that others equally ignorant, who see things only through words, will deem his words most excellent" (*Rep.*, 601a). *Who see things only through words*: here is the crux of the critique. In his *Seventh Letter*, Plato says that he has never written down his true philosophy. This, of course, raises the question, What are those thousands of words we have been reading? What, apart from words, are we to see? Philosophy can never fit within language with its changeable and slippery words. Socrates was a master of demonstrating this slipperiness, often in striking and amusing ways, making good use of laughter to prod at words claiming to contain the truth. But though language cannot fully contain the truth, it is not merely through such false claims that it deceives but also through the spell wrought by the poets through rhythm, meter, and harmony, techniques that lure the unaware into accepting the poets' accounts and tales. At times the spells created by the poets seem almost akin to the state we see in children watching television and listening to commercials, and accompanied by the same sorts of dangers that any parent can attest to who has countered with their own insistence that there is not a necessary connection between human flourishing and the purchase of the latest electronic game set or consumption of a new fast-food item. Take away these alluring features, and what remains in such poetic utterances is compared by Socrates to "the faces of adolescents, young but not really beautiful when the bloom of youth abandons them" (*Rep.*, 601b). This image is telling, for there is a way to achieve a beauty more lasting than the bloom of youth. This hope is bolstered by the *image* of the true philosopher, Socrates, whose physical homeliness and satyrlike appearance did not diminish the godlike beauty that led the military genius Alcibiades to attempt to seduce him.

As book 10 progresses, Socrates shows that the mimetic poet neither knows nor forms opinions rightly regarding the beauty of imitation or its lack (*Rep.*, 602a). The poets have nothing except other poems against which their work is measured to determine beauty or lack of beauty. But even such judgment among poets requires something that is not itself poetry. As the poet C. Day Lewis said, "No poem ever contradicts another poem anymore than one experience can be contradicted by another. Contradiction only comes when we begin to make deductions from our experiences or judgments on poetry."[3] Socrates' definition of mimetic poetry helps to clarify why he insists on his critique. Mimetic poetry "imitates human beings acting under compulsion or voluntarily and as a result of their actions supposing themselves to have fared well or ill, and in all this feeling either grief or joy" (*Rep.*, 603c). But when one supposes fate to be good or ill, such a supposition assumes knowledge of what really is good or evil in such things as calamity. How could the poets know such a thing? Socrates himself argues for agnosticism regarding the true good or evil present in such events, and he even goes further saying that "nothing in mortal life is worthy of great concern" (*Rep.*, 604c). Whatever the true state of such events might be, Socrates is ultimately more concerned with the poets' representation and manipulation of those emotions that are engendered in the citizens of Athens by the acts of fate. The poets claim to represent something real and true regarding events brought about through fate, and they present their claims in language that moves the heart and captivates the listener. But before making use of such powerful and persuasive means of presenting such a claim, Socrates wants to know how the poets are so sure of what is true or real. If they cannot account for the veracity of their claims, their claims might be false or, worse, dangerous to the human soul. In that case, linking such claims to the powers of poetry is as dangerous as linking some other powerful force such as sex to false pictures of human flourishing and well-being. Again, the case Socrates is making is one that easily resonates with those living in the age of advertising.

So poetry can elicit feelings in response to the imitative portrayal of apparently tragic events brought about through fate, but such feelings, Socrates insists, are an obstacle to the very things needed in calamity – deliberation and the exercise of reason to heal the injured and raise up the fallen. The grief that follows tragedy is a waste of time (*Rep.*, 604c–d). Unfortunately, the imitation of the steady and intelligent and

---

[3]  C. Day Lewis, *The Poetic Image: The Creative Power of the Visible Word* (Los Angeles: Tarcher, 1984), 15.

temperate person makes bad theater for the mob. To win favor, the poet must be "devoted to the fretful and complicated type of character" (*Rep.*, 604c–605e). This sort of poet does not appeal to the better parts of the soul and leaves us reveling in the spectacle of an unbalanced person totally controlled by ambition, greed, anger, or lust.

Socrates is making serious charges against the poets. But none of this constitutes the deepest foundation for the quarrel between poetry and philosophy, centering as it does on the influence of poetry on the multitude. The chief accusation is that poetry has the power to corrupt even the *best* sort of person (*Rep.*, 607b). When, at the hand of the poet, the very things that are to be ruled in an ordered soul – pity, sex, grief, and anger – become instead the rulers, poetry yields a different kind of citizen and soul from that advocated by the philosopher. Plato himself began as a poet: he knew the lure of poetry firsthand, and it was Socrates who drew him away and showed him philosophy as a way of life. But, as Nietzsche argues, Plato did not so much leave poetry as rechannel poetry into the service of philosophy, creating a new poetry and indeed creating the novel, a move that Nietzsche regretted – but that is a story for much later in this book. The place of poetry, then, is by no means tangential to the discussion of the city or the soul, and the stakes of the quarrel are high. Socrates finally says, "Let us, then, conclude our return to the topic of poetry and our apology, and affirm that we really had good grounds then for dismissing her from our city.... For reason constrained us" (*Rep.*, 607b).

The "ancient" quarrel is being created before our eyes as Socrates labors to wake up the Greeks from the slumber induced in part by the poets. The real quarrel is not between individual people but rather points beyond itself. Even the greatest of the poets, Homer, is not identified as the focus of the quarrel but as an *interpreter* of some independent thing – *poetry* as such. Should poetry be willing to take up its proper place in the city, says Socrates, it might be invited in again, though it would have to be a special poetry to be sure. Chief among the required characteristics is that it must not distract a person with an immortal soul from righteousness, excellence, and the truth. Throughout the *Republic*, the well-ordered soul has been directed toward the eternal world of the forms transcending this world of particulars. A poetry proper to the well-ordered soul must finally derive its propriety from its own relationship to this transcendent world. But however much it submits to the law of order, poetry is revealed only through words marshaled by those interpreters of poetry – the poets. Can poetry have another relationship to the transcendent forms beyond merely finding its proper place in the city ordered by reason? The mimetic poets invite us to heightened emotion – pity, grief, desire, fury. The poets are known to lie. Reception and contemplation of the forms are a different thing entirely – serene, calm. Is Plato a "poet of the forms"? If he were such a poet, why should we trust him any more than we trust the mimetic poets? After all, his "dialogues" look a lot like *imitations* of dialogue. This is the question toward which we move.

For Plato, true knowledge is possible only within the purview of reason. Unfortunately, according to Socrates, poetry cannot be composed by the poet until reason is no longer in him, "for a poet is a light and winged thing, and holy, and never able to compose until he has become inspired and is beside himself."[1] The acknowledgment that poets are holy and inspired looks like a compliment on the surface. The poets speak with the veritable voice of a god. Surely if anyone knows the truth, it is the gods. If we want the true starting points, the firmest of axioms from which to structure our lives, build our cities, write our philosophical treatises, and judge all things human and divine, from what better place could we start than with the voice of a god?

In the *Ion*, Socrates suggests that the poets bereft of their senses by the deity serve as ministers so that we listeners might know "that it is not they who utter these precious revelations while their mind is not in them, but that it is the god himself who speaks, and through them becomes articulate to us" (*Ion*, 534d). If the gods are the best foundation for true starting points, and if the poets give us access to the god's voice, this seems promising. However, Socrates shows in the *Euthyphro* that something is not good simply because the gods approve it (as though the gods could approve injustice and it would thereby become good), but rather that they approve something because it is good and worthy of being approved. Its goodness is independent of the god's utterance, and if a god says that injustice is good, so much the worse for that god. And so, even the voice of a god may not help us judge reality. If we are to see the goodness of what the gods say, we must already have some idea of what the good is. If goodness does not follow purely on the fact that something (including an idea) came from a god, then the voice of a god will not suffice to teach us to see goodness. So even if the greatest of poets speaks the words of the gods, there is still work to do before we

---

[1] Plato, *Ion*, trans. Lane Cooper, in Hamilton and Cairns, *The Collected Dialogues*, 534b, hereafter cited in text as *Ion*.

know we have arrived at the truth of the thing, and the work of the poet cannot be accepted uncritically.

Uncritical acceptance of such a poet's utterances is explored in the *Ion*, a dialogue that is lighthearted in part because Ion himself is an image of a likable fool. In the *Republic*, Socrates called Homer an *interpreter* of poetry. Ion, then, is the interpreter of the interpreter, and so worse off than the poet himself, in the parlance of Platonic proximity to what is real. Though he is a rhapsode who keeps the poet's voice and poetry alive in the city, whatever Socrates may say about poetry, he is the kind of character who must be dealt with gently. And so Socrates begins with praise and asks about his area of expertise. "Homer," Ion answers, adding that the poetry of Homer is surely enough for any one rhapsode to know (*Ion*, 531a). Not so, says Socrates, for the subject matter of which Homer treats has been treated also by other poets, and insofar as this is true, Ion is a specialist in those poets as well. Socrates begins to draw Ion away from the particulars of Homer and toward more generalized knowledge. Ion has a rejoinder available to him: Homer treats those common subjects in a superior way (*Ion*, 532d). And yet, Socrates points out, to make a judgment between the superior poet and the inferior poet concerning a particular subject, the judge of the poet must already have *knowledge* superior to that of either poet. One who judges among poets has moved a step across the divide separating the poets from the philosophers.

Up to this point, Socrates has avoided the actual experience of listening to the rhapsode so that he can pull Ion into a dialogue. But Ion suggests that if Socrates actually heard him speak the words of Homer, he would not attribute this power of speech to madness. So Socrates agrees to listen, but he allows Ion to recite only enough poetry to provide him with material for his next point, and then he interrupts. He looks at the various particular topics expressed through the poetry of Homer, of which Ion's short passage is an example, and argues that once the topics have been raised by the poet, prompting us to ask about what we know regarding war, medicine, and so forth, the rhapsode's art is no longer required. We want to get to the truth of things, and though poetry might have a role in getting us started, once the truth of a thing has been communicated – whatever the form of communication – the vehicle for communication is irrelevant.

Throughout, Socrates acknowledges that the poets can provide starting points for philosophical inquiry, can offer particulars among which we judge, especially the particulars of feeling. For one who is a lover of wisdom, feeling seems relevant. But there is a difference between "feeling" and the driving force behind philosophy. Poetry is relegated by Socrates to the domain of emotion, but it is *wonder* that primarily marks the lover of wisdom.[5] Nonetheless, there is a motivating force in the act of philosophy that might properly be called a feeling and which is very close to a certain experience that can be provoked and inspired by some poetry – what J. A. Stewart has called *transcendental feeling*, "a sense of that which was and is and ever shall be – a sense of Timeless Being. As a normal experience of our conscious life it is the conviction that 'life is good.'"[6] No doubt Plato did not share this view of poetry – at least as poetry thrived in the days the quarrel was born. But the writing in which Plato himself engaged might fruitfully be understood in light of this central and common experience of wonder.

If a poet does make a claim to induce any sense of "life as good," the philosophical rejoinder Socrates offers is that such recognition requires some *concept* of what goodness is. But the converse might be argued: to begin a discussion about goodness, one must first experience something *as* good in order to question the nature of that experience. Philosophical thought must have some fundamental experience with which to begin, an experience that is in some sense necessarily unreasoned, prior to reason's work, which occurs while the questioning mind is "absent" or at least precedes the activity of questioning and analysis. What is prior – the *experience* of goodness or recognition of the experience of goodness *as* an experience of goodness?

In the myths of the theological poets, before the development of philosophy, we find open to us concrete materials that, in the hands of the philosophers, become some of our most fundamental philosophical images. Hesiod gave an account and genealogy of the gods and everything needed to make a world in the *Theogony*, where we find chaos, light, dark, eros, war, time, evil, fate, resentment, truth, and justice with a mythic account of each. Consider the images in the following passage: "And there are the sources and extremities of dark earth and misty Tartarus, of the un-draining sea and the starry heaven, all in order, dismal and dank, that even the gods shudder at; a vast chasm, whose floor a man would not reach in a whole year if once he got inside the gates, but storm wind upon terrible storm wind would carry him

---

[5] Plato, *Theatetus*, trans. F. M. Cornford, in Hamilton and Cairns, *The Collected Dialogues*, 155d.
[6] J. A. Stewart, *The Myths of Plato* (Whitefish: Kessinger Publishing, 2007), 20.

hither and thither. It is a cause of fear for even the immortal gods, this marvel. And there stands the fearful house of a gloomy night shrouded in clouds of blackness."[7] A myth may be susceptible to critique revealing factual error, evaluative error, conceptual error, moral error. But at least there is an account of the whole – in this case, a mythopoeic account – from which we can move. This point is at the crux of the quarrel between philosophy and poetry, and it arises repeatedly throughout the history of the quarrel: though mythic thinkers do not question myth and though the work of the poets such as Hesiod and Homer are embraced uncritically as authoritative, the philosopher incurs debt to such poets by being born into the middle of a complete world with a complete language and an account of the totality of that which is, with a place even for the darkness and the vast chasm that makes the gods shudder. Before the first philosophical question is ever uttered, there is already in place a full account of what humanity is, what the world is, why we are here, what we ought to do, and who the gods are. And it is precisely this account of the whole that gives the philosopher both the starting points for questioning the account and the language with which to ask such questions.

Despite such indebtedness, Socrates argues in the *Ion* that the poets are not qualified to evaluate their myths. Socrates insists that he has given the poets a real chance to defend themselves and they have been found wanting. Likewise in the *Apology*, he says that his experience with the poets leads him to conclude "that it was not wisdom that enabled them to write their poetry, but a kind of instinct or inspiration such as you find in seers and prophets who deliver all their sublime messages without knowing in the least what they mean."[8] Inspiration that intuits reality without apprehending its nature through the philosophical question is not knowledge but rather mere opinion, blather about this or that part of the world with no actual connection to reality, no critical effort to move past the stories and get to the truth of things so that we can tell a story about reality that counts as knowledge. He says, "Opinions divorced from knowledge are ugly things" (*Rep.*, 506c). The poets are not trustworthy guides to the truth – not even to whatever truth is contained in their own poetry.

---

[7] Hesiod, *Theogony and Works and Days*, trans. M. L. West (Oxford: Oxford University Press, 1988), 25.

[8] Plato, *Socrates' Defense (Apology)*, trans. Hugh Tredennick, in Hamilton and Cairns, *The Collected Dialogues*, 22c.

It is not entirely clear that the poets disagree with Socrates on this point. In the opening of the *Theogony*, Hesiod identifies the Muses as his inspiration, his teachers, the origin of his own song. Then the goddesses open their mouths to speak: "Shepherds that camp in the wild, disgraces, merest bellies: we know to tell many lies that sound like truth, but we know to sing reality when we will."[9] The poet argues that the gods can speak lies that look like the truth, but he gives no means for discerning truth from falsehood. This bespeaks of possible poetic folly – and fodder for Socrates' critique.

A more urgent motivation for Socrates' critique has already been touched on: beyond mere folly, the poets can become frankly dangerous if, lacking discernment, they nonetheless claim to be wise. In the Greek literary tradition, the claim to wisdom among the poets was common. H. S. Thayer says that this claim to wisdom did not derive merely from their artistic skill, as though wisdom was limited to excellence in a craft, but rather it derived from two other sources. The first was a claim that the *sophoi* have a divine "sense" in addition to the five physical senses – a special means of gaining information.[10] Again, on the surface this notion that poets somehow speak for the gods or from the gods seems to be a compelling reason for someone to embrace their wisdom, and it is just such claims that Socrates has been at pains to dispatch, not by denying them, but by showing that, even if they are true, the poets are still not to be embraced uncritically. Second, the poets' substantial claims to wisdom rested on the art of memory, an art exemplified by Simonides, who invented a mnemonic system correlating images and phrases with names and descriptive terms.[11] But here, too, Socrates, despite agreeing with the value of memory, says that even memory requires discernment, for not everything is equally worth remembering (*Rep.*, 486d). Something is true not because its source is the gods or memory ("this is how we have always thought of things"), but rather because it stands up to questioning, indeed, is revealed as true through the philosophical question.

If the poets, though inspired by gods and drawing on long memory, are not trustworthy guides to wisdom, but if nonetheless there is a kind of power and wealth in poetry that philosophy can mine, what has philosophy learned from poetry, and how, in the midst of the quarrel, can philosophy make use of poetic tools?

[9] Hesiod, *Theogony*, 3.
[10] H. S. Thayer, "Plato's Quarrel with Poetry: Simonides," *Journal of the History of Ideas* 36 (1975): 6.
[11] Ibid., 9.

The case for philosophy is made in the medium of language, dialogue, storytelling, and mythmaking, and the irony of Socrates' poetic critique of poetry grows most vivid in the *Phaedrus*. Part of Socrates' critique of the poets is the observation that they are taken by a divine madness. But in the *Phaedrus* we learn that the first step toward philosophy is love as a kind of divine madness. The conversation about love begins with a poetic account of love from Phaedrus's friend Lysias. What is enacted after Phaedrus gives the account is a philosophical drama using the very tools of poetry along with those of philosophy to show what it looks like for a mind to be pried out of the limits of a single poetic account, and it is a struggle indeed, but one between friends.

Socrates begins his critique by presenting other voices besides that of Lysias. He presents the perspectives of a couple of poets and a prose writer, who might well have produced a better account of love than either of the poets. It does not matter to Socrates whether the account is delivered in verse or prose. He is after the truth of the thing. Nor does it matter who wrote the piece – he cannot remember the names of the authors anyway, and he supposes that, given his ignorance of the source, the account must have "been poured into me through my ears, as into a vessel, from some external source, though in my stupid fashion I have actually forgotten how, and from whom, I heard it."[12] The content and truth of the account are what matter, not the deliverer, the personality, or the form into which the account is cast.

This is a difficult point to make well in a culture where the poets hold such power over accounts of the gods and the tales of the people, over history and language. So Socrates must plunge in as the poets themselves do before he can show how philosophy is superior to poetry, and this he does, invoking the Muses for his speech and warning Phaedrus, "Listen to me in silence." He goes on, "For truly there seems to be a divine presence in this spot, so that you must not be surprised if, as my speech proceeds, I become as one possessed: already my style is not far from dithyrambic" – not far, that is to say, from the choric hymn used to honor Dionysius (*Phaed.*, 238d). Indeed, at the end of his first discourse on love, he does break out into verse (*Phaed.*, 241c).

Because the work of the poets deceives people into thinking it is the way of truth, Socrates must uncover how its tricks work, first nearly falling into the hands of the nymphs as he delivers his discourse, and then

---

[12] Plato, *Phaedrus*, trans. R. Hackforth, in Hamilton and Cairns, *The Collected Dialogues*, 234c–d, hereafter cited in text as *Phaed.*

drawing a contrast between poetry and philosophy by showing what the ideas mean when viewed through the philosopher's prism. The fact that poetry and philosophy are similar in so many ways is what makes poetry such a great danger for true lovers of wisdom, and Socrates demonstrates the danger by nearly succumbing to it. Carried on the wave of his own near-dithyramb, he has erred in his discourse against love. But the way in which he recognizes his own error does even more to make us wonder at the strange relationship between poetry and philosophy, for his recognition of error does not follow upon a careful exchange of reasoning, but rather, he says, "there comes to me my familiar divine sign – which always checks me when on the point of doing something or other – and all at once I seem to hear a voice, forbidding me to leave the spot until I had made atonement for some offense to heaven" (*Phaed.*, 242b–c). By indulging in a poet-like activity, he spoke against love. A spell was upon his lips (*Phaed.*, 242e). But convicted of his error by a divine sign that is his guide, and which appears at many points in Plato's portrayal of Socrates, he recants.

What is this madness that takes hold of a mind? And why is understanding its nature and origin so important? Socrates claims that madness in and of itself – whether it be that of love or that of poetry – is not a reason for fear. Madness, when sent from heaven, can be a great blessing: it is the madness of the seer and the prophet (*Phaed.*, 244b–c). And madness, when sent by the Muses, is also considered a benediction because it is inspiration that allows the poets to compose. For all his skills, a poet who does not surrender to the Muses will perforce write poetry that comes to naught (*Phaed.*, 245a). But if such madness can yield good things, where does the problem lie?

As always, Socrates searches for the answer by first returning to the fundamental questions of self-knowledge, "to discern the nature of the soul, divine and human, its experiences, and its activities" (*Phaed.*, 245c). When he embarks on this investigation, he learns first that whatever madness comes from heaven's engendering a poet's power, there is something beyond these heavens that has not been the subject of any poet's production, and which, even if it was, would remain beyond the power of the purest poetry to sing in a worthy manner (*Phaed.*, 247c). A poetry reaching for this point will always have to aim beyond itself, and this need is the crux of the philosopher's reinvention of and victory over poetry. The new poet will sing about what lies beyond the heavens where true being resides in a manner touchable only by reason, pointing the seeker toward that which nourishes the minds of gods and which is the only proper food for the immortal soul. The new poet is Plato. Being the true poet and the poet of truth, even as he sings he says that no poetry, including his own, will be adequate to the task of saying what is true about this realm. Here is the centerpiece of the argument: no poetry that calls itself finished can contain the truth. And yet, by its very nature, poetry yields finished poems, whole tales, and complete mythic accounts of things human and divine. The moment a poem is finished is the moment a poem begins to deceive, whether that poem belongs to Homer, Hesiod, or Plato. However, just as Socratic ignorance is the hallmark of his wisdom, so this very awareness of the limits of language that is at the heart of Plato's own poetry makes it different. Though it has a beginning, a middle, and an end, it remains open, pointing beyond itself and making use of many voices and open questions to resist any false closure, any appearance of being the whole of wisdom. This poetry is always on its way. It is the poetry of the threshold, pointing beyond the gods themselves and opening new paths for the lover of wisdom.

The poets' claims to wisdom were founded on access to the voices of the gods and memory. Regarding the former, the philosopher also turns out to have a divine voice, but one that leads more certainly toward what lies beyond the heavens where the very gods nourish themselves. The philosopher's voice turns out to be a reclaiming of memory as well, memory of what has been seen before arriving on earth: the soul, which has seen the most, upon entering the body, "shall grow into a seeker after wisdom or beauty, a follower of the Muses and a lover" (*Phaed.*, 248d). The Muses are the daughters of Zeus and Mnemosyne, the goddess of memory. According to Socrates, the fullness of memory is the measure of the nearness of the philosopher's soul to the gods whose minds feed in the meadows of reason and true being beyond the heavens (*Phaed.*, 249c). Memory derives from the *soul's own vision* of true being. It does not require that one be possessed by a god, for the soul sees on its own, and this vision, for the short time the soul is in a body, is accessed through memory. The poets' sources of inspiration – memory and proximity to the gods – are both now claimed as the gifts of the philosopher. Such a one might well be thought mad. But the philosopher's "madness" is not that of a witless and deprived reason, or the madness of the mimetic poet or the rhapsode, but rather the madness of the lover who has beheld and loved true beauty. Memory of this vision, even if for a time it is not recognized as such, is nonetheless what compels the soul toward the noble and philosophical life.

Such is the philosophical life. But, as mentioned before, Plato claims that he never wrote down his philosophy, and indeed he questions whether philosophy can be written down at all. Philosophy cannot be written down, he claims, but poetry can be written down, and what Plato has given us in the thousands of pages he wrote is an *image* of philosophy, as Stanley Rosen has rightly argued.[13] In the *Symposium*, Socrates goes even farther and stretches the notion of the poet in the *true* sense to include all those "calling something into existence that was not there before, so that every kind of artistic creation is poetry and every artist is a poet."[14] Plato, writer of dialogues, is to be counted among the poets, and poetry shall be put to a new use at the hands of the lover of wisdom. But all making, all art, all poetry, including the written dialogues of Plato, can only be semblance, and semblance is never the thing itself. A vision of beauty or of the good is precisely that – a vision. No likeness can substitute, and the vision cannot be fit into a poem. At the same time, a vision is approached in a stepwise manner, and the poem, which is merely a semblance, must yet have some contact with true being, with what is real, if it is to be a signpost pointing the lover in the direction of the beautiful and the good.

Just as poetry cannot deliver on the final vision of beauty and the good, and cannot get us to the land of the gods, neither do the methods of philosophy used by Socrates in his pursuit of wisdom constitute the vision. The methods may train the soul to be loyal to the truth. The method of *analogy* might open our eyes to new connections. The method of *collection and division* can do the same. *Hypothesizing* gives us experience in drawing inferential or deductive connections. Above all, the method of *elenchus*, of inquiry and cross-examination, can, by the law of noncontradiction, give us that barest of insights that two contrary particulars cannot both be true, and such vigilant opposition to inconsistency might provide a way for the soul to develop a habit of truthfulness.

The use of these methods is not without risk because we are in danger of a kind of misplaced faith. If we are to persist in the training of the soul, we must believe training is for some end. But until the soul has actually reached the final revelation, it cannot be certain that the goal toward which it is working is actually reachable. Indeed, it cannot be certain that the goal is real at all. This is why we value the experienced teacher who tells stories, who writes dialogue, who lives life in a certain way.

[13] Stanley Rosen, *The Quarrel between Philosophy and Poetry: Studies in Ancient Thought* (New York: Routledge, 1998), 12.
[14] Plato, *Symposium*, trans. Michael Joyce, in Hamilton and Cairns, *The Collected Dialogues*, 205b, hereafter cited in text as *Symp.*

This is also why it is important that the role be assumed by the proper person. Socrates said that philosophy is preparation for death. So death is a fitting cauldron in which the teacher, Socrates, is tested. Socrates faces death with disarming calmness amid the tears and mourning of his friends. But death is a unique threshold, an extreme test case for the power of words to bring us to peculiar openings. Here, above all, the dying philosopher is alone in wisdom, for no one with whom he might converse has died, nor can they die his particular death.

From outside Socrates appears calm, his demeanor touched with humor even at the last moment of his life. As he speaks to his friends, he reveals that his outward expression manifests an inward truth, a truth that can *only* be inward. We cannot have this truth in words, for to have this truth that is residing in Socrates would be to have the soul of Socrates, to *be* in this particular way. The closest we can come is friendship, love, and following after his example. That is, after watching Socrates we might move through our own death with a different attitude, a kind of courage we might have lacked were it not for Socrates. This in turn sets us on the path toward becoming the kind of person who inhabits the final moments of life with assurance founded on truth.

When has the situation been otherwise? The Platonic poems have brought us to the threshold where we can watch the *image* of Socrates bearing witness to the transcendent, truth, beauty, justice, and the good. This example prods us to persist along the way. At the final revelation, the procession from ignorance to full knowledge is not guaranteed by poetic starting places or philosophical methods. The path is neither inevitable nor marked with certainty. Attaining a true vision does require training of the soul. Until our souls are trained to see truth as truth, we are more like children who tussle about pretending to be great warriors in imitation of the real warriors, but who would be consumed with fear if faced with an actual enemy. But life is not long, and if we are to live well, to live the best life, we need someone to show us the way, to help us move in the right direction. We want to trade our irrecoverable days for something worth the trade. The terrible risk is that our teacher is a bad one, for if that is so, we will squander our lives. No wonder Plato was so concerned with false claims to wisdom.

Even if I am fortunate enough have a great teacher, some very important things will not be said by the teacher simply because they are unsayable. These I will have to find myself. For example, the highest form toward which philosophical inquiry aims is the form of the good. And yet when the dialogue in the *Republic* reaches this pinnacle, Socrates refuses to talk about the good. "Nay, my beloved," he says, "let us dismiss for the time being the nature of the good in itself, for to attain to my present surmise of that seems a pitch above the impulse that wings my flight today. But of what seems to be the offspring of the good and most nearly made in its likeness I am willing to speak" (*Rep.*, 506e).

Attaining to the nature of the good shall always be a pitch above the impulse that wings his flight. But apparently there is some value in approaching the unsayable through that which is most nearly like it. One thing most *like* another – this is a mimetic endeavor of a new sort, now with knowledge of the limits regarding what can be said, a knowledge that also redeems the value of what can be said because of its ability to usher us toward the thing itself. This, ultimately, is the meaning of "poetic openings" and it is the very purpose of the quarrel that must continue for the sake of poetry, philosophy, and that which transcends both toward which we are moving.

We want to see. We want a vision of the thing itself. Even the true name of the thing, though it may reveal something about the thing in a way that false names cannot, remains nonetheless a name. "My dear Socrates," Diotima says in the *Symposium*, "if a man's life is ever worth living it is when he has attained this vision of the very soul of beauty.... It is only when he discerns beauty itself through what makes it visible that a man will be quickened with the true, and not the seeming, virtue – for it is virtue's self that quickens them, not virtue's semblance" (*Symp.*, 211d–212a).

The poet sees but does not retain reason. The unpoetic philosopher reasons but cannot move beyond the methods and truly see. Diotima tells us about a third option. When the eyes have been opened and the lover of wisdom gazes upon the transcendent, upon beauty or the good in true contemplation, such a vision remains *one's own* forever. The beholder experiences a vision without becoming ecstatic or possessed by a god, without losing reason. Indeed, the vision is attained in part through reason properly used. This is the source of a new and better type of poetry, the sort of poetry Plato writes.

The writing itself is an issue with which Plato struggles. In his *Seventh Letter*, he discusses those who have written books on philosophy. Of them, he says, "Such writers can in my opinion have no real acquaintance with the subject. I certainly have composed no work in regard to it, nor shall I ever do so in the future, for there is no way of putting it in words like other studies."[15] That words and names are slippery and unstable,

---

[15] Plato, *Epistle VII*, trans. L. A. Post, in Hamilton and Cairns, *The Collected Dialogues*, 344c, hereafter cited in text as *Epistle*.

susceptible to a variety of interpretations, is not a contemporary discovery. The great mistake – one made by Plato's own contemporaries – is to forget the distinction between the name, the description, the image, knowledge of an object, and the object itself. To demonstrate the slipperiness of the word or phrase is not to have said a thing about what the soul knows, or about the object known. Knowing is an *activity* of the soul, of my soul. This may seem to tend toward a kind of solipsism, but there is a remedy for this sort of solipsism, and it is friendship – indeed, love. If philosophy is the love of wisdom, and love is an activity of the soul rather than something that occurs on the page, there may be a sense in which all of the writing of books occurs in the cave.

At the end of the *Phaedrus*, Socrates tells a story about writing. Theuth, who invented writing, visits the king to show off his various arts. The king answers him, "Oh man full of arts, to one it is given to create the things of art, and to another to judge what measure of harm and of profit they have for those that shall employ them" (*Phaed.*, 274e). Theuth is attached to his creation in such a way that he cannot judge its potential for good or ill rightly. He thinks writing will aid memory, but he is corrected by the king, who sees that collecting marks external to the soul and using them as a repository for things worth remembering is only the *appearance* of wisdom, a substitute of *semblance* for true memory. The same might be said for the written portrayal of Socrates pursuing wisdom among the people of Athens. The *Phaedrus*, in diminishing the value of a poet's literary works "on whose phrases he spends hours, twisting them this way and that, pasting them together and pulling them apart," is also commenting on the Platonic dialogues, resisting the reduction of true philosophy to a written image of philosophy. True knowledge requires a different kind of writing, a sort growing from discourse and written on the very soul of the learner (*Phaed.*, 276a). Living discourse must always be allied to such a soul. The soul is the immortal part of the human that views truth as gods view truth – if it goes along the right path with the right teacher. The soul is the only ground in which the seeds sown through dialectic can grow.

Throughout the rest of this work, Plato's image of the quarrel will be the guiding metaphor. This image has three parts – the image of the philosopher, the image of the poet, and the image of the quarrel. Neither the image of the philosopher with his various methods for testing and critiquing ideas nor that of the poet singing out of his mind completes the true story of the philosopher and the poet. The quarrel is an image of the living power that allows the poet to rush forward in song and which keeps the philosopher from being overcome, whether by gods, madness, or the lure of critique and questioning detached from a true vision of goodness. It is an image of the soul's battle against half truths. It is also an image of the living power that, because it maintains the distinction between poetry and philosophy and makes clear the dangers of confusing the two, opens the possibility of a new poetry, which in turn opens the possibility of leading minds to the love of wisdom. The quarrel is the image of the very power that allows Plato, the philosopher-poet, to produce this new poetry without confusing his own poetry with true vision. It allows the work of the new poetry to bring us to thresholds we might not otherwise have reached. Producing such poetry in a good and beautiful way can now be a unified act arising from the soul of the lover of wisdom. Plato is clear that if anything is to be written about philosophy the writer should take care that it not be folly: "I should be very sorry to see such a treatise poorly written" (*Epistle*, 7.341d).

As the apostle Paul says of faith and hope in 1 Corinthians 13, once we see God, neither will be necessary anymore, though love will remain. If transcendent truth is available only to the wise and to the gods, nothing that is made (*poiesis*) can embody or contain it. Poetry is entirely a creature of this world, the immanent world, however inspired it may be by the transcendent. But neither is there room or need for the philosophical question among the Forms as they are in themselves. Socrates distinguishes between the one who is wise and the one who is the lover of wisdom, a philosopher. It is the former who sees as the gods do. The philosopher is every bit a part of this world as the poet. They each have an oar, and via the quarrel they bring each other, and us, to new thresholds.

All art is artifice, and the philosopher-poet – the self-conscious, self-knowing lover of wisdom who teaches and writes – will be careful to remember this. In doing so, irony will arise. Socratic irony aims its force and stings not against the truth, or against the effort and possibility of seeing truth, but rather against the finishing of truth, the false completion. Socrates, written into a poem, a *made* thing with a beginning, a middle, and an end, must be ironic to avoid being a false image. Socrates *written down* is not Socrates the living soul in search for wisdom. Irony, properly wielded, is always directed against false completion. At the same time, irony detached from the possibility of finding truth becomes cynicism or, worse, sin.

Wittgenstein gave the famous ending to his *Tractatus Logico-Philosophicus*: "6.54 My propositions are elucidatory in this way: he who understands me finally recognizes them as senseless, when he has climbed out through them, on them, over them. (He must so to speak throw away the ladder, after he has climbed up on it.) He must surmount these propositions; then he sees the world rightly. 7. Whereof one cannot speak, thereof one must be silent."[16] True poetry and philosophy are only necessary in this worldly struggle to find all of wisdom. But when one sees as the gods see, one is no longer a lover of wisdom – one is wise. Though Plato, the true poet and lover of wisdom, did not write down his philosophy, when he did write he did so in a way that might have concluded each time with Wittgenstein's words. For those who have not attained the true vision spoken of by Diotima, what is available is a guiding image in the poem. The starting point for these seekers is the new poetry read with a true love of wisdom.

A poem written by a true poet points beyond itself. If it cannot make us wise, perhaps it can at least goad us on toward wisdom and make us feel that Diotima was on to something of the highest importance in saying, "When he has brought forth and reared this perfect virtue, he shall be called a friend of god, and if ever it is given to man to put on immortality, it shall be given to him" (*Symp.*, 212a). Love is the activity that brings us to wisdom. Love begins with what is only an image of the true, final, fitting object of love. The task of the true poet is to make an image that sparks love, without becoming itself the false object of that love. The ancient quarrel allows poetry and philosophy to have their proper places, though there is always the danger that even a true poem will fall into the wrong hands and be made a false idol, made a substitute for the real thing.

Plato makes a powerful case. If language fails us, it fails us because we asked the wrong things of it. True poetry is about something besides itself – indeed, about anything and everything besides itself. In poetry, as in philosophy, there is room for the whole world. This is the meaning of the poetic opening. This is the task of discovery as true poetry creates the starting points from which philosophy proceeds. It is this relationship between poetry and philosophy that is made possible and sustained by the ancient quarrel. No doubt it is at least in part this victory of self-knowledge, awareness, and the love of wisdom wrought by Socrates and Plato that allowed Plato's student Aristotle to critique in turn the very case made by Plato.

---

[16] Ludwig Wittgenstein, *Tractatus Logico-Philosophicus*, trans. C. K. Ogden (London: Routledge, 1992), 189.

# 2

# Aristotle, Poetry, and Ethics

When we step into the lecture hall with Aristotle, we quickly sense that we are in a different arena. There are a few echoes of Plato's judgment on poetry, as when Aristotle, discussing the education of children in the *Politics*, says, "The legislator should not allow youth to be spectators of iambi or of comedy until they are of an age to sit at public tables and to drink strong wine; by that time education will have armed them against the evil influences of such representations."[1] But Aristotle embraces the whole range of poetry as valuable in the right setting, and he spends most of his effort trying to understand the elements of great poetry in order to teach the poets.

Plato found a fair amount of overlap between poetry and metaphysics, motivating the quarrel as philosophy made its foray into domains dominated by the theological poets – the realm of truth, the good, the gods, being and access to the mysteries of the universe and the heavens. In all of this, poetry and philosophy occupied similar territory. In order for philosophy to do its work, the quarrel had to become trenchant indeed, Plato's three-part strategy being, as we have seen, to exile the poets; to create a new poetry that is capable of serving philosophy; and to tuck the real philosophy into the realm of silence, inaccessible to the best tools of the poet's trade.

Aristotle's approach is quite different. In *The Metaphysics* he does begin with the theological poets and acknowledges that philosophers are lovers of myth to some extent, as both philosophy and the myths of the poets begin in wonder.[2] But shortly after this observation,

[1] Aristotle, *Politics*, in *The Complete Works of Aristotle*, ed. Jonathan Barnes (Cambridge: Cambridge University Press, 1988), 1336b15–20, hereafter cited in text as *Politics*.
[2] Aristotle, *Metaphysics*, in Barnes, *The Complete Works of Aristotle*, 982b11–21, hereafter cited in text as *Meta*.

he dismisses the poets' representation of the gods as envious, reminds us of the proverb "The poets tell many lies," and moves on to explore the topic of "being as such" with no apparent need to argue further against the poets (*Meta.*, 982b30–983a3). Indeed, in a later passage he says bluntly that it is not even worthwhile to inquire into the subtleties of the myths of these theological poets. The only writers and thinkers worth engaging seriously are those who use the language of proof (*Meta.*, 1000a5–20). In short, Aristotle seems much less worried over the poets, because, unlike Plato, he sees them as much less of a threat. Certainly he offers practical advice for the production of great poetry (especially advice for the production of epic and tragedy) and the appropriate use of such poetry. But even the portrayal of the fall of a relatively good man has its place, and far from being the threat Plato said it was, this sort of poetry can have positive benefits and is to be welcomed.

Part of the difference is that Aristotle tends to find more overlap – very suggestive overlap – between poetry and ethics. The *Nicomachean Ethics*, the *Politics*, and the *Poetics* are usefully read in series as books informing and illuminating each other.[3] Aristotle judges tragedy by the standard of his ethics. The philosopher always judges the moral dimensions of poetry rather than poetry challenging and changing the ethics of the philosopher. That said, tragic reversals can indeed be ethically illuminating. This back-and-forth between ethics and poetry (as it evolves in technique and approaches its "natural form") is found throughout Aristotle's works. The poets can be drawn upon for illuminating illustrations of a point, but the choice of how the illustration is used and which parts of the poet's work can best serve the point being made remains subject to the judgment of the philosopher.

To understand how poetry ought to be written, how it is to be judged, and how it relates to the work of philosophy, the first tools that are needed are those found in a map for self-knowledge in the *Nicomachean Ethics*. Tragedy reveals the need for self-knowledge, xe "knowledand philosophy provides the means. For humans, the starting place for self-knowledge is not with the highest, most divine (and most useless) study – metaphysics – but rather with the most immediately relevant and practical study that begins with who we are and how we ought to *act*.

---

[3] *Nicomachean Ethics* employed action, and especially action following from a person's choices and revealing virtuous character, or its lack. In the first part of the *Poetics*, Aristotle shows why this work follows the *Ethics* and the *Politics* naturally: the objects the poets imitate are "actions, with agents who are necessarily either good men or bad."

Here we find the most important set of clues about how poetry should be written – especially tragedy, which is composed of *actions*.

Aristotle – a man with an earthly curiosity about fish, bees, meteorology, the ways in which constitutions are structured, and innumerable other facets of life – is at home in the world and embraces with wonder its *reality*. He is a practical man willing to offer practical advice. So, in the making of virtuous citizens, the *polis* aims for people who wish "to learn and to become habituated to judge correctly and to delight in decent character and fine actions" (*Politics*, 1340a15). How this comes about – the range of useful things that can achieve this end – reveals an important difference between Plato and Aristotle. For while Plato's artist is several rungs removed from Truth and correspondingly inferior to it, in Aristotle's view, becoming habituated to appropriate feeling or pain in response to something *like* the thing itself is similar to doing so in relation to the thing itself. This underscores Aristotle's recognition that most people are not swayed to virtue by a philosophical argument. The basest among us respond to the stick, but for the majority of nonphilosophers, presenting common models that evoke right feeling (including fear and pity where fitting) is a useful way to shape the community. Again, it is not that poetry serves merely as a means to shaping a moral community. But the measure of a good tragedy will be its ability to evoke pity and fear, where pity and fear are appropriate. The appropriateness is measured in relation to virtue fitting to humans.

In order to show how poetry, in the form of tragedy, can lead us to knowledge of good and virtuous action, Aristotle explains how tragedy works. The perfect tragic plot has three ingredients – a single issue, an agent with a fault, and a change of fortune from good to bad – and its goal is catharsis in all who behold its action. By presenting the responses of the tragic hero, whether he be a man who is noble and magnanimous despite distress or one who is undone by what transpires, poetry can reveal the ethical structure of events to which we are all vulnerable and, thus, can allow us to experience the suffering of another in a way that makes us aware of structures we might otherwise ignore. When we witness a tragic choice devised by a poet, we become more immediately aware of a possibility that exists and that bears on our perceptions of vulnerability and value in a finite domain. Although poetry is not merely a primer for ethical activity, the pedagogical role of tragedy does allow us to learn from a hypothetical "if…then" by watching a character cry out from the middle of things, "If only…." The *paideia* of the poets is catharsis.

As I have already stated, Aristotle emphasizes the importance of beginning our inquiry into the good and the true with that which is accessible. For humans, the starting place is not with metaphysics, but rather with the most immediately relevant and practical study that begins with who we are and how we ought to *act*. In the *Poetics*, the presence of human-size characteristics, virtues, and actions draws us into the action, even when the character is a better version of ourselves – more courageous, more attractive, more magnanimous. Actions are not entirely under our control. They are "out there" in the world where other factors can influence them. This is in part why tragedy portrays actions rather than persons.[4] Actions are vulnerable to the world, while the magnanimous person might remain good-tempered. One question addressed in the *Ethics* is whether and how shaping my character can affect my response to events beyond my control, the question whether the irrational (*alogon*) forces can somehow be redeemed by my own participation in the ordered and rational (*logos*) world. Tragedy might well prompt me to change my response to the reality of my own frailty and of chance. We are able to observe the actions and consequences of actions of our neighbors better than we are able to observe our own.[5] So also in tragic poetry when actions are staged, we can observe in a way we might not from inside the events.

Virtue is concerned both with feelings and with actions, and specifically with the intermediate state between excess and deficiency, either of which is morally blameworthy (*NE*, 1106b25–8). At this stage, whether speaking of feeling, decisions leading to action, or intelligence, Aristotle is clear that he is speaking about the human world, and about virtue as a mean between two vices. This is a mean relative to us, discernible to the reason of an intelligent person (*NE*, 1107a36). Intelligence is not the same as wisdom. Wisdom is unchanging, wonderful, and divine, but it is also somewhat useless because it is not about human goods (later in the *Metaphysics* it will become clear that this most "useless" activity is also the best, and even here in the *Ethics* Aristotle makes it clear that it is absurd to think of intelligence, which is indeed very useful, as the best thing because humans, though they may be the best among animals, are not the best thing in the universe) (*NE*, 1141a20–b17). One interesting point about the relationship of this practical aspect of intelligence

---

[4] Aristotle, *Poetics*, in Barnes, *The Complete Works of Aristotle*, 1450a16–21, hereafter cited in text as *Poetics*.

[5] Aristotle, *Nicomachean Ethics*, trans. Terence Irwin (Indianapolis: Hackett, 1985), 1569b33, hereafter cited in text as *NE*.

that allows us to make a decision about the mean and virtue is that the decision about the mean requires intelligence, and intelligence in turn requires virtue. Aristotle says that "we cannot be intelligent without being good" (*NE*, 1144a29–36).

When the poets write tragedy and show us characters like ourselves, or like better versions of ourselves, the events that cause us to pity the person and fear for our own well-being gain traction precisely because the reality against which such tragedy occurs is familiar to us: it is a reality in which human happiness depends in part on the stability of character throughout life (*NE*, 1100b20–1101a10). And it is not necessarily that the good person becomes miserable through misfortunes as great as those of Priam – the character cited by Aristotle to tether his point – but rather that even if he is not miserable, such a one can be robbed of blessedness by misfortune.

And when the poets portray a good character robbed of blessedness because of fortune and ill choice, how great is the loss? What are the stakes when we talk about the loss of fortune? For Aristotle, the loss so portrayed is enormous because the truly happy life is superior to the merely human and is, in fact, lived not insofar as we are human beings, but insofar as we have a divine element in us.

The divine element in human character makes the undoing more poignant. This divine aspect, as opposed to the human element, is what makes the life of contemplation accessible. How does the divine element in us that allows contemplation compare with the manner in which the theological poets were said to have the gods in them? Possession of the poets by the gods was hard to distinguish from madness, and it required that the poets become not more themselves, but less, being beside themselves. In contrast, Aristotle says that the divine spark makes us more ourselves. So the divine must be present to the mind of the philosopher, though the awareness of such a possibility came first from the theological poets, not the philosophers.

In light of this, the inscription on the temple of Apollo, "Know thyself," takes on new meaning. It was first understood to mean "Know that you are human, and that you are not a god." Socrates introduced a new level of meaning, namely, know that you do not know, and in so knowing achieve a new kind of self-awareness born of this ignorance, yielding the philosophical question that tests and challenges and so threatens the established starting points of the theological poets. Aristotle – this sane, careful, attentive philosopher – has yet another perspective on the dictum. Far from accepting that we should know that we are not gods – or, as the proverb writer he cites says, "think human since you are human" or "think mortal since you are mortal" – Aristotle says that we should think "immortal." Do whatever it takes to live a life that most fully experiences the divine element, the supreme element of our being, "For however much this element may lack in bulk, by much more it surpasses everything in power and value" (*NE*, 1177b27–1178a1). This life will lead to the work of the metaphysics, which, of all pursuits accessible to human beings, concerns itself with the divine knowledge proper to God, a pursuit that is less necessary than all others, but which is also more excellent than all others (*Meta.*, 983a4–11).

Wherever the gods are located in relationship to the events of a poet's tragedy, tragedy itself will portray action, and the action in the tragedy will involve fault, and that fault will involve a decision by a character who is sufficiently good (and so, intelligent as well) for us to feel pity and fear as a result of the reversal of fortune. The Greek word for this is *proairesis*, action taking the form of a decision and dependent on the two faculties that function in moral action – the desiring part of the soul and practical intelligence.[6] It is this kind of decision making, more so than action, that best distinguishes the virtuous character from others, because actions, though they can be voluntary like decisions, do not always follow from decision, as with those actions we do on the spur of the moment (*NE*, 1111b5).

These points are fundamental for the poet who would produce the best tragedy. Virtuous actions are concerned with promoting an end, and it is precisely deliberation (using the intellect, or *nous*, in its practical aspect) and decision making that direct us toward actions that will best promote the ends. Virtue is up to us, and so is vice, both following from decisions leading to action to promote some end. Nor does it matter if the means to the end following upon deliberation is actually refusal to act, "For when acting is up to us, so is not acting, and when No is up to us, so is Yes" (*NE*, 1103a15–20). The poet who wants to make use of the third element of the perfect plot (that change in fortune results from some great fault) does well to understand this part of the *Ethics*.

The goal is to *be* good, which means to *act* virtuously. All the knowledge in the world about virtues does not measure up against this goal, not merely to know about virtue but rather to act in accordance with virtue. The arguments of the philosophers will not bring most people

---

[6] J. P. Vernant, "Myth and Tragedy," in *Essays on Aristotle's Poetics*, ed. Amelie Oksenberg Rorty (Princeton: Princeton University Press, 1992), 40–1.

to the threshold of virtue. Aristotle is fairly pessimistic here: "The many naturally obey fear rather than shame" (*NE*, 1179b1–20). In the same passage, he suggests that we ought to become good by any other means as well. There is an important sense in which people with the capacity for good choice and bad choice might be directed toward virtue in many ways. For some, philosophical argument will indeed yield virtuous action. For the basest among us, perhaps only fear of punishment will nudge character toward virtuous action. Tragedy is intermediary between the treatise and the stick in the sense that we can actually *experience* fear and pity associated with great fault on the part of a person not so different from ourselves. In this way we are made aware of capacities within us that we might not otherwise acknowledge, as when we awaken shocked from a dream of great error with doubled determination to remain virtuous.

Paying attention to our fear and pity, and becoming thus aware of our own capacity for bad choice and vulnerability to reversal of fortune (without which capacity we could not enjoy the pleasure of good tragedy) do not make us bad. According to Aristotle, not only the good person but even God has the *capacity* for bad things inconsistent with character.[7] Moreover, he thinks it is desirable to have such capacities, and capacity as such is never the origin of evil. But it is tragic ignorance indeed to live unaware both of our capacities and powers and of the right ways to mold character virtuously along with the consequences of not doing so. The answer to such tragic ignorance is education. But moral education requires legislative science, which in turn, Aristotle says, requires both theory and experience. The *Nicomachean Ethics* is theory, as is the *Politics*, but tragedy allows a certain kind of "experience" in areas that, if *actually* experienced in life, would be harmful and immoral (*NE*, 1180a35–1181b5).

Our character does not develop in isolation from that of our neighbors and fellow citizens. This legislative science occurs in the political realm, and in such a realm, concern for the development of virtuous citizens is of great importance. Therefore, in the political halls the philosopher will advise politicians to pay attention to such things as language, rhythm, music, and tragedy. Tragedy works and is of benefit when, in the middle of the well-structured *polis* made up of virtuous citizens, we see and hear the truth of our vulnerability to poor choice and bad fortune

---

7 Aristotle, *Topics*, in Barnes, *The Complete Works of Aristotle*, 126a35–126b3, hereafter cited in text as *Topics*.

and our occasional experience of moral luck of a better variety in which tragedy is averted.

We have seen that Plato claimed that imitation, which is at the heart of poetry, is dangerous, and is so for several reasons. First, it is three removes from the real: it is neither the thing *in itself*, a particular instance of the thing, nor a complete representation of a complete instance of a thing; rather, it is one appearance of a particular instantiation of a form and so represents only a partial truth. Second, it makes unwarranted claims to wisdom, being only an imitation made through words. Poets may understand words but not what the words refer to (poets can portray a physician healing but cannot heal themselves). Through such imitation poets make judgments about good and ill, without providing a good reason why we should believe that a poet knows good from bad. Third, by eliciting feeling in response to mimetic events, imitation interrupts philosophical questioning and panders to the stimulation of emotions through creation of characters and actions that appeal to the mob and are entertaining rather than educational. Fourth, poetic mimesis can deceive us through the seeming beauty wrought by rhythm, meter, and harmony. In short, Plato viewed mimesis as removed from the truth and – insofar as it is distant from the real – distracting the mind from what is best. Plato strove to save people from poetry so that they might be better.

Perhaps the most important way in which Aristotle differs from Plato on these points is that for Aristotle the emotional effects in poetry that come about through mimesis (by which he understood imitation as *true*) function as a threshold and opportunity to acquire habits of appropriate (virtuous) response. For this reason Aristotle instructed the poets on how to use *all* forms of poetry to make people better, insofar as innocent pleasure and appropriate emotions contribute to virtuous character.

True imitation is fundamental to Aristotle's conception of poetry, just as it was to Plato, though to different effect. While Plato argued against the poets that it was not good to devote effort to imitating bad fortune, undesired events, and imperfect character, Aristotle recognized that poetry, being grounded in human nature, could provide an opportunity for instruction that all humans, as human, could readily grasp. This recognition, in turn, relates to the very origin of poetry rooted in human nature, for imitation is natural to people from childhood, and it is natural for people to delight in works of imitation (*Poetics*, 1448b5–10). Starting with these natural capacities and inclinations, and armed with a voice, rhythm, and meter (as discussed in the *Rhetoric*)[8] – poetic elements that naturally appeal to human nature – the poets began this work, and moving from their first improvisations, they improved bit by bit until they hit upon the natural forms of poetry set out in the *Poetics* as an answer to those who would limit poetry. The limitations of poetry should not arise from the potential uses of poetry but rather from excellence internal to poetry well practiced, and imitation should be imitation of things as they are, in which poets use techniques that allow the right emotions to be felt in response to the things represented. The ham-fisted poet might bungle the representation of action, but that problem is with the practice of poetic techniques, not the portrayal of a character acting through poor choices. Good imitation is a response to things as they are. This is the deep connection between the work of learning and exploring the world (as philosophy does) and the work of the poet who, like the philosopher, begins in wonder. Aristotle's inclusive approach to the full range of poetry is fitting, given his capacious interest in everything from politics and dreams to the genitals of insects, the nests of birds, and the generation of bees without copulation.[9]

Whereas Plato gave Homer a rather harsh critique in dialogues such as the *Ion*, Aristotle's stance toward the poet is different. For Aristotle, what is important about Homer is, in part, his role in the progression of poetic development, from poetry's early dithyrambic improvisation and gradual improvement until it reached its natural form. Aristotle provides a definitive discussion of this final and most excellent form in the *Poetics* (*Poetics*, 1449a10–15) . He does not rehearse the whole history leading up to this form because "it would probably be a long piece of work to go through the details" (*Poetics*, 1449a30). To be sure.

Importantly, in this final natural form tragedy imitates not persons but action and life (*Poetics*, 1450a16–21). The characters are there to make action possible, not the other way around. This is why plot is most important, followed by character, thought, and then, least artistic of all, spectacle. Indeed, spectacle is not necessary, has the least to do with the art of poetry, and is something devised more by designers than by poets (*Poetics*, 1450b16–20). Those who use spectacle to share the merely monstrous rather than evoking the proper emotions of pity or fear are out of touch with tragedy (*Poetics*, 1453b1–12). In the *Rhetoric* he says that

---

[8] Aristotle, *Rhetoric*, in Barnes, *The Complete Works of Aristotle*, 1404a20–40, hereafter cited in text as *Rhet.*

[9] Aristotle, *History of Animals*, 615a1, and *Generation of Animals*, 760a1–5, in Barnes, *The Complete Works of Aristotle*.

"in most respects the future will be like the past has been," and on this point he seems especially correct (*Rhet.*, 1394a2–9).

Poetry, then, should not rely on monstrosities, but neither should it rely on merely everyday occurrences. Here Aristotle makes a vital distinction. Historians, he says, describe something that has happened, which, like all historical events, might have ten thousand details. But poets should represent the kind of thing that *might* happen. History presents singular events, but poetry can present universals. For this reason, Aristotle says that "poetry is something more philosophic and of a greater import than history, since its statements are of the nature rather of universals, whereas those of history are singulars" (*Poetics*, 1451a37–b10). It deals with kinds every bit as much as philosophy. Does Socrates want to get at the universal definition of justice? Poetry shows forth a universal type, saying "Behold, the just man." And poetry names the character – as did Plato in presenting his own types. But in presenting such universals, there is in poetry, as in philosophy, no room for the apparently extraneous detail. In both, unlike the reports of history or science where collecting details down to the width of the butterfly's wing is crucial, "that which makes no perceptible difference by its presence or absence is no real part of the whole" (*Poetics*, 1451a35). When Aristotle says that poetry shows forth a universal type and is more philosophical than history, he hits upon a theme that will recur throughout the history of the quarrel – the exercise of both poetic and philosophical gifts constitutes a feeling after and a reaching for patterns, connections, meaning. When plots are constructed to imitate complex actions, the poet is judged to have done well if the action evokes pity or fear through events that follow upon one another (rather than being randomly inserted) but which nonetheless surprise us (*Poetics*, 1452a2–10). One way to put this is to say that the finest plots feel real and seem to be meaningful, with the meaning drawn from the presence of pattern or design.

Aristotle argues that one cannot reason deductively without universals, raising the question, What is the relationship between poetry's use of universals and that of philosophy (*Topics*, 164a10–11)? Universals function at many levels – from that of abstraction to that of sense perception of things as the things are. Stephen Halliwell has argued that universals "inhere, so to speak, as categories of discrimination and understanding, in perceptual cognition. The poet does not deal in abstracted universals, as the philosopher does....Universals should enter into poetry...in a way or on a level which is somewhere between abstraction and common sense experience."[10] We can see universals functioning in poetry, as Halliwell suggests, when we, along with Aristotle, analyze the poetry. But this is a conscious response in thought to universals. Universals emerge in other ways, however, especially among the theological poets. For example, Hesiod places love as a principle among existing things. Others introduce friendship and strife in nature, while others a *deus ex machina*. But though they seem to be getting at points that Aristotle himself writes about in the *Physics* ("The mode of existence and the essence of the separable it is the business of first philosophy to define"),[11] they do so "vaguely…and with no clearness, but as untrained men behave in fights; for they go round their opponents and often strike fine blows, but they do not fight on scientific principles, and so these thinkers do not seem to know what they say" (*Meta.*, 985a11–17).

Another difficulty with poetry is that the early poets told stories and made claims that were simply not true. For example, in their "improvisations," they seemed to be *aiming* at knowledge as Aristotle conceives it, which is in one sense universal and in another sense not. Hesiod and the mythologists assert what is plausible to their own minds, but they leave Aristotle baffled. They assert, for example, that the first principles who are gods and born of gods would become mortal without nectar and ambrosia. But if their existence is dependent on tasting such comestibles, Aristotle points out, how can such gods be thought of as eternal? The quarrel is clear, and here is settled thus: "But into the subtleties of the mythologists it is not worth our while to inquire seriously; those, however, who use the language of proof we must cross-examine and ask why, after all, things which consist of the same elements are, some of them, eternal in nature, while others perish" (*Meta.*, 1000a5–20). This is the starkest dismissal of the early poets that I can find in Aristotle. No doubt he took more seriously some later poets who came after the theological poets. And, indeed, this might simply be a moment of taking the good from among the poets' contradictions, which they seemed to allow themselves.

Elsewhere, though, his tone toward the theological poets is much more patient. In *Movements of Animals*, for example, he takes the images from myth as worthy of serious consideration when he wrestles with the immovable mover of the heavens. There are only two options. The mover of the heavens might be moved itself, in which case it must touch

---

[10] Stephen Halliwell, "Pleasure, Understanding and Emotion," in Rorty, *Essays on Aristotle's Poetics*, 249.

[11] Aristotle, *Physics*, in Barnes, *The Complete Works of Aristotle*, 194b15.

something immovable to get the movement going, or else the mover is indeed immovable, in which case it cannot be part of what is moved – neither in the heavens nor in a part of the heavens, but somehow outside of and other than the heavens. Arguments concerning this question meet problems. It is at this point that he turns to the poets saying, "And the mythologists with their fable of Atlas setting his feet upon the earth appear to have based the fable on intelligent grounds."[12] So Atlas, with feet set on the earth, twirls the heavens around the poles. But the awkward position the poets find themselves in is that the earth ends up not being a part of the universe. With a marvelous Newtonian-sounding observation in physics, Aristotle says, "As the pusher pushes so is the pushed pushed, and with equal force" (*Movements of Animals*, 669b5). So, if Atlas is going to get the whole moving it will have to be with an overcoming force, and unless the immobility of the earth matches that of the whole heavens, when Atlas plants his feet on the earth and pushes hard enough to get the heavens moving, the earth will be pushed out of its place in the center of the universe. And that is a mess. There must be an unmoved mover outside the universe to get the movement going. And for those who insist on keeping the mover inside the universe, Aristotle offers the words of the poet Homer: "Nay, ye would not pull Zeus, highest of all, from heaven to plain, no not even if ye toiled right hard" (*Movements of Animals*, 699b36). Even later in the *Metaphysics*, after the subtleties of the mythologists have been dismissed as unworthy of the labor of close examination, they are found, for better or for worse, to agree with some of Aristotle's contemporaries on the issue of when the good and the beautiful appear and who is first in time (*Meta.*, 1091a30).

Thus, although the early poets might have been in error, their work provided a step in the right direction. Myth provided a whole world in which there was an accounting for all things human and divine, including the forces of the irrational. "Even the lover of myth is in a sense a lover of wisdom, for myth is composed of wonders," and it is also wonder that sets people on the road of philosophy (*Meta.*, 982b5–15). Aristotle as the philosopher clarifies the groping questions, observations, and speculations of these early poets. It is clarity that the philosophical sentence offers, achieved through the philosophical question. The philosophical question is the knife with which the philosopher carves truth from the

---

[12] Aristotle, *Movements of Animals*, in Barnes, *The Complete Works of Aristotle*, 669a27–8, hereafter cited in text as *Movements of Animals*.

vagaries of these early thinkers. And it was Socrates who introduced the dialectical power of the philosophical question, Socrates to whom is ascribed the discovery of inductive arguments and universal definitions (*Meta.*, 1078b25–30). Thus, when the forefathers in the most remote ages tell us through their myths that the whole of nature is enclosed by the Divine, many additions were made about the gods in human or animal form to persuade the masses. But, says Aristotle, "if we were to separate the first point from these additions and take it alone – that they thought the first substances to be gods – we must regard this as an inspired utterance" (*Meta.*, 1074b1–14).

Clarity and the testing of ideas with an eye to achieving truth is the purview of the philosophical question. Stating the truth is the purview of the philosophical sentence. But engaging in that gift of connecting, making metaphors, seeing likenesses – this gift is well exercised in both poetry and philosophy, and it may well be that the philosophers learned the skill from the poets. In the *Topics*, Aristotle instructs that likenesses should be studied first. This habit of using analogy to explore (as one thing is to one thing, so another is to another) is intimately related to the use of metaphors to discover fresh ideas. It is a short leap indeed from the likeness, "as sight is in the eye, so is intellect in the soul," to the metaphor of "the mind's eye." And just as good metaphor brings together apparently disparate things in a meaningful and illuminating way, so "practice is more especially needed in regard to terms that are far apart" (*Topics*, 108a7–15). It is this habit and gift that moves us away from the particular world – of this, then this, then this – to the world of the universal, which is a comprehensible world.[13] In philosophy, this is the search for the middle term, which makes things comprehensible. Socrates is a man. All men are mortal. Therefore Socrates is mortal. This middle term, "All men are mortal" allows us to move from the particular of Socrates before us to deeper knowledge of Socrates, namely, realization that Socrates is mortal. Without the middle term, we can never connect Socrates with mortality. We advance in understanding via the middle term, and just as being a master of metaphor is the greatest thing, in the arena of philosophy "acumen is a talent for hitting upon the middle term in an imperceptible time....For seeing the extremes we become familiar with all the explanatory middle terms" (*Post. Anal.*, 89b10–15).

---

[13] Aristotle, *Posterior Analytics*, in Barnes, *The Complete Works of Aristotle*, 86a30, hereafter cited in text as *Post. Anal.*

During the evolution of the form, there is plenty of room for missteps, and there are pitfalls along the way. Because "the poets tell many lies," it falls to the philosopher to avoid such errors. Within the effort to find what is common among disparate particulars, the philosopher must avoid errors such as homonymy, for this leads to false connections. Skill and understanding are needed as, through experience, universals come to rest in the soul. To describe this process, Aristotle uses a metaphor of his own, though he ends up not being extremely satisfied with it: "The states [of skill and understanding] neither belong in us in a determinate form, nor come about from other states that are more cognitive; but they come about from perception – as in a battle when a rout occurs, if one man makes a stand, another does and then another, until a position of strength is reached. And the soul is such as to be capable of undergoing this.... When one of the undifferentiated things takes a stand, there is a primitive universal in the mind" (*Post. Anal.*, 100a10–15 and 100b1).

The importance of taking such care is that as the philosophers seek their middle terms and abstract universals, and as the poets seek their middle universals (e.g., through metaphor), not all players are equally concerned with what is true, and false connections can pass all too easily for meaningful insight. Consider the topic of dreams. In dreams everyone makes connections between disparate things – the images of the sleepy night world and the events of the world in action. What does Aristotle say about these connections? "Most dreams are...to be classed as mere coincidence, especially all such as are extravagant, and those in fulfillment of which the dreamers have no initiative, such as in the case of the sea fight, or of things taking place far away."[14] Because animals have dreams also (who has not watched the dog seem to run in its sleep?), dreams are not sent by God. Their mystery derives from nature, not divinity, for nature is itself mysterious. The support Aristotle marshals for this conclusion is that the people who actually do foresee the future are of an inferior type, so it cannot be the case that God is responsible for their dreams.

Here the work of the philosopher in abstract universals, the poet in middle universals and metaphor, and the slipshod connections made in the common interpretation of dreams sufficiently resemble each other that it is useful to identify the qualities of each and the

[14] Aristotle, *On Divination in Sleep*, in Barnes, *The Complete Works of Aristotle*, 463a30–463b1, hereafter cited in text as *On Divination in Sleep*.

reasons for the weakness of the inferior type.[15] Aristotle does not disappoint: "Atrabilious persons, owing to their impetuosity, are, when they, as it were, shoot from a distance, expert at hitting; while owing to their mutability, the series of movements deploys quickly before their minds. For as even the insane recite the poems of Philanenis, so what they say and think is connected by mere similarity – e.g. 'Aphrodite, phrodite' – and thus they go on stringing things together" (*On Divination in Sleep*, 464a30–464b5). Given the importance of the abstract universal and the middle term to the philosopher, and the metaphor to the poet, we must maintain a balanced perspective and make intelligent distinctions in order to avoid conflation of such gifts with the utterances of the insane reciter of poems and the "expert" interpreter of dreams whose skill rests on the faculty of observing resemblances.

The *Poetics* follows the *Ethics* and the *Politics* in rational sequence. Tragedy is judged by the standards of the *Ethics*, but it is also true that the poets provide Aristotle with the palette of images and situations from which he draws in elaborating his ethics, his politics, the starting points of his metaphysics, and even his economics. Poetry is poetry, not a primer to ethics, and the pleasure we get from poetry is its own good, but it can be the occasion for encountering interesting ethical structures in human experience, including the experience of God and both fortune and misfortune. So, Aristotle, rather than worrying over whether the citizens are encountering diluted truth, sees the pleasures the poets bring and asks a practical question: how did they do it? Aristotle's manual and taxonomy is still astonishingly useful to the writer.

As with other inquiries, Aristotle "follows the natural order and begins with first principles" (*Poetics*, 1447a13). We need not legislate to correct and overcome the potential bad effects of the poets. Rather, we can educate the poets. It is easy to wonder if the concern Plato had with prying the minds of the Greeks off the luring and alluring effects of the poet to make room for conscious analysis, judgment, and the philosophical question might be answered by Aristotle this way: "Here is how

---

[15] Aristotle ends *Metaphysics* with an exercise in eye rolling at tiny false connections that only *seem* to be in the same category of activity as the discovery of abstract universals and types of great and illuminating metaphors. For example, he finds absurd the connection of sevens: seven vowels, seven strings, seven animals who lose their teeth, seven champions, and so on and so forth. Every seven has an alternate explanation that undoes the sevenness. In fact, some of the sevens are accidental: maybe the Pleias consists of seven stars because we choose to count that way, and indeed other people count more. The insult Aristotle responds with is this: "These people are like the old Homeric scholars who see small resemblances but neglect great ones."

it is done – first this, then that. And see: well structured, the portrayal of tragedy brings us relief and insight." The broad view is presented in the *Rhetoric*, and the nuts and bolts of getting good poetry written are presented in the *Poetics*.

In discussing speech and language, whether in the theater or the court, Aristotle has a clear optimism: things that are true and things that are just tend to prevail in the natural order over things that are untrue and unjust (*Rhet.*, 1355a20). Consider the presentation of a case in court. Rhetoric teaches us that we ought not to appeal to anger or prejudice within the judge (as these have no connection to the facts of the case), but rather should consider actions that are *chosen*, because, as we learned in the *Ethics*, a person and a person's actions are judged well only if based on the fact that the person chose the action (*Rhet.*, 1354a13–20 and 1367b21–5). When we choose actions, we must, to some extent, see the actions as good or as pleasant (*Rhet.*, 1369b20–5). This almost sounds like Socrates' idea that we never choose evil and, perhaps cannot choose evil – but not quite. The difference between Aristotle and Socrates comes in Aristotle's understanding of what constitutes pleasure: "Pleasure is the consciousness through the senses of a certain kind of emotion" (*Rhet.*, 1370a27–30). Pleasure can certainly be linked to wonder, learning, and even the mere state of being free from evil (*Rhet.*, 1370b7). But, though it may be that the world of goodness, if fully comprehended, can consistently be desired whole and without contradiction, when the formula for choosing is that we choose what seems pleasant, choice has been untethered from the good as such. The pleasant can be willed apart from willing the good, and we know about this possibility from tragedy. The tragic character – like ourselves – will choose only what seems pleasant. But the set of things that can seem pleasant includes plenty of room for tragic choice.

In the *Mechanics*, Aristotle quotes the poet Antiphon: "Mastered by nature, we overcome by Art."[16] This is relevant to Aristotle's project, as he draws on the poets in the *Rhetoric* to marshal evidence in support for his discussion not only of pleasure but also of anger, fear, and pity. Pity and fear are symmetrical emotions related to the same events – in the first case, the event as related to others; in the second case, as related to ourselves. When we consider what may cause pain, harm, or destruction at some point in the future, we feel fear, and when we see the same threatening others, we feel pity (*Rhet.*, 1382a22–30 and 1382b26). For

---

[16] Aristotle, *Mechanics*, in Barnes, *The Complete Works of Aristotle*, 847a20.

pity to be pity, the harm must also in some way be undeserved – we do not properly pity the knave undone as a consequence of his knavishness (*Rhet.*, 1385b13–19). This in turn requires that we believe that at least some people are good – otherwise everyone deserves the evil that comes their way (*Rhet.*, 1386a1–4). The philosopher (who wants to understand justice, virtue, and the truth of things as they are) and the poet (who wants to produce great art and achieve a desirable effect) both benefit from understanding these ingredients.

Aristotle offers instructions for the poet who would write a proper tragedy capable of evoking fear and pity, and those instructions are closely linked to the discussion in the ethics regarding what constitutes the goodness and the vulnerability (and resources in adversity) of the good person. Following on this, he says that if you want to write a good tragedy, avoid plots in which a bad person moves from good fortune to good or from good to bad because neither of these evokes fear or pity. Likewise, do not have a truly and thoroughly good person go from good fortune to bad. Rather, a plot should have a character who is sufficiently good that we can identify with him or her, but who is nonetheless capable of making the poor choices that will bring about a change in fortune linked to great fault. Aristotle adds that a good tragedy will not have reversals of fortune diminished through such events as enemies becoming friends, "with no slaying of anyone by anyone" (*Poetics*, 1453a30–7). This blunts tragedy, and it is not only a poetic blunder for failing to evoke pity or fear but also a blunder in truth (because such happy endings are not what we find when misfortune visits us) and a pandering to a weak audience.

Another powerful tool for both poetry and prose is metaphor. Metaphor provides a way to get to new ideas and new facts (*Rhet.*, 1410b10–20). It can allow us to get hold of fresh ideas and a new understanding of things. In his discussion of poetry, he says that "the greatest thing by far is to be a master of metaphor. It is the one thing that cannot be learned from others; and it is also a sign of genius since it implies an intuitive perception of the similarity of dissimilars" (*Poetics*, 1459a5–7). Metaphor addresses things related to some original thing, but in a way that is not obvious, and this aspect is what makes metaphors capable of showing forth both new ideas and facts in a fresh way, "[just] as in philosophy an acute mind will perceive resemblances even in things far apart" (*Rhet.*, 1412a10–12). Indeed, metaphor is even more important to the prose writers because they have fewer resources at hand than the poets. Unfortunately, the use of metaphor cannot be taught, so if you do not have the gift, you do not have the gift. By opening up the arena, writers and poets can most clearly prove their art, or else most miserably fail (*Rhet.*, 1404a5–10 and 1413a9–14).

Despite its importance, metaphor does not get universal praise from Aristotle. In the *Topics* he says bluntly that "metaphorical expression is always obscure" (*Topics*, 139b35). Likewise, in the *Posterior Analytics* he says that one should not argue in metaphors, nor should one define by metaphors, for then one will necessarily argue in metaphors (*Post. Anal.*, 97b36–8). Nevertheless, if a poet, a prose writer, or even a philosopher wants to use metaphor for expression or explanation, there are some guides for its use. The proportional metaphor is the liveliest type. Among Aristotle's many examples is this one: to his fellow Athenians, Pericles says that the vanishing from their country of the young men who fell in battle was "as if the spring were taken out of the year." A good metaphor helps people to see things by showing things in a state of activity, and it surprises people by presenting ideas they were not expecting, the way riddles do, and jokes and lively remarks such as that of Anaxandrides: "Death is most fit before you do deeds that would make death fit for you." Besides the proportional metaphor, there is the simile, the proverb, and the hyperbole, all of which are metaphors of a sort.

Though Aristotle's focus is primarily on poetry, he offers a related discussion of music as an art that is also able to shape character (*Politics*, 1340a5–15). In many ways the language Aristotle uses to discuss music is very similar to that with which he discusses poetry. Not all music is properly expressive of character, however, and his instructions regarding the role of music in the education of citizens sound more like Plato's discussion of the poets. For example, the only music that is to be allowed in education is that which makes people intelligent students of music and so forth; he recommends eliminating the flute, which, because it is so exciting, cannot be expressive of character (an argument bolstered by examples from history and myth, including the observation that the playing of the flute makes the face ugly and contributes nothing to the mind) (*Politics*, 1341a17–1341b7). And yet, though insisting on this in regard to education, Aristotle fully acknowledges and even embraces the fact that the *polis* is made up of not only the free and educated type but also the vulgar, and for these latter it is fine for musicians to perform perverted music that fits their perverted minds so that they too might have the pleasure of relaxation (*Politics*, 1342a17–27).

He says in the *Politics* that music has several purposes and can be studied for the goal of education, intellectual enjoyment, relaxation, recreation, or catharsis (*Politics*, 1341b35–1342a1). There are some associations made in relation to music that are useful for understanding catharsis in the setting of tragic poetry. One association is with healing. Some people are more susceptible to feelings such as pity, fear, and enthusiasm. They can fall into mystic frenzy and then, through sacred melodies, be restored "as though they had found healing and purgation" (*Politics*, 1342a6–11). So it is with melodies that inspire pity and fear (the two feelings most relevant to tragic poetry), and those who go through the experience "are in a manner purged and their souls lightened and delighted." The pleasures brought about by this purifying of the passions (passions that were looked on with suspicion by Plato) are counted as innocent by Aristotle (*Politics*, 1342a15).

As we have seen, Aristotle embraces the poets. However, he also claims that the activity of the intellect is best, and it is this that constitutes the substance of the good life that Aristotle describes in the *Nicomachean Ethics*: "So if among excellent actions...the activity of intellect, which is contemplative, seems both to be superior in worth and to aim at no end beyond itself, and have its pleasure proper to itself (and this augments the activity) and the self-sufficing, leisureliness, unweariedness (so far as this is possible for man), and all other attributes ascribed to the blessed man are evidently those connected with this activity, it follows that this will be the complete happiness of man, if he be allowed a complete term of life (for none of the attributes of happiness is incomplete)" (*NE*, 1177b15–25).

But what exactly is the impact of the poets on that highest subject for contemplation, metaphysics? One is tempted to step out of the poetry-philosophy dichotomy and suggest that each reveals some aspect of the whole called thinking or contemplation. Metaphysics is not a practical endeavor. It is an endeavor that begins in wonder, which is why the philosopher has some affinity with that other form of wonder, the myth. Here again one must be careful – and the one who must be careful is the philosopher. The poets tell many lies, asserting, for example, that the deity is naturally envious, which is not appropriate for a deity (*Meta.*, 982b30–983a10). The point is important because metaphysics is the most honorable science, dealing as it does with divine objects – explanations of first principles and the cause of all things. Though the poets are perhaps listened to, and their suggestions, images, and insights considered, judgment resides with the philosophers. This attention to first principles and to the divine is the finest pursuit available to us: "All the sciences, indeed, are more necessary than this, but none is better" (*Meta.*, 982b30–983a10).

In the end, though it is philosophy that gains access to the highest object of contemplation, Aristotle values the poets and considers tragedy to be a useful part of the *polis*. Tragedies require a character that is sufficiently good, appropriate, real, and consistent (*Poetics*, 1454a16–28), acting among events that are themselves necessary or probable, with the denouement arising out of the plot and not dependent on stage artifice or spectacle (*Poetics*, 1454a38–b6). The poets who are fit to produce such tragedies that evoke such emotions may be unusual: "Poetry demands a man with a special gift for it, or else one with a touch of madness in him" (*Poetics*, 1455a29–39). Aristotle is comfortable with this. He compares through understanding, and he uses taxonomy and observation to instruct the poets without dismissing them from the city, diminishing the need for their "touch of madness," or eliminating the pleasure of tragedy. He embraces Homer, who "more than any other has taught the others the art of framing lies in the right way" (*Poetics*, 1460a19–20). If Plato confronts the poets directly, conquering their poetry with a poetry of his own, Aristotle plays judo, using the momentum of the poets to overcome the poets, without the appearance of "overcoming." He draws from the poets their most useful images and ideas, he advises the poets on how best to practice their art, and he maintains an openness to the possibility that there is an inspiration in poetry that touches importantly on things human and divine. But he is not a poet. Aristotle seems to be a friend to the poets, but one who calls their bluff when they distract from the truth. That said, some of the tasks of the philosopher (in the shadow of the great tragedies) can seem laughable. Aristotle reminds us that "it is the function of the philosopher to be able to investigate all things." Noble indeed. But he then goes on to give an example of the inquiry that falls to the philosopher: "For if it is not the function of the philosopher, who is it who will inquire whether Socrates and Socrates seated are the same thing," to which the poet concerned with tragic life might respond, "And who else, besides the philosopher, cares" (*Meta.*, 1004b1)? In short, Plato answers the poets with a poetry of his own. Aristotle answers the poets (and Plato) with taxonomy, judgment, and instruction. In the work of Aristotle, the poets and philosophers have much to say to each other regarding all things human and divine.

# 3

# Plotinus, Augustine, and Strange Sweetness

"Through a man puffed up with monstrous pride," Augustine writes in his *Confessions*, "you brought under my eye some books of the Platonists, translated from Greek and Latin. There I read, not of course in these words, but with entirely the same sense and supported by numerous and varied reasons, 'In the beginning was the Word and the Word was with God and the Word was God.'"[1] Saint Augustine says that he met Christ, the Logos, in the work of Plotinus and that of his disciple Porphyry. Much later he encountered head-on both the pagan philosophers and the poets in light of this encounter. Indeed, the ancient quarrel between poetry and philosophy is at the heart of the young Augustine's own life and is at the heart of the mature Augustine's encounter with all Greek and Roman literature and philosophy in *The City of God*, where the poets' need for the corrective response of philosophy is rooted in the active malevolence of the demonic. Given the impact of Augustine on subsequent thought and the impact of Plotinus on Augustine, it is worthwhile starting with a brief look at the work of Plotinus.

Addressing the accusation that poetry obstructed the view of truth required that philosophy intervene, yet the intervention has shown that poetry has contributed positively to the ways in which questions are posed in philosophy, especially metaphysics and ethics. Plotinus is an example of how the efforts of philosophy impact the seeing, the knowing, and the speaking of the poet. Among the many ways in which the work of Plotinus has intersected with that of both poets and philosophers is through his offering of a foundation for the training of poets and other "children of the muses" for higher work. He had a genius for

---

[1] Augustine, *Confessions*, trans. Henry Chadwick (Oxford: Oxford University Press, 1991), VII, ix, 13, hereafter cited in text as *Conf.*

metaphor and yet, according to Porphyry, he had bad handwriting and spelling and did not want to reread his own work even once after it was written. He cared for the idea only. In Plotinus we find the philosophical soil in which was grown a poetic strain (in the sense of a type as well as a struggle) that included poets such as Dante, Spenser, Goethe, Wordsworth, and Coleridge.

What constitutes the proper act of the philosopher, what constitutes the proper act of the poet, and how do these differ? In the highest act of contemplation, the work of the philosopher and the work of the poet might seem to converge, making the distinction less sharp. Contemplation requires training. Plotinus instructs the poet, the musician, and the lover on such things that will carry them beyond the appearance to real being. He instructs them in such a way that the local universe is transformed. For one who asks the question how the quarrel manifests itself in Plotinus, the guiding thought and starting place is his statement, "All that is Yonder, is also Here." This is one of the ideas that emerge so powerfully in the works of Dante, Goethe, Coleridge, and Wordsworth. Achieving this sort of vision does not necessarily mean an escape from "Here" but rather a transformation of how we view our local world, a true seeing that is of interest to the philosopher, to the poet, and to the one who climbs the ladder of poetry and philosophy with gratitude toward something that is more than either.

Though many poets have grappled with Plotinus, as Plato and Aristotle have done at the front end of the quarrel with the theological poets, the only poet Plotinus himself grapples with deeply is Plato as myth writer. Plotinus takes on the myths of Plato as myths indeed – as places where truth breaks through uniquely in myth – setting a precedent for the striving of the contemplative who moves from philosophy to poetry and back, all with an aim of getting to something more ultimate. Not so other poets and mythmakers. Plotinus's work is suffused with the tone and timber of those poets grounded in wonder, but despite the many periphrastic passages that incorporate magic, music as sorcery, and prayer as responsive to a universe in which true magic is internal to the whole, specific mention of the work of the poets is rarely made, and when he does quote the poets to his own purposes, he usually does not identify the poet. For example, speaking of a state of the soul before it is lifted up to blessedness, Plotinus says it is stark body, blankness of matter, the absence of being, and "as an author says, 'the execration of the Gods.'" Here, "an author" is Homer, from the

*Iliad* (20.65).[2] Although Socrates humorously claimed to forget where he heard certain phrases, making the point that he cared only about the truth, not about the origin of the statement, in Plotinus one gets the sense that there is no irony at all in the vagueness of "an author" – it just does not seem that important to him. Or again, in writing of the nature of the Good and the vision of the intellectual principle, he says, "We must not run after it, but fit ourselves for the vision and then wait tranquilly for its appearance, as the eye waits on the rising of the sun, which in its own time appears above the horizon – out of the ocean, as the poets say – and gives itself to our sight." In this case too, "the poets" refers to Homer's *Iliad* (*Enn.*, V, 5, 8). He lived among the truths of a higher world, and whatever poetry may do to point toward it, it does not carry the weight of either danger (as for Plato) or usefulness (as for Aristotle).

Plotinus often uses metaphor to reveal something important about the "seeing mind" searching, a posteriori, for images to express something accessed a priori. The "beyond," which opens up so fully in Plotinus, and his deep embrace of Platonic myths as sources of mystery and wisdom are both a kind of *poetic a priori*, a disposition toward finding and expressing meaning in the world, whether from clouds, stars, a beautiful face, an action, a feeling, or a sudden insight – a faculty for opening up new ideas for philosophical contemplation and new means for expressing these ideas. Philosophical contemplation restores the poet to true poetry, recognizing as it does that art arises from the same originals as nature and, indeed, adds where nature is wanting. In sharp (and rare) distinction from Plato, Plotinus sees art not as merely imitating nature but as flowing in parallel from the same source (*Enn.*, V, 8, 1). For this reason, art itself can be a means of exploring what is real as much as nature can. What we find in nature flowing from the higher stages of reality, we find flowing in art as well. Plotinus tends to focus on the *mousikos* as a representative of those who are devoted to fine arts.

For Plotinus, the Truth, which is the whole of truth, layers out into Matter, the Soul, the Intellect, and the One – combining the Good, the demiurge of the *Timaeus*, Aristotle's active intellect, and the Platonic realm of ideas. The One is beyond. Beyond what? Very nearly beyond anything that can be called the "what." Intellect is the realm of real being, Platonic ideas, whatever is as itself, rather than being through

² Plotinus, *The Enneads*, trans. Stephen MacKenna (London: Penguin Books, 1991), V, 1, 2, hereafter cited in text as *Enn.*

something else. The soul is divided into a world soul and individual souls, each of which have an aspect operating through the body, and an aspect that does not operate through the body. At the bottom is the curious category of matter.

What is the highest phase of life? Plotinus answers "intellection," an act that combines all that is characteristic of our individual souls with the character of Divine Mind as we move toward it (*Enn.*, I, 1, 13). The highest gift in this highest life is the Socratic gift of Dialectic (*Enn.*, I, 3, 4). Through this gift, the soul is able to traverse the intellectual realm, distinguishing all forms until, having made this wide-ranging journey, it arrives at an awareness of the unity of all things and takes this as its new object of contemplation. All the stepwise approaches available to science and reasoning may carry on as they wish – this soul has found the better fruits and, by attending to these, can rise higher still. The soul moves forward, and in moving forward, in finding the edge, the clue, the scent, it comes to an awareness of the journey and the very fact of the journey as having a goal, an end, and a fulfillment. Then, it journeys in a new way.

Dialectic as wisdom deals with being, but as intellection it transcends being. This is where philosophy earns its place, and where the absence of philosophy most poignantly underscores the resulting diminution of the training of minds and souls. Dialectic is the best part of philosophy. When a person has reason enabling such intellection, that person has the perfect life. This thing that constitutes happiness is potentially and effectively accessible to all human beings (*Enn.*, I, 4, 4). How do we get to the higher state? The metaphor Plotinus uses to describe the path to this life is that of a road ascending upward with movement that is both metaphysical and moral, an ever-maturing journey inward reaching toward the pure and inmost self that is the interior sanctuary where one returns to one's origins, origins conceived as metaphysical in the sense of principle or cause. All of these lead to "conversion." Undergirding this movement toward conversion is not some fiction that is a joy to play with but rather a real goal, a real union of the soul with the One, the Good. This is where Augustine senses the same presence that he finds in the first chapter of the Gospel of John – "In the beginning was the word."

The Good was that which Socrates found so hard to address directly in the *Republic*. For Plotinus, insofar as anything partakes of ideal form and has a degree of unity and existence, it has something of the Good. This Good is beyond beauty. Even our own intelligence is alien to the deep nature of the Good (*Enn.*, I, 8, 2). Because our intelligence must proceed along the lines of reasonable steps, logical demonstration, and a kind of piecemeal assembling of the whole, we come up against the reality of Being only a bit at a time, and we try to connect the dots. No lifetime is sufficient to the task of connecting the dots. But there is a better way. Plotinus is at pains to pry the mind off the laborious connecting of dots at the expense of grasping fundamental order. The world of the philosopher (and of the poet, the artist, the musician, and the sane person in contact with "common sense") is a world of order and pattern. As humans we are in a rather strange situation because we are half-way between the gods and the beasts, and some of us are more beast-like, others more divine (*Enn.*, III, 2, 8). But even the brutish among us who are weak in that contemplation capable of grasping the highest vision are nonetheless moved by compulsion toward the vision. The move toward this vision animates all. Even when we play, we are working toward the vision. Indeed, when we are engaged in contemplation, this is a kind of play (*Enn.*, III, 8, 1). Some are not capable of this play of contemplation and find themselves hurried along in actions that are yet another version of connecting the dots. But even here, in the pursuit of actions that must finally leave a void, it is the inward longing to see the ultimate, to see that which might be most fully grasped by intellection, which motivates action upon action upon action (*Enn.*, III, 8, 4). Much might be said about this notion of contemplation and play, especially as it contrasts with the feeble alternative of making a way toward the vision through mere action. Work multiplies, and the space for play and for contemplation can be swallowed up by the world of work.

At the top of this hierarchy grasped in contemplation is the Good. At the bottom is Matter. A deep order works in our universe making it "a wonder of power and wisdom, everything by a noiseless road coming to pass according to a law which none may elude" (*Enn.*, IV, 4, 45). Because of this link from the top to bottom, the sense world is transformed and its beauty redeemed by virtue of its relation to the intellectual sphere. Even though attaining the life of the gods means leaving the things of earth behind, on the way it is right to see the sense-realm as "an index of the nobleness of the intellectual sphere, displaying its power and goodness alike" (*Enn.*, IV, 8, 6). Plotinus allows the possibility that, though the earth can distract some from the best life, it can also facilitate advancement and serve as the steps on which we rise toward the higher truth of the intellectual sphere: "There are souls to whom earthly beauty is a leading to the memory of that in a Higher Realm, and these love the earthly as an image [of the Other]" (*Enn.*, III, 5, 1). In this arena, the true poet can advance, using the things of earth to point us toward the things of the Higher Realm.

Purity and completeness of vision is the goal. As we move toward the higher advanced stages of contemplation in the Intellectual Principle itself, the object contemplated becomes progressively a more and more intimate possession of the Contemplated Beings, until finally there is, in the Intellectual Principle, "complete identity of knower and known, and this not by way of domiciliation, as in the case of even the highest soul, but by Essence, by the fact that, there, no distinction exists between Being and Knowing" (*Enn.*, III, 8, 8). As this level of being is approached, there is no limit to the possible objects of contemplation, and so the soul is universal, with "vision not cabined within the bournes of magnitude" (*Enn.*, III, 8, 5).

Plotinus strains toward the Good. Socrates said that he was hesitant to speak directly of the Good because he lacked the wings that might carry that high. But he was willing to discuss what is most *like* the Good. In the same spirit, Plotinus draws on the experience we have in the sense-world as a source for clues regarding how and toward what we proceed in the intelligible world. When we look up to the glory and beauty of the stars and long to search for and find the Maker, we are compelled to ask, in our contemplation of the Intelligible universe, "what Being raised so noble a fabric." This is what leads toward the Good: the source of the Intelligible universe is not an intellect, but rather is before intellect. It is not power, but rather before power. This Maker, which is before power and intellect, "neither needs nor possesses anything, since, needing or possessing anything else, it could not be what it is – the Good" (*Enn.*, III, 8, 11). Not even definitions that are *true* get to it wholly. Whatever true things we might say about the Good, our words and ideas still fall short. What is needed, Plotinus says, is a *direct* intuition of It. This we reach only "by virtue of what in ourselves is like It.... The Intellectual Principle [Divine Mind] in us must mount to its origins" (*Enn.*, III, 8, 9). As he approaches the One, Plotinus finds it necessary to offer images and ever more metaphors, so hard it is to say the thing. One of his most important and central images that captures the vision he is trying to convey is this: "Imagine a spring that has no source outside itself; it gives itself to all the rivers, it is never exhausted by what they take, but remains always integrally as it was; the tides that proceed from it are at one within it before they run their several ways, yet all, in some sense, know beforehand down what channels they will pour their streams.... We form a conception of Its authentic Being from the image of Itself which It has communicated to the Intellect that contemplates It. Yes, this Divine Mind – how beautiful, most beautiful!" (*Enn.*, III, 8, 10).

For those who are not so far along the path, Plotinus says there is room for instruction. How do we get at the Good? The effort requires a great deal of letting go. If one wants to transcend the world of sense and move toward the world of the intellect, all representation of the senses must be put aside. The Good is higher than the intellect, and so, when one wants to transcend the world of the intellect, an analogous requirement holds, but now, rather than putting aside sense represen-tation, one puts aside everything that is of the intellect – no definitions, no sound, presumably no word, which makes the movement exceedingly difficult to write about. He says, "We are in agony for a true expression; we are talking of the untellable; we name, only to indicate for our own use as best we may" (*Enn.*, V, 5, 6).

As a good teacher, Plotinus gives exercises to help the student along the way. He returns again and again, first from this aspect, and then from that aspect. He instructs us to begin by making a mental picture of the universe. Everything in this picture remains what it is (again, all that is Yonder is Here), each thing fully itself and distinct from each other thing, but with all together forming a whole on a single plane – the stars, the earth, the sea, "and all living things as if exhibited upon a transpar-ent globe" (*Enn.*, V, 8, 9).

Once the globe is in sight, imagine now another sphere while hold-ing the first in the mind's eye, but remove magnitude, remove Matter completely. Once this image is in the mind, "call on God, Maker of the sphere whose image you now hold, and pray Him to enter. And may He come bringing His own Universe with all the gods that dwell in it – He who is the one God and all the gods, where each is all, blending into a unity, distinct in powers but all one God in virtue of that one divine power of many facets" (*Enn.*, V, 8, 10). Our own movement depends on understanding that this universe stands as a copy to the original (*Enn.*, VI, 7, 12). Straining toward a better way to express the point, Plotinus says that the Intellectual Principle, through what it receives from above, from the Good, results in, yields, and is bound up with intense Love (*Enn.*, VI, 7, 21). The Beings of this Intellectual Realm received their light from the Good even as the material forms of this world receive their light from the Intellectual Realm.

Plotinus, like Plato, is fairly clear that in speaking of such things, the things spoken of are necessarily diminished. But despite this acknowledgment, it is probably fair to say that even for those who find these strange ideas beautiful in some way, the ideas prompt skepticism. Plotinus is aware of this and says that "we must not overlook what some surly critic will surely bring against us: what's all this: you scatter praises here, there, and everywhere: Life is good, Intellectual Principle is good: and yet when the Good is above them; how can the Intellectual Principle be good?" (*Enn.*, VII, 7, 24). "Etc., etc.," Plotinus might add. For there is no other answer for the surly critic simply because surliness nearly guarantees that the vision will not take, that the necessary conversion will not occur. Conversion is a fundamental characteristic of authentic knowing. The great error that blocks us from this kind of authentic knowing is to think of knowledge as "a mass of theorems and an accumulation of propositions" (*Enn.*, V, 8, 4). This is a kind of knowledge that has its place, but which obscures more than it reveals if it is thought to exhaust the meaning of authentic knowing.

If the question, then, is how to begin, where to start, and by what power the ascent is to be made, Plotinus answers, "The guiding thought is this: that the beauty perceived in material things is borrowed" (*Enn.*, V, 9, 2). This is where the poet finds a tethering point, for the very beauty of the world is a kind of beckoning to which the true poet can give voice. If philosophy reminds the *mousikos* that the beauty here is not to be taken as the end of the story, the poets remind of the beginning, which, even if it is a ladder to elsewhere, is a start, and the journey must start somewhere. The world here can be transformed, as we discover that the very Ideas of which the sense-world is a reflection reside not in some particular place but rather wherever there is a soul, including myself as soul. "Whatever the free soul attains to Here, that is There.... if in the content of the cosmos we mean to include Soul and the Soul-things, then all is Here that is There" (*Enn.*, V, 9, 13). We are already There, if only we knew it. Nor is contemplation of even the highest something reserved for the few; rather, "any conscious being, if the Good come to him, will know the Good and affirm his possession of it" (*Enn.*, VI, 7, 26).

Plotinus knows that there are fully conscious people who, when they hear about the Good, will feel nothing, either because of a lack of understanding or because they are distracted by such things as the pursuit of wealth. What is to be said of such a one? "The answer is that even in his disregard of the good proposed he is with us in setting a good before him, but fails to see how the good we define fits into his own conception" (*Enn.*, VI, 7, 29). And for those who are not distracted by a false view of the things of this world? For these, "Things here are signs; they showed therefore to the wiser teachers how the supreme God is known; the instructed priest reading the signs may enter the holy place and make real the vision of the inaccessible" (*Enn.*, VI, 9, 11).

Such is the world of Plotinian philosophy in brief. What about art and myth in that world? There is beauty that addresses itself to sight and beauty, which, by its melodies and cadences, addresses itself to hearing (*Enn.*, I, 6, 1). There is also beauty of content, action, character, and intellect. And there is a highest beauty in the Good. The Soul has a faculty that perceives, responds to, and affirms beauty (*Enn.*, I, 6, 3). As mentioned earlier, Plotinus identified one who is particularly responsive to beauty as a *mousikos*, which means "of the Muses" and which can refer both to a musician and to a poet (*Enn.*, I, 3, 1). Such influence by the Muses is most relevant when Plotinus addresses harmonic beauty and the cadence arising from "harmonies unheard," which are "determined by the principle whose labor is to dominate matter and bring matter into being" (*Enn.*, I, 6, 3). The artist starts with what is seen and heard in this world, and this points toward a beauty beyond this world. He goes farther, saying that everything, because of its unity and existence, partakes of the good and so has value and can serve to point toward that highest which is the Good (*Enn.*, I, 7, 2).

Plotinus embraces this world as wonderful, despite the "jarring notes" we find in it. He asks, "What reflection [of the Intelligible Realm] could be conceived more beautiful than this of ours? What fire could be a nobler reflection of the fire There than the fire we know Here?...And for a sun figuring the Divine Sphere, if it is to be more splendid than the sun visible to us, what a sun it must be!" (*Enn.*, II, 9, 4). Such is the world transformed and witnessed by converted poets who would catch and sing the sun in flight. The work of the *mousikos* becomes, in this world, a *threshold* to the divine world, the true wisdom, beckoning and reminding even as it points past itself. The one who truly perceives the harmony of the Intellectual Realm cannot fail, if he has any bent toward music, to answer to the harmony in sensible sounds (*Enn.*, II, 9, 14). It would take a dullard to fail to be "gripped by reverent awe" at the order in this lovely world. One who sees the world rightly must conclude that only from Greatness could such greatness spring. The wonder of the poets and philosophers necessarily begins in this world of sense and local beauty, but it does not stop there, or else even the local beauty disappears in a clash of meaningless matter.

When the meaning and structure of the world are seen in the right way, we can view the world as a play written by a poet. "In the dramas of human art the poet provides the words but the actors add their own quality good or bad....As the actors of our stages get their masks and their costumes, robes of state or rags, so a Soul is allotted its fortune and not at haphazard but always under a Reason" (*Enn.*, III, 2, 17). If an actor is "murdered" in a play, no matter: the actor simply changes makeup and takes on the next role. "All human intentions are but play...death is nothing terrible...to die in a war or in a fight is but to taste a little beforehand what old age has in store" (*Enn.*, III, 2, 15). It is not enough that raining atoms suddenly swerve, by chance, and bring about the order and coherence in variety of this world. Plotinus is at pains to pry the mind off of numbing materialism, just as Plato wished to pry the mind off the powerful but lulling rhythms of the poets. In both cases, the aim is to wake up the mind to what is real and true. And so this world is as structured and ordered as a play but is also as light as a play: it is as if we walk out of a tragedy moved, but moving on, we see the world rightly, and the same should happen in life.

Like a pantomimic dancer, life aims at a pattern (*Enn.*, III, 2, 16). Conflicting elements are brought into harmony. Even the damned are "blessed" for being part of a good and just universe – which is no doubt difficult to hear if you happen to be one of the damned. But again, like actors in a play written as an ordered whole, if your role is to exist in the utter darkness and dread of Tartarus, that is part of the overall goodness of the universe in which "everyone throws in his own voice towards a total harmony, singing out a life – thin, harsh, imperfect though it be" (*Enn.*, III, 2, 17). Inequality and suffering are local, but the whole is good. The Intellectual Principle is one and good even as the hooded executioner raises the ax over the neck of a husband and father unjustly convicted of a crime by the state: "Even as things are, all is well." Look around and see the details not as following from chance but as authored in a divine act. See "the marvelous art shown not merely in the mightiest works and sublimest members of the All, but even amid such littleness as one would think Providence must disdain" (*Enn.*, III, 2, 13). This concept of the world animates the poet, pulling animals, insects, waterfalls, mountains, stars, leaves, and "the diversity of exquisite Bloom" into a kind of poetry and art that cannot be exhausted or finished. Ideas such as this deeply impacted Augustine in his understanding of a providence that reaches all the way down to the most frail and perishable of things.[3]

---

[3] Augustine, *The City of God*, trans. R. W. Dyson (Cambridge: Cambridge University Press, 1998), X, 14, hereafter cited in text as *City*.

Before moving to Augustine's thought, there is a bit more to say about conversion of the poet. There is a gap between the sensible world and the intelligible world. The gap is one that reaches the roots of being. One comes to see this rightly through conversion. The power driving this conversion is something active we discover in our souls to which we must pay attention. "As speech is the echo of thought in the Soul, so thought in the Soul is an echo from elsewhere: that is to say, as the uttered thought is an image of the soul-thought, so the soul-thought images a thought above itself and is the interpreter of the higher sphere" (*Enn.*, I, 2, 3).

The *mousikoi*, those artists who are "of the Muses," must be led upward, and so they require conversion. The poet, the musician, and other artists who are *mousikoi* are "exceedingly quick to beauty, drawn in a very rapture to it" (*Enn.*, I, 3, 1). The starting points for such a one are harmony, rhythm, and design. The poet must be converted from the lower world, and then travel along the path toward a vision of the Good. The poet does not know at the outset that Absolute Beauty draws the soul toward local beauty in the production of art. As is true for the true lover, a poet must not be "spellbound" and "bewildered" by some single embodied form but through conversion be led toward the wider presence of beauty, and then toward what is Absolute (*Enn.*, I, 3, 2). Even the metaphysician, "winged already and not, like those others, in need of disengagement," nonetheless needs a guide (*Enn.*, I, 3, 3).

The poet starts with local form, local beauty, and this local beauty becomes the starting point, when philosophy as the love of wisdom is planted in the poet's soul. The poet is still drawn toward beauty, but when instructed by the true philosopher, the poet can begin to see through local beauty to the Absolute Beauty. In producing art, music, or poetry, the *mousikos* reveals the Absolute Beauty and the harmonies from There, just as nature does, and sometimes better than nature does. From the poet we learn through parable, as when he tells about Calypso, "not content to linger for all the pleasure offered to his eyes and all the delight of sense filling his days," and instructs us to "flee then to the beloved Fatherland" (*Enn.*, I, 6, 8). Plotinus then interprets the point to us saying this Fatherland is "There," the place from which we have come, the divine world. In this way poetry can prepare the soul for vision. The soul begins in a state of weakness that makes it unable to "bear the ultimate splendor." But it progresses by being trained through noble tasks and true works of beauty made by people with good souls and, then, by looking into the souls from which this beauty emanates. Conversion involves turning round your own soul, and if that beauty is not apparent, then shaping your soul until it is beautiful (*Enn.*, I, 6, 9): "Never can the soul have a vision of the First Beauty unless itself be beautiful. Therefore let each become godlike and beautiful who cares to see God and Beauty.... The Primal Good and the Primal Beauty have one Dwelling Place, and thus, always, Beauty's seat is There" (*Enn.*, I, 6, 9). The lesser beauties are training for the soul ultimately to see the Primal Good and Beauty.

This effort of fleeing, however, must be rightly understood. It is not a matter of fleeing the earth and our life here. Rather, it is a matter of living our lives here well (*Enn.*, I, 8, 7). Dwelling in the divine world is something that can happen on earth and can transform our vision of our earth. As we move toward this highest realm, our poetry and music are likewise transformed, and "we hymn the Divinities of the Intellectual Sphere, and, above all these, the Mighty King of that dominion whose majesty is made patent in the very multitude the gods" (*Enn.*, II, 9, 9).

Poetry of the sort we usually find in the world makes use of metaphor, but it also functions as a metaphor in the work of Plotinus. So considered, we know that actors ought not to add words to a poet's drama, an act that would suggest that the poet had not done an adequate job of writing the play in full. And if the actors do add words, they cease being actors and become the poet – a very different role because the poet foreknows the words of all the actors, whereas a character within a play knows only his or her own words (*Enn.*, III, 2, 18). So, act the part you are given, for without being the poet, you cannot know the truth of the play as a whole – as noble princes may be the yield of adultery, and noble cities follow the wicked destruction of our own.

The poet and the poem are an image of the whole. And the very act of imaginatively producing worlds in words is a power beyond nature but still only intermediary. Nature merely produces – it neither knows nor imagines. Imagination is inferior to intellection, and it is not the highest power of the soul, but is rather on the way from nature to the highest realm of intellection. This intermediary power can be altered, shaped, and in some sense converted and redeemed by the soul's exercise in the Intellectual Realm (*Enn.*, V, 8, 1). Aristotle identified two kinds of imagination – that which depends on sense perception and that which depends on thought.[1] Likewise, Plotinus conceives of this intermediary

---

[1] Aristotle, *Movement of Animals*, in *The Complete Works of Aristotle*, ed. Jonathan Barnes (Cambridge: Cambridge University Press, 1988), 702a18.

faculty as functioning in two distinct ways. It looks below itself and receives images of matter, and it looks above itself to receive images of thought. Though it is the case that the imagination is intermediary, it is also true that some artists are better, some worse, and imagination is better off converted and transformed so that a higher art is made: "In the end, the sorriest craftsman is still a maker of forms, ungracefully" (*Enn.*, III, 8, 7).

In a passage that intrigued Coleridge,[5] Plotinus has nature tell us why it brings forth its work, beginning with the statement, "It would have been more becoming to put no question, but to learn in silence just as I myself am silent and make no habit of talking" (*Enn.*, III, 8, 4). Nature sees and in that silent gaze brings forth the natural world. "As with my Mother (the All-soul) and the Beings that begot me so it is with me: they are born of Contemplation and my birth is from them, not by their act but by their Being; they are the loftier Reason-Principles, they contemplate themselves and I am born" (*Enn.*, III, 8, 4). A study of nature shows that contemplation is the process of coming to be. This view of nature can improve the poetic imagination for those like Coleridge who look to such philosophical insights, aware that "it is neither possible nor necessary for all men, or for many, to be philosophers. There is a philosophic (and, inasmuch as it is actualized by an effort of freedom, an artificial) consciousness that lies beneath or (as it were) behind the spontaneous consciousness natural to all reflecting beings."[6] This is the sage, and the sage "is the man made over into Reason; to others he shows his act, but in himself he is vision; such a man is already set towards what is one and at rest and finds all things within" – especially as the knower's faculty, in knowing, becomes one with the object of its knowledge (*Enn.*, III, 8, 6).

So the imagination of the artist has the outward-looking phase and the inward-looking phase, and to one who understands, insofar as knowing makes the knowing faculty one with the known, even the knowledge of the outer world is inner knowledge. Plotinus says, "The sensitive principle is our scout; the Intellectual Principle our King" (*Enn.*, V, 3, 3). The highest principle, the Good, if it can be spoken of at all, cannot be spoken of as the object of a pursuit, placed in among other things which come from here and go to there, toward which we may be active in our striving after. Rather, we do what preparative work we can, the work

5 Samuel Taylor Coleridge, *Biographia Literaria*, ed. H. J. Jackson (Oxford: Oxford University Press), XII, 284.
6 Ibid., XII, 283.

of conversion, "and then wait tranquilly for its appearance as the eye waits on the rising of the sun, which in its own time appears above the horizon – out of the ocean, as the poets say – and gives itself to our sight" (*Enn.*, V, 5, 8). The conversion is a conversion to true seeing as well as a conversion to readiness, patient anticipation, and a willingness to stake a life on the possibility of a vision that, though neither guaranteed nor in our control, is above all else that might be accessible to a life. Beyond Beauty, understanding the nature of the Good can help the converted poet toward the serenity of contemplation. And then something remarkable occurs, and we no longer need to strive. "The Good is gentle and friendly and tender, and we have it present when we but will. Beauty is all violence and stupefaction; its pleasure is spoiled with pain, and it even draws the thoughtless away from the Good....the Good is the older – not in time but by degree of reality" (*Enn.*, V, 5, 12). Beauty can distract, or it can enable. The works of the *mousikos* can hinder by directing the vision earthward without reference to the higher realm or, in the work of the converted, point one toward what transcends even the intellectual realm, in which case all of earth is thrown in as well.

Here all human striving after images to express what is most real reaches its limit, for all images are necessarily less. As gold can be represented only by gold, so with this primal Beauty. "In the same way we learn in this matter from the purified Intellect in ourselves, or, if you like, from the gods and the glory of the Intellect in them" (*Enn.*, V, 8, 3). This is a godly inspiration, a *theia mania*[7] that may yield a poetry able to wing the soul higher, looking further into heaven. Socrates said, "Of that place beyond the heavens none of our earthly poets has yet sung, and none shall sing worthily,"[8] but philosophy presses poetry toward this unattainable speech and even takes on the language of poetry as poetry takes up the content of philosophy. The whole of wisdom is the truth by which we can best understand the work we do here, whether it is the work of the philosopher through dialectic or that of the poet writing a play, the musician writing music, or the sculptor shaping stone. Wisdom presides over all of these activities, and as the philosopher moves toward wisdom through dialectic and the soul is trained to see, the artist draws on a wisdom that, like the wisdom of the whole, "is not a wisdom built-up of theorems, but one totality; not a wisdom consisting

---

[7] Plato, *Symposium*, trans. Michael Joyce, in *The Collected Dialogues*, ed. Edith Hamilton and Huntington Cairns (Princeton: Princeton University Press, 1963), 218e5.

[8] Plato, *Phaedrus*, trans. R. Hackforth, in Hamilton and Cairns, *The Collected Dialogues*, 247c.

of manifold detail coordinated into a unity, but rather *a unity working out into detail*" (*Enn.*, V, 8, 5; emphasis added). This is the fundamental aesthetic principle governing the relationship of the *mousikos* (and art in general) to philosophy. Primal Beauty itself is a unity, "entire and omnipresent as an entirety" (*Enn.*, V, 8, 8). And so, when the works of the artist are made, through these occur discovery, uncovering, revealing. And when any unity deriving from wisdom breaks into the world, the philosopher will do well to pay attention. A poetic vision, then, is this thing that gives access to and clues about a unity, and it is worthy of testing with the philosophical question.

When Porphyry observes the somewhat careless and offhanded way that Plotinus writes, refusing to revise and craft language, perhaps he writes this way because he is less tempted than was Plato to view language as anything more than an image of the true, a tool in service to the path toward truth. And again, perhaps the quarrel of philosophy and poetry was so strident in Plato precisely because Plato was so drawn to the language of poetry. But Plotinus, when he writes, treats language as a slightly blunt instrument, inadequate for the task at hand, and yet the best we have at the moment; thus, "we must be patient with language; we are forced for reasons of exposition to apply to the Supreme terms which strictly are ruled out; everywhere we must read 'so to speak'" (*Enn.*, VI, 8, 13). So it is that the spirit of Plato's *Seventh Epistle* shows up again. "'Not to be told; not to be written': in our writing and telling we are but urging toward it" (*Enn.*, VI, 9, 4). All language is only pointing down the road. But the aim is neither the questioning and testing of philosophy nor the image, rhythm, metaphor, or tale of poetry. The point is rather seeing as an act of one who has chosen to step forward from the threshold toward which poetry, philosophy, and the quarrel between the two has led. And Plotinus tells us that when we reach this Supreme height, having stepped up on the rungs given to us in music, art, poetry, dialectic, and love, and having chosen the act of seeing, "this is the life of gods and of the godlike and blessed among men, liberation from the alien that besets us here, a life taking no pleasure in the things of earth, the passing of solitary to solitary" (*Enn.*, VI, 9, 11).

So we reach toward the gods. But there is a surprise in store among those deeply influenced by Plotinus when God likewise reaches out, and while we strive to be like the gods, God becomes a man. This is the point at which Platonic philosophy as presented in Plotinus meets Christianity in the mind of Augustine.

Augustine was a professor of grammar and literature, trained in rhetoric, a writer who used rhythm in his prose and who saw skill with words as a gift from God, but one that could be used instrumentally and deliberately. For him, not only can *words* serve as signs, but so can all the world – all things are full of signs pointing beyond themselves. This is a notion rooted in Plotinus as read and received by one who knows God. In *Confessions*, where Augustine shows us a way to think about and live conversion rooted not in myth, poetry, or fable but in the very truth of God who is the origin of all that is while being personal, the influence of Plotinus shows up in the very first paragraph where God makes us such that our deepest desire is to praise God, and as with Plotinus, for whom the soul rests in the One, "our heart is restless until it rests in you" (*Conf.*, I, i, 1). Again, in the very last paragraph, we hear that God is good, and that only God enables us to understand this, as we in our longing stand on the threshold: "Yes indeed, that is how it is received, how it is found, how the door is opened" (*Conf.*, XIII, xxxvi, 51).

Augustine hated Greek literature when he was taught it as a boy. But he loved Latin literature, learned to write whatever he wanted, and found himself moved most deeply by poetry – weeping over the death of Dido while shedding not a tear for his own lost soul (*Conf.*, I, xii, 19). Literature can distract from more useful studies, and when it does, it becomes sin (*Conf.*, I, xii, 22). But it is not merely when poetry distracts from useful study that it is sin: its content likewise can be sin, as when Homer portrays the gods as committing immoral acts – an argument that is central to his quarrel with the poets in *The City of God* (*Conf.*, I, xvi, 25). The words themselves are not the problem, and indeed they are "like exquisite and precious vessels, but the wine of error is poured into them for us by drunken teachers" and these are "poetic fictions" (*Conf.*, I, xvi, 26). Mythological pictures are formed by an extension of our imagination's power to make images of real objects, but these great mythological entities do not exist and are "empty phantoms" (*Conf.*, III, iv, 10). When verses and poems are seen for what they are – stories that may delight, but which we do not take as fact – they can be valuable. It is when these myths are actually believed that they become dangerous, and this is how Augustine ended up believing the false myths of the Manichees (*Conf.*, III, iv, 11).

When Augustine was younger, he wanted to write poetry according to rules of meter that were "same rules at all times" (*Conf.*, III, vii, 14). He even won a poetry contest, in which the crown was awarded by a proconsul and physician named Helvius Vindicianus, who also attempted to persuade Augustine that astrology was bogus (*Conf.*, IV, iii, 5). Unfortunately, the only formal poetry of Augustine's that we have now is in *The City of God*, a poem in praise of the Paschal candle: "These are Thy gifts: they are good, for Thou who art good hast created them. Nothing in them is from us, apart from the sin which arises when we neglect the right order, and love that which Thou hast made instead of Thee" (*City*, XV, 22). He won this poetry contest despite rejecting the aid of a soothsayer who offered to ensure victory for a fee (*Conf.*, IV, ii, 3). Of course, much of what he wrote outside the formal limits of poetry is, in the deepest sense, poetic.

In his youth, Augustine began to think about beauty, and even wrote a book called *The Beautiful and the Fitting* which, unfortunately, he somehow lost (*Conf.*, IV, iii, 20). But in thinking about beauty, though he was, as he says, far from truth, the older Augustine recognizes that the younger Augustine was "straining, sweet truth, to hear your internal melody" (*Conf.*, IV, xv, 27). Meanwhile, he encountered the philosophers known as the Academics, who taught that everything is a matter of doubt and that truth lies beyond the capacity of human understanding (*Conf.*, V, x, 19). This skepticism gave him the tools to question (and leave) the Manichees, but it left him in a state of fluctuating doubt. It was in the middle of this tension between his "listening" for an internal melody and the power of philosophical doubt that he decided to become a catechumen of the Catholic Church "until some clear light should come by which I could direct my course" (*Conf.*, V, xiv, 25).

In this journey, Augustine discovered the inward turn. An interesting observation on his part is the silent reading of Ambrose, the reasons for which Augustine and his friends did not understand (*Conf.*, VI, xvi, 26). Nor was he yet capable of embracing that beauty which is accessible only through inward discernment. But he was ready to meet Plotinus through whom a peculiar conversion was made possible. Here, though not in the same words, he found expressed the Son of God, the Logos, although the books only approached the threshold because the full knowledge of Jesus was not present (*Conf.*, VII, ix, 14). That said, the Platonists turned Augustine inward, where he found an immutable light above mind and soul that was his maker and source. "The person who knows the truth knows it, and he who knows it knows eternity. Love knows it" (*Conf.*, VII, x, 16). With this discovery, a new world opened for Augustine, and he would come to read the physical world, as well as the thoughts and words of the philosophers and poets, in a new way. Although at first he was not stable in his enjoyment of God, his new inward awareness of the transcendent helped him to ascend from "swarms of imaginative fantasies" to the power of reasoning and to affirm the unchangeable as preferable to the changeable (*Conf.*, VII, xvii, 23).

He was ready to turn to a study of sacred writings. God wanted Augustine to encounter Plotinus before he encountered Paul the apostle (*Conf.*, VII, xx, 26). When he did encounter Paul, he found all of the truth of Plotinus, redeemed and made full by the grace of God. Now he understood the Good, but far from the character of the Platonic Good, here the Good was revealed as God, one to whom Augustine might sing hymns and psalms and in whom he might find salvation (*Conf.*, VII, xxi, 27). For conversion to occur, he needed to reach a crisis of will. He found his very bones yearning to enter into a covenant with this God, and he was distressed that he had not yet done so. "But to reach that destination one does not use ships or chariots or feet" (*Conf.*, VIII, viii, 19). When finally the answer comes to the question "how long, how long is it to be? . . . Why not now?" the conversion is accomplished through a confirmation of what Augustine takes as a divine oracle through a child's voice from a nearby house – "pick up and read, pick up and read" – and using a practice that was close to the sortilege used by pagans with the poetry of Virgil and by Christians with the Bible (often to the discomfort of church leaders, including Augustine), he opened the Bible and read the first passage that his eyes fell upon: "Not in riots and drunken parties, not in eroticism and indecencies, not in strife and rivalry, but put on the Lord Jesus Christ and make no provision for the flesh in its lusts" (*Conf.*, VIII, xii, 29). Thus was it done.

This conversion and what followed in Augustine's process of discovery deeply affected the tenor of the quarrel between poetry and philosophy in his work. He decided to retire from his work as a "salesman of words in the markets of rhetoric" (*Conf.*, IX, 11, 2). His lungs had weakened because of teaching too much literature (*Conf.*, IX, ii, 4). A new silence became his desire, in which flesh, birth, water, air, and even the heavens themselves fall quiet, and without tongues, angels, thunder, or symbolic utterances, without mediation, "we extended our reach and in a flash of mental energy attained the eternal wisdom which abides beyond all things" (*Conf.*, IX, x, 25). Unfortunately such flashes do not last long – a regret Plotinus shared. But like Plotinus, having caught a glimpse, the world was transformed for him and the wind, the heavens, the sun, the moon, the stars all pointed beyond themselves to God who made them. In one of his finest sentences, Augustine says, "My question was the attention I gave them, and their response was their beauty" (*Conf.*, X, vi, 9).

But Augustine then asked the same question Plotinus had asked: why isn't everyone spoken to in the same way by this beauty? The world does not change, and the voice of the created world, which is its beauty, is always the same. It is not change in the world that accounts for the difference. "It is rather that the created order speaks to all, but is understood by those who hear its outward voice and compare it with the truth within themselves" (*Conf.*, X, viii, 10). The repository of this truth for which we search is found in "the fields and vast palaces of memory" (*Conf.*, X, viii, 12). Here all perceptions of the senses are preserved – shape, light, sound, smell, taste. All the skills learned in the liberal arts are stored in the mysterious cavern of memory. Indeed, "what literature is, what the art of dialectical debate is, how many kinds of question there are – all that I know about these matters lies in my memory in this distinctive way" (*Conf.*, X, ix, 16). Learning and thinking constitute an ordering of what we find in memory (*Conf.*, X, xi, 18). He tells us that memory is not independent of the mind, and when he tries to explain the relation of the mind to memory, he trips a bit on a silly illustration, calling memory "the stomach of the mind" where experiences such as sadness and gladness are stored but not tasted, like bitter and sweet foods we have swallowed: "It is ridiculous to think this illustration offers a real parallel; nevertheless, it is not wholly inapposite" (*Conf.*, X, xiv, 21). Humility and a sense of humor are useful in these sorts of endeavors.

The fascinating thing about the conundrums and mystery regarding memory is that the mystery is not something located in the remotest heaven – the mystery is me. "It is I who remember, I who am mind. But what is nearer to me than myself? Indeed the power of my memory is something I do not understand when without it I cannot speak about myself" (*Conf.*, X, xvi, 25). Nonetheless, this mind is I myself. But this inward mystery, this mind which is I, is the scaffolding we scale to reach the God who is our source and our deepest longing, the one who transforms and redeems all the world, all images and all the content of memory by revealing, and indeed being, the purpose of it all. Mystery with purpose, aiming at something true and finding joy in the effort, is the mystery Augustine has discovered. Now what is unknown beckons, but the calling is farther in and farther up. "Here I am climbing up through my mind towards you who are constant above me. I will pass beyond even that power of mind which is called memory, desiring to reach you by the way through which you can be reached, and to be bonded to you by the way in which it is possible to be bonded" (*Conf.*, X, xvii, 26).

This is the conversion from the inside, which is why it is so useful to have *Confessions* as a preface to *The City of God*, where – especially in the first half – the quarrel between poetry and philosophy is central. In a passage known (in Latin) for its beauty, rhymes, and poetic rhythms, Augustine captures the heart of the confessions: "Late have I loved you, beauty so old and so new: late have I loved you. And see, you were within and I was in the external world and sought you there, and in my unlovely state I plunged into those lovely created things which you made. You were with me, and I was not with you. The lovely things kept me far from you, though if they did not have their existence in you, they had no existence at all. You called and cried out loud and shattered my deafness. You were radiant and resplendent, you put to flight my blindness. You were fragrant, and I drew in my breath and now pant after you. I tasted you, and I feel but hunger and thirst for you. You touched me, and I am set on fire to attain the peace which is yours" (*Conf.*, X, xxvii, 38).

He was now liberated. Even toward what he called "the pleasures of the ear," which had earlier subjugated him, he was now free, able to enjoy "the sounds whose soul is your words," but to walk away when he wished. Chant became the servant of God and moved the soul to piety (*Conf.*, X, xxxiii, 49). Even then the old dangers lurked, and he tended sometimes to be rather severe. In the end, the middle way was struck because "through the delights of the ear the weaker mind may rise up towards the devotion of worship" (*Conf.*, X, xxxiii, 50). Emerging again was the theme (and guiding principle) that the poets (and musicians and artists) get at something important and valuable but do not, within their art, find the truth that leads to right use. As with Plotinus, Augustine agreed that the work of the artist comes from that very beauty, higher than the soul, for which the soul longs. This higher beauty provides the criteria for artistic judgment, "but [the artists] do not draw from there a principle for the right use of beautiful things. The principle is there, but they do not see it" (*Conf.*, X, xxxiv, 53).

Small things of the world – a lizard catching flies or a spider waiting in its web – first fascinate and then provoke praise (*Conf.*, X, xxxv, 57). Everything points toward and leads to God. There is a flavor to the truth just beyond the threshold of these many things that usher us toward God. Again, it is transient, but for those who have tasted it, all the world becomes a poem, and even the experience of no longer tasting it provokes the experience of longing, which is second only to the experience of tasting. "And sometimes," Augustine says about this inner awareness of what Plotinus called "There," "you cause me to enter into an extraordinary depth of feeling marked by a strange sweetness. If it were brought to perfection in me, it would be an experience quite beyond anything in this life. But I fall back into my usual ways under my miserable burdens" (*Conf.*, X, xl, 65). A person so converted turns back to the world with a new way of seeing and can explore the world anew, which Augustine does.

Words can bring us to the threshold of truth about God and about the "heaven of heaven," compared to which "the heaven of our earth is earth" (*Conf.*, XII, ii, 21). But words never get us past the threshold. Some things cannot be said in words, which can only point, approximate. "Human thinking employs words in this way; but its attempts are either a knowing which is aware of what is not knowable or an ignorance based on knowledge" (*Conf.*, XII, v, 5). From such starting points, reason questions, tests, and abstracts. But no progress toward the truth of God can be made if the words and images are mistaken for the truth. Even sacred words from Scripture – about which Augustine says the author reveals truth that is never incorrect – are still words that we interpret as well as we can with sincerity, though an interpretation does not hold the weight of Scripture (*Conf.*, XII, xviii, 27). The sacred mysteries conveyed by the words of Scripture are not finally mysteries that can be fully contained in words. And so these words have a special role in human seeking and are open to a variety of interpretations.

The gap between words about God and the truth of God is what makes searching possible and interpretation necessary. But it is a redeemed back-and-forth between the words and the truth that the words are about: "My weight is my love. Wherever I am carried, my love is carrying me. By your gift we are set on fire and carried upwards: we grow red hot and ascend" (*Conf.*, XIII, ix, 10). God is the Good. This highest truth is accessible to us only through the enabling of God. Philosophy and poetry go back and forth in the grappling ascent up the mind toward God. But in the end we are still brought only to a new threshold. How do we ever truly cross? "Only you can be asked," Augustine ends in praise, "only you can be begged, only on your door can we knock" (*Conf.*, XIII, xxxviii, 53).

It was a long journey for Augustine. But once fully converted, he could revisit the entire world of poetry and philosophy, first traversed in sin and blindness, and understand it in a new way. In this redeemed vision, the quarrel has a renewed tension and urgency, and this renewal of the quarrel is central in the first half of Augustine's massive work, *The City of God*.

In *The City of God*, the quarrel becomes a spiritual battle, and the stakes are high, eternal. In contrasting the city of God, which transcends time and space, with the earthly pagan city, it is not surprising that the poets show up early in the fight – indeed, Virgil shows up on page one. Virgil fares pretty well. Not so the earlier poets who, Augustine says, speak with the voices of demons. The latter are unfavorably compared to the prophets who become the poets of the city of God, playing the role the theological poets once played, making available in the language of humanity the very voice and will and character of God.

The quarrel centers on truth and falsity, the true God and the false gods, and finally happiness and the relationship of happiness to the true God. Virgil tells us that Diomedes and Ulysses slayed the grandsons of the topmost citadel, seized the sacred image, "and with bloody hands [dared] to touch the fillets of the virgin goddess" (*City*, I, 2). Believing in such gods who, far from protecting humanity, actually need soldiers to protect them is imprudent. Why did the Greeks believe in such gods, and why was Rome entrusted to these gods? When the poets spoke about these vanquished gods, they "were not merely lying to serve their own purposes. Rather, they were men of intelligence whom truth had compelled to make confession" (*City*, I, 3). Virgil is taken seriously when he speaks of these gods, and Augustine supposes himself to be doing something meaningful when he considers all that has been said about these gods and ultimately about the true God. That is, for Augustine there is something important occurring in poetry that must be examined thoroughly and attended to, but with caution, for these waters are treacherous and one's very soul is on the line, as he showed in his *Confessions*.

Book I confronts these vanquished gods and is immediately suffused by confrontation with the poets, for it is among the poets that these gods tend to show up. The gods that show up in the theaters of Rome are not fictional, according to Augustine, and this is what makes them even more dangerous. These gods are, in fact, "noxious demons," and far from disapproving the vain and lustful acts depicted on the stage, they actually command the poets to write these plays (*City*, I, 32). And so the poets *must* be challenged, and Augustine will spend hundreds of pages doing so. There is a shorter route to truth and redemption: if humanity, whose understanding is weak, would "submit that weakness to wholesome doctrine as to a medicine, it would, with divine aid, be healed by the intercession of faith and godliness" (*City*, II, 1). But because this does not happen as it should, the poets must be refuted through long discussion about matters that should already be clear. This is the task of philosophy.

Augustine notes that "the philosophers at least tried to discover the means by which a good life is to be lived and blamelessness attained. Surely, then, it would have been more just to vote divine honors to them rather than to the gods" (*City*, II, 7). Better to praise Plato than the deeds of Jupiter. This is not so easy when the gods demand otherwise: for example, "it was not merely by their own ignorant submission that the Romans introduced into the rites of their gods those displays in which the fictions of the poets hold sway. Rather, the gods themselves, by imperious commands and, in a certain sense, by extortion, caused these things to be solemnly performed for them and consecrated in their honor" (*City*, II, 8).

Cicero in *De Republica* reports that one reason the shameful acts in the theater won approval is that "the manner of the times already accepted such things" (*City*, II, 9; Cicero, *De Rep.*, 4.10.11). The poets could not say such things about people – this was a capital offense. However, "the gods not only patiently, but indeed willingly, suffered themselves to be lashed by the slanders and maledictions of the poets" (*City*, II, 12). In Rome, the actors who portrayed the gods in this way were considered infamous, and yet the poets were honored. Augustine thinks we should "award the palm" to a Greek, to Plato, who would not tolerate the corrupting influence of the poets on the citizens and who threw the poets out as the root cause of the problem. The Romans did well in not allowing the poets to bring disgrace on people, and in excluding actors from membership in the city, but they did poorly insofar as their law allowed the poetic deception and disgrace in theatrical performance demanded by their gods. Augustine again quotes Cicero: "When the poets win the applause and approbation of the people as if it were that of some great and wise master, what darkness falls, what fears burst in, what desires they kindle!" (*City*, II, 14; Cicero, *De Rep.*, 4.9.9). In response to all of this debased activity of the gods, the poets with their stories of gods having intercourse with humans and the rousing support of the citizens for it all, Augustine echoes Plotinus in entreating them to "seize now the Heavenly Country," to leave their gods and enter a sanctuary where there is no vestal flame and no statue of Jupiter, but where the one true God dwells, ready to forgive their sin. This God, he says, quoting the poet Virgil for his own need, "will set no bounds or duration to your state, but will grant empire without end" (*City*, II, 29; Virgil, *Aeneid*, 1.278). Though he quotes a poet – *the* poet – to make his point and to persuade that the false and deceitful gods should be despised, he still has a long battle to do with the poets and their stories.

"Someone will say: 'do you really believe all this?' Of course I do not believe it. After all, Varro himself, our adversaries' most learned man, comes close to admitting that these stories are false.... He asserts, however, that it is advantageous for states if brave men believe, albeit falsely, that they are offspring of the gods" (*City*, III, 4). If these lies are advantageous to the citizens, it is reasonable to consider them intended for this purpose. Varro is a very useful guide, and it is important for the thinker and seeker after truth to stay open to the truth from any quarter. "Though fabulous, the songs of the poets nonetheless described the behavior of the demons in a way that is not always at odds with the truth" (*City*, III, 11). The challenge is to sort out what is true from what is false. Because Augustine is responding to the sack of Rome (resisting the idea that it was the Christian Church that brought this about), the scale of the quarrel is enormous, now being between, on the one hand, the false gods responsible for Rome's fall and portrayed in the poetry of the empire and, on the other, Christian philosophy, which hears truth where it dawns (as it often does in Virgil) calling us to the higher power, the true God. Varro wrote about things human and divine, and he placed the theatrical work of the poets among the divine. Augustine used Varro (cataloger of the gods and their activities) as a guide. And what a catalog it is. There are so many gods, each doing some little specialized task, and Augustine admitted to being bored by the review of the full list. The simpleton can function as a doorkeeper, but among the Roman gods there is a god for the doors (Forculus), one for the hinges (Cardea), and one for the threshold (Limetinus). "Forculus, then, was not able to guard the door, hinges and threshold all at once!" (*City*, IV, 8). And if one cannot ask for bread from one God or wine from another, how can we be reasonable in asking for eternal life from such gods?

Varro was also unhappy with the ways in which the gods were treated by the poets, and though he was subject to his own culture, he thought that images of the gods diminished reverence. He had a rich notion of the gods' presences and thought that Jupiter was worshiped even by those who do not call him Jupiter – including monotheists, an idea that had some traction for Augustine as well. "The Romans publish a saying concerning this god which, though that of a poet, is nonetheless most apt: 'all things are full of Jupiter'" (*City*, IV, 9; Virgil, *Ecl.*, 3.60). Though "all things are full of Jupiter," there is a contradictory multiplying of gods so that Juno gets a part, and Neptune, and Pluto, and the wives of the gods – "Our adversaries seek a way to patch up their fables, but they do not find one" (*City*, IV, 10). Augustine picks at Vesta, Venus, and

Virginity. He knows well that a critic will say, "Again you revert to fables." His rejoinder is to repeat, "But what kind of justice is it to reproach us for speaking thus of their gods, yet not to reproach themselves for taking such great pleasure in witnessing the crimes of those gods in the theaters?" And, again, "no wonders and no vices, however far removed from the nature of the gods, can be imagined which are not found in the details of the poets" (*City*, IV, 27). If the city wishes to put its trust in the poets to present the gods, that city must be prepared for the philosopher. So Athens, so Rome.

Varro not only named the gods but also described their tasks. This categorizing was a very practical task with the goal of leading a good and useful life: if you do not know the particular power of a god, you will not know which god to call on for which task (*City*, IV, 22). The problem, Augustine saw, was that the attributes identified as gods are in fact gifts of the one true God, but the gift itself is identified as a god. Felicity is called a god and worshiped as such. But a person will not be closer to true happiness by worshiping felicity as a god while forsaking the God who also gives true happiness, "just as he cannot escape hunger if he likes a picture of a loaf instead of asking for a real one from someone who has it" (*City*, IV, 23). But classification of the gods is an important step in the philosopher's response to the poets and to the institutions that house and affirm the poets' fables. The poets write for amusement. Varro says that "the writings of the poets are less than the people ought to follow, whereas those of the philosophers are more than it is profitable for plain folk to investigate," and though Varro thinks civil theology is conditioned by both the mythical and philosophical, he suggests that "we must keep company more with the philosophers than with the poets." Augustine's own argument will first unite the poetic and the civil and then side with philosophy against both in his move toward deepest truth.

There are three accounts given of the gods corresponding to the three kinds of gods: the mythical approach used by the poets, the civil approach used by the people, and the natural approach used by the philosophers. The mythical approach is best adapted to the theater, the civil to the city, and the natural to the world (*City*, VI, 5). But Varro fails to see that, while the world is a divine work, both the theater and the city are human works, and "the gods laughed at in the theater are none other than those who are adored in the temples" (*City*, VI, 6). The poets and the priests are thus united, and both are wicked. Augustine argues for a much stronger connection between the mythical and the civil, and a much clearer separation of the philosophical from either. Both the poets and the priests alike "represent Priapus as having enormous private parts" (*City*, VI, 7). Because the civil and the mythical both contain such vanities and obscenities, and because both show up in the divine rites of the cities, "the civil and the mythical theologies are both civil and mythical" (*City*, VI, 8). The effort to which Augustine responds thus is that effort which teases out distinctions between cities and theaters, temples and stages, pontiffs' rites and poets' songs – all to suggest that the frivolity of the poets' work is to be distinguished from the work of the cities as honest, serious, and desirable. However, Augustine does not let the Romans untether themselves from the poets: "They know that the theatrical and mythical theology derives from the civil and is reflected, like an image of it in a mirror, by the songs of the poets" (*City*, VI, 9). This confluence of the poetic and the civil is what he contrasts with the work of the philosophers (natural theology) on the way to that final truth of the one God, most fully revealed in Christ.

The quarrel between poetry and philosophy is at the heart of *The City of God*: "I am here endeavoring most diligently to uproot and extirpate depraved and ancient opinions which the long-continued error of the human race has implanted deeply and tenaciously in the dark places of the soul" (*City*, VII, preface). Poetry is the home of these deep-rooted ideas, these myths of the gods. So Augustine first connects the civil and mythical in order to dismiss the first by refuting the second. Then the gods of the philosophers are hit one by one as he moves ever closer to the true God. Twenty of these gods (twelve male and eight female) are identified as "select" by Varro, and so god by god Augustine offers arguments and opposition. This is a preface to the history of philosophy. His strategy is to demonstrate how the gods became not gods but concepts. Jupiter is genius (*City*, VII, 13). Mercury is the faculty of speech, and the same god (in Greek) Hermes is interpretation (*City*, VII, 14). Mars is no god, but only war. The sun is the sun (not Apollo), the moon is the moon (not Diana), and neither fire (Vulcan) nor water (Neptune) is a god. In the progress of *The City of God*, then, the quarrel is yet again recapitulated, and we are readied by and for philosophy through a transformation of the world from a mythical confluence of many gods into a world of ideas, things, and the actions of people and animals. The poets invented all sorts of things, but philosophy frees us to use poetry to new ends: "Saturn devoured his children, as the poets tell; and the natural philosophers interpret this story in whatever way they wish" (*City*, VII, 26).

The Platonist philosophers were able to move closer to the truth than even Varro was because they conceive of a God over all: Augustine says, "The true philosopher is a lover of God" (*City*, VIII, 1). Plato leads philosophy in this direction. "Let what is contained in these two theologies, then, the mythical and the civil, give place to the philosophy of the Platonists, who have said that the true God is the author of all things, the illuminator of truth, and the giver of happiness" (*City*, VIII, 5). This is an important move forward: the poets offer the starting points by portraying the gods, the concepts are abstracted from the characters of the gods, and the obscenities demanded from the demons who are the "gods" are put aside so that now in a world once crowded with myth there is room for philosophy and, most especially, for the Platonists to whom the true and highest good is God: "Philosophy [for Plato] aims at the happy life, and he who loves God is happy in the enjoyment of God" (*City*, VIII, 8).

Plato said there are no bad gods (*City*, VIII, 13; Plato, *Rep.*, 379a). But the "gods" celebrated by the poets in the theater are, at the gods' command, portrayed as immoral. Furthermore, Plato, as we know, banished the poets from the city. There seems to be a contradiction here, which Augustine addresses by saying that Plato "in detesting poetry and prohibiting works of fiction, deprived not the gods, who are entirely good and exalted, but the demons, of their pleasure in theatrical displays" (*City*, VIII, 14). Plato deprived the demons of poetic pleasure in order to "admonish the mind of man, even while still confined within those dying members" and so uphold virtue and reject the uncleanness of the demons. Who are these demons who seem to play such a central role for Augustine in the quarrel between poetry and philosophy? The Platonist Apuleius says the demons are midway between the gods and humanity, eternal in time, animal in genus, with rational minds, passive souls, aerial bodies (*City*, VIII, 16; Apuleius, *De Deo Socr.*, 13). He also says that these demonic intermediaries move between the gods and people, carrying messages back and forth. But again, if this is true, it puts Plato in a bind because the poets defame the gods whom Plato praises, and the demons take pleasure in the poets' defamation.

Augustine says that the only way to reconcile Plato's praise of the gods and his rejection of the poets is to say that the demons who so compel the poets "are spirits whose sole desire is to harm us: who are entirely alien to justice, swollen with pride, livid with envy, and subtle in deceit" (*City*, VIII, 22). There are other theories about these demons, such as that of the Egyptian Hermes Trismegistus, who thought that humans had a great and wondrous power to make gods in imitation of the highest God, who made the celestial gods (*City*, VIII, 23). But "the god of Socrates, if he had a god, cannot have belonged to this class of demons" (*City*, VIII, 27).

So it cannot possibly be that the demons are friends who "reconcile good men with good gods" because demons rejoice in "sacrilegious tales told not of men, but of the very gods, by the poets" (*City*, IX, 1). And, indeed, Apuleius says that the poets make demons into gods (rather than intermediaries) "under the protection of poetic license." The gods are off in heaven, blessed, far from the demons. "This, then, is a poetic fiction, to say that those demons are gods who are not gods" (*City*, IX, 7). Augustine observes repeatedly that Apuleius wants to make certain that details of the poets are not to be believed of the gods themselves but of the demons in the middle region.

Why this emphasis on demons? Why are they necessary? Apuleius thinks it is because the gods would be contaminated if they mingled with humans, and so an intermediary is needed. The argument has centered on poets' demons as intermediary between gods and humanity. As the argument extends to Christianity (the topic of the remainder of *The City of God*), Augustine says demons are not the intermediary we need: "Rather, we need a Mediator who is united with us in our lowest state by bodily mortality, yet who, by virtue of the immortal righteousness of His spirit, always remains on high: not in terms of temporal location, but because of the excellence of His resemblance to God" (*City*, IX, 17). In this sentence, where the intermediaries of the poets with their portrayals of the gods and the counterpoint of the ineffable God of the philosophers are in tense contrast, the resolution of this quarrel, for Augustine, is Jesus Christ. In many ways the poets with all their bawdiness, sex, drinking, and so forth are straining to bring the gods to Earth. And the philosophers, who have seen the fleeting vision of God, strain to resist the corrupting influence of the poets, who, with their obscenities, would diminish the wise person's vision of the true God. The only answer, Augustine says, is the centerpiece of history – for God to dwell in human form.

This incarnate Christ is "the True Light which lighteth every man that cometh into the world," that light by which the intellectual soul identified by Plotinus derives its light (*City*, X, 2). Likewise, Jesus says of lilies that "Solomon in all his glory was not arrayed like one of these. But if God so clothes the grass of the field, which today is, and tomorrow is cast into the oven, how much more shall he clothe you, oh ye of little faith?"[9] With this He confirms Plotinus's view of providence, which extends from the supreme God down to the lowliest flower, bestowing upon it perfect, intelligible, ineffable beauty and form (*City*, X, 14).

This Christ, then, came to free humanity from "the Lordship of demons." In Christ, the mind, the body, and spirit are cleaned. By taking on the whole of human nature, a whole person can be cleansed of sin. So pervasive is this redemption that the seeker Augustine can find Christ even among the pagan poets: "The most noble of poets has said of him – poetically indeed, for it was another portrait that he sketched; but the words are true if you refer them to Christ – 'With you as our guide, if any vestiges of our crimes remain, they shall be obliterated, and the Earth released from its perpetual fear'" (*City*, X, 27; Virgil, *Ecl.*, 4.13–14). This "poetical speaking" is in the arena of poetry in which the philosopher listens for truth. Because he is speaking of the incarnation of the Logos who was "in the beginning," the Christian Augustine can take a poem from a poet who died twenty years before the birth of Jesus and use it to say of sinners that "these can be healed only by that Savior of whom this verse speaks." The poets are redeemed, but now it will be the voices of the psalmist and the prophets that generate the poetry that the Christian philosopher mines for truth more faithfully. Of course, even the poetry of the psalmist must be interpreted: "What is expressed in the Psalms, then, is often something obscure and figurative; but however it be understood, our interpretation must beyond doubt be consistent with these things which are very obviously true" (*City*, XVII, 16).

Virgil also earns praise when he fits Platonic doctrine into his poetry. Plato thinks it high reward for people who have lived well to be separated from their bodies and join the gods, who never forsake their bodies, "so that, unremembering, they may again behold the vault on high and once more desire a return to bodies," to which Augustine says, "Virgil is congratulated for expressing a Platonic doctrine in these words" (*City*, XIII, 19.; Virgil, *Aeneid*, 6.750–1). Or again, "Virgil...seems to be expanding Platonic teaching in his magnificent verse when he says, 'the force of those seeds is fiery, and their sources heavenly to the extent that they are not impeded by harmful bodies nor enfeebled by earthly limbs and dying members'" (*City*, XIV, 3).

Augustine, like Plotinus, also draws on the character of great poetry to explore theodicy. From poetry, he says, we can learn something of

9  Matthew 6:28ff.

the complex beauty of this world God created. God created the world as it is, foreknowing the people and angels who would become wicked only because this might be put to use on behalf of the good, "thereby adorning the course of the ages like a most beautiful poem set off with antitheses. For what are called antitheses are among the most elegant figures of speech....Just as the opposition of contraries bestows beauty upon language, then, so is the beauty of this world enhanced by the opposition of contraries composed, as it were, by an eloquence not of words, but of things" (*City*, XI, 18). Thinking of the world as a poem of things illuminated Augustine's understanding of evil in the world and the ways in which providence functions even at the lowest level and with the smallest things. Nothing is evil by nature, and "'evil' is the name for nothing other than the absence of good" (*City*, XI, 22). God works no less in little things than in great. Little things are not measured by their littleness but by the wisdom of their creator. "Take, for example, the visible appearance of a man. Suppose we shave off one eyebrow: how nearly nothing is taken from the body, but how much from its beauty! For beauty is not constituted by size, but by the balance and proportion of the parts." So with existence itself. Merely existing is so pleasant that, though the miserable wish for the causes of misery to be removed from them, they do not want to escape misery by having themselves removed from the causes through death. "Do not even all the irrational animals, to whom the power of thought is not given, from immense dragons down to the smallest worms, all shows that they desire to exist, and therefore avoid death by every movement that they can make?" (*City*, XI, 27). So the world is a world made better by antithesis, a poem of things, in which beauty and the pleasure of mere existence are not trivial even in relation to things as small as an eyebrow or a worm. This vision of the world opens the soul and mind to a poetry of praise approximating in words that which angels know without the sound of words, for angels know God "by the very presence of the immutable truth: that is, of His only begotten Word" (*City*, XI, 29).

Christians who are citizens of the Holy City of God do not bother with the conflicting controversies of the philosophers but rather "feel fear and desire, pain and gladness, but in a manner consistent with the holy scriptures and wholesome doctrine; and because their love is righteous, all these emotions are righteous in them" (*City*, XIV, 9). Scripture is the standard by which these feelings are judged and understood, including such feelings as modesty among those who practice philosophy naked (*City*, XIV, 17). Having made the journey through the ancient poets and philosophers, we come to understand through Scripture that "the supreme task, in this world, of the pilgrim City of God, its whole task during this mortal life, is to call upon God" (*City*, XV, 21). Knowing that it is possible to revisit the pagans with an ear newly tuned to truth is something that will become important through the Middle Ages when the prophets take on the voice of God and become the standard by which the philosophers are judged. The theological poets started the journey with their poems concerning gods. "It may be that, in the midst of all their vanities and falsehoods, these poets have something to say of the one true God" (*City*, XVIII, 14). The problem of the mingling of false tales with whatever truth is present in the poetry can be answered by throwing the poets out of the city. But Augustine would have us rather "cling to the Mediator through whom we climb from the depths to the heights" (*City*, XVIII, 18).[10]

---

[10] From such a perspective in which we cling to Christ as mediator, Augustine says, all stories can be judged. Of course, there are tales that should be approached with skepticism, such as the reports of female innkeepers who give poison cheese to unwary travelers to turn them into beasts of burden. But other stories come from sources sufficiently reliable that they must be explained, as with stories about the frequent transformation of men into wolves by Arcadian demons, or as with Virgil's account of Circe, "who by her chanting changed the companions of Ulysses." For Augustine, such stories from a poet of Virgil's stature must not be merely dismissed. The demons are responsible for such apparent transformations, but the mechanism is complex. A demon cannot create a real nature. Rather, people have phantoms that, in their thoughts or dreams, can assume different forms, and the sorts of forms our phantoms assume can be influenced by many things, including demons. And though a person will physically be present in one place in a deep sleep, deeper than normal, this phantom can be present in bodily form to others while their physical senses are asleep. To complete the deception – as when the phantom seems to become a beast of burden after eating poison cheese – demons will sometimes actually carry the objects themselves so that it seems that they were carried by the transformed phantom. One who would not be deceived must be cautious indeed in this complex world. If there are demons, and if the demons used the poets and can even influence our phantoms, the world is a dangerous place.

The Christian philosopher navigating these waters from this new perspective must stay aware of places where truth breaks through. For example, around the time of Rome's founding, when Hezekiah was the king of Judah, there was a prophet, the Sibyl of Erythraea, whose utterances Augustine takes to be references to Christ. This was shown to him in a manuscript of a poem from the Sibyl in which (read in Greek) the order of the initial letters is ICHTHUS, which comes from the five Greek words Iesous, Cristos, Theou, Uios, Soter, meaning Jesus Christ, Son of God, Savior. This word *ichthus* is Greek for "fish," "and this name is a mystic symbol of Christ, who was able to remain alive – that is, without sin – in the abyss of this mortality, as if in the depths of the sea" (*City*, XVIII, 23). In the recording of these Sibylline testimonies, details such as these are important. Augustine is, for example, careful to distinguish the individual testimonies by capital letters between them, "which copyists should not neglect to retain."

The philosophers aimed to discover how life should be lived in order to attain happiness. The problem is that the disciples disagreed with the masters and with each other about how happiness is to be attained. The reason they disagreed is that they depended on human reason alone, and what is available to the human senses. Without divine authority, it does not matter what direction the philosophers go in – they will not reach the goal. "As to our own authors, however, God forbid that they should disagree with one another in any way!...when those authors wrote their works, God himself was speaking to them, or through them" (*City*, XVIII, 41). For Augustine, the holy now breaks through not in the poets, to whom the philosophers carefully respond with human reason, but rather through the prophets. "In that City of ours...it was by prophecy – that is, by the divine voice speaking through men – that such things were commended to the people: they were not inculcated by controversy and argument. This was done so that anyone who came to know them should fear to despise that which was not the mere cleverness of man, but the utterance of God." The earthly city and the heavenly city are "mingled together from the beginning to the end" (*City*, XVIII, 54). The earthly city serves – and even creates – false gods sung by the poets. The heavenly city is made by the true God and sung by the prophets. "Both cities alike make use of the good things, or are afflicted with the evils of this temporal state; but they do so with a different faith, a different hope, a different love, until they are separated by the final judgment, and each receives its own end, to which there is no end" (*City*, XVIII, 54).

The topic of *beginnings* belongs to the poets, whether through true or false myths, and this is one meaning of "poetic openings." But the topic of *ends* belongs to the philosopher, whether it is consideration of the ends of the earthly city, or the heavenly city. Regarding the philosophical study of Supreme Good and Supreme Evil, Varro through "diligent and subtle study identified a range of teachings so broad that, by employing certain principles of differentiation, he found it easy to distinguish 288 sects in all" (*City*, XIX, 1). But of these 288 sects, only the Old Academy of Plato "was as free from error as from doubt." There was no purpose in practicing philosophy except to attain happiness, and the only thing that makes the philosopher happy is the Supreme Good. After this, Varro, our philosophical historian of the earthly city, embraces as the Supreme Good for humanity, which leads to happiness, a combination of goods for both soul and body: "This, therefore, is the life of man which is properly called happy: a life which enjoys virtue and the other goods of soul and body without which virtue cannot exist" (*City*, XIX, 3). And the happy life is social, loving the good of friends as much as its own. These friends may include a spouse, children, servants, fellow citizens, other nations, or even angels.

Such is the character of the philosophers in the earthly city. But those in the city of God, the Christians, differ from the philosophers of the earthly city in a very important way, for the earthly philosophers suppose that the Supreme Good lies within themselves, while the Christians say that "eternal life is the Supreme Good, and eternal death is the Supreme Evil, and that to attain the one and avoid the other we must live rightly" (*City*, XIX, 4). There, in this eternal life, "everything will bestow ineffable delight upon us." The earthly philosophers cannot believe this because they cannot see it, and so "they endeavor to continue for themselves an entirely false happiness, by means of a virtue which is as false as it is proud" (*City*, XIX, 4). But in regard to the philosopher's view of the wise and good life as a social one, "this is a view of which we more readily approve" (*City*, XIX, 5). For the city of God can progress and achieve its proper end only if the life of the saints is social.

Nor does it matter what dress or manner of life the Christian embraces as long as it is not immoderate. "[Once] philosophers become Christian, they are required to change their false doctrines; but they are not compelled to change their dress or customary mode of life, for these are not an impediment to religion" (*City*, XIX, 19). If such a one is compelled by love to engage in active life, such a life should be carried out not for honor or power but for the well-being of those affected by this active life. But if one is not compelled to pursue an active life, then the love of truth may compel that one to preserve a holy leisure, a leisure that is not idle but is devoted to seeking the truth and sharing it when it is found.

The Christian philosopher, then, working in a holy leisure, will find the world and history transformed and may interpret back to the citizens of the earthly city their own stories. The gods portrayed by the poets are now interpreted by those who know the true God, truly proclaimed by the prophets. The earthly philosophers respond to the poets, the Christian philosophers respond to the prophets, and in doing so they change how the poets and philosophers of the earthly city are understood. This true God spoken of by the prophets "is the God whom Varro, the most learned of the Romans, supposed to be Jupiter.... He is the God whom Porphyry, the most learned of philosophers (though the bitterest enemy of the Christians) acknowledged to be a great guide, even according to the oracles of those whom he supposes to be gods"

(*City*, XIX, 22). Wherever truth is spoken, if it be truth, it is the truth of the true God. But this truth will continue to be found in many different forms, coming from many different sources. In Boethius, Philosophy is personified and has her say in verse and prose only after dispatching the Muses, and in Dionysius, mystical contemplation replaces poetry as the oracle or channel for the voice of God, in contrast to the voices of the philosophers and nonmystical theologians. So to these two writers who carry on the Neo-Platonic tradition, we now turn.

# 4

## Boethius, Dionysius, and the Forms

Anicius Manlius Severinus Boethius sat in prison at the age of roughly forty-four, condemned by Theodoric, king of the Ostrogoths. He awaited execution, which came around the year A.D. 525 – he was tortured and bludgeoned to death in Pavia. In the time between his imprisonment and his death, he was able to write *The Consolation of Philosophy*, one of the central texts bridging the classical and medieval worlds. When Lady Philosophy visits Boethius in prison, the urgency of Boethius's struggle is rooted in his strange circumstance. Facing death by bludgeon in the not-too-distant future hones his ear as he listens to Philosophy's counsel and to her carefully crafted cure. The book follows in the tradition of Menippean satire. The poetry is not where consolation is found, though often the poems are used to refresh Boethius after a difficult course of treatment by Philosophy in her attempt to cure him. He goes through the curative rigors and is then allowed a draft at the fountain of poetry for relief. Other times poems do carry forward an idea presented in the prose argument or else sum up what she has said. No longer does poetry find itself struggling against philosophy. Poetry is very nearly subsumed by Philosophy, who speaks in poems at various junctures in the work of helping Boethius make the ascent from the earthbound grief he starts with in the first poem to contemplation of the mind of God, even approaching in the final chapter (which is all prose with no poem) the very ideas of the nature of God's knowledge, time, and eternity – a fitting place to end before exiting this life at the hands of a tyrant.

Once taken over by philosophy, poetry is no longer a threat. It is often offered to sweeten things, to cover the bitter medicine with honey, as Philosophy takes Boethius toward true consolation in the face of death. Boethius is facing death, and soon. This is not a time for splitting hairs merely to split hairs. It is a time for philosophy in its most powerful form.

Death is about to arrive, but not naturally. It is about to be imposed. No lightweight philosophy can bear the image of Socrates in the *Phaedo*, one moment singing philosophy, the next being uncovered by the executioner for examination and found with eyes dead, mouth open. Boethius values the image of Socrates before his death when he talks with his friends and, like the swan, sings for joy most especially at the time of death because of the good things that await him in the unseen world (*Phaedo*, 85a–b). Socrates gently chides his friends for weeping loudly after he has drunk the hemlock. The death as narrated is calm, and his last words are buoyed by a glittering and humorous irony as he gives a task to Crito – sacrifice a rooster to Asclepius, something for Crito "to do" as we often want "to do something," even when it is time to lie back and let go.

Yes, it is all well and good to die calmly and in joy if you are Socrates. But what about me – Boethius? This is no longer a story, no longer history – this is my flesh, which is now alive but which, on a particular day, at a particular moment, will be lying in the particular dust of Pavia in a courtyard, while particular men with bludgeons in their hands catch their breath after carrying out the order of King Theodoric, whose judgment was confirmed by a timid, frightened Senate. Can Philosophy answer that?

At first Boethius does not ask anything of Philosophy. Prematurely white-haired bone-bag that he is now, he sits in a prison with the Muses, trying to hide in songs of sorrow. While he cries and moans in a very un-Socratic way, Philosophy glides up, seeming sometimes of human size and sometimes so great her head is lost to human sight for dwelling in the heavens. Her first act upon arriving is to dispatch the Muses of Poetry who were hovering around Boethius's head, reciting mournful poems to him that threaten a false consolation. She asks, "Who has allowed these hysterical sluts to approach the sick man's bedside?"[1] With that question she makes it clear that while Boethius may be vulnerable to these poetic whores who mislead, she is not afraid of them. She says that these Poetic Muses – better called sirens – kill reason with passion and enable people to persist in sickness of mind rather than embracing the cure. She would not worry if Boethius was one of the hordes who had never tasted philosophy. But he has feasted upon philosophy, especially in the work of Plato, and she will not allow this to be undone.

---

[1] Boethius, *The Consolation of Philosophy*, trans. V. E. Watts (New York: Penguin Books, 1969), I, 1, hereafter cited in text as *Consol.*

The Muses of Poetry will be replaced, she says, with "my own muses to heal and cure," the "True Muse" (*Consol.*, I, 1; Plato, *Rep.*, 607a). The Muses of Poetry depart immediately because, centuries into the quarrel, Philosophy has acquired an "imperious authority." Her first words were directed to these Muses, and she spoke in prose. Her first words to Boethius are poetry.

She is sad over his confused mind, which has been darkened by his recent misfortune. He used to joyfully explore nature, asking questions about the sun, moon, planets, seas, seasons, and any other secret that crossed his path. But this once free mind is now in shackles (*Consol.*, I, m2). Under the benighted weight of worldly cares, he has forgotten who he is, but she will restore him. Philosophy now replaces his exploration of external nature, and in the confines of a prison cell, Boethius turns to a new study, which can be pursued freely even with iron shackles on his hands and feet. Through philosophy, he will again come to know himself and to gain access to the highest, inward truth.

When his eyes are opened to her presence and he realizes that she is his physician, she reminds him that she has fought this battle before, when Socrates was put to death. She knows that these tyrants and wicked people who put the likes of Socrates – and Boethius – to death are actually powerless, their rage impotent. They are in fact blown about by random winds, scuttling around to amass even more of useless fame, wealth, and power while ignoring the real treasures accessible through philosophy (*Consol.*, I, 3).

Of course, no physician can help until the wound is exposed (*Consol.*, I, 4). And so Boethius gathers himself and reviews the charges unfairly brought against him. He is astonished less at the fact that wicked people have pitted crime against virtue than at the fact that, by doing so, they have apparently succeeded. The wicked rejoice while the innocent lie in fear. It is unfair. His anger breaks loose into poetry against the corrupt who sit on thrones despite the cosmic band holding the universe together with fixed laws (*Consol.*, I, m5). He bemoans the fact that, despite the steadiness of the law that guides the stars, on earth things are less stable, less fixed. This is core of his wound.

"Throughout this long and noisy display of grief, Philosophy remained unperturbed" (*Consol.*, I, 5). In his passion, swinging from grief to anger, he was in danger of losing his true mind every bit as much as a tyrant full of greed and lust for power. And so she starts with gentle medicines, and when these have brought him a little ways along, he will be ready for stronger medicines. Like any good physician and diagnostician, she will deliver the proper medicines in the proper order based on the condition of the singular patient before her. After gentle prodding, she reaffirms the major reason he is so sick: "You have forgotten your true nature" (*Consol.*, I, 6). Even though he knows that the world government "is subject to divine reason and not the haphazards of chance," his sense of injustice results from his failure to understand the purpose of things and the means by which the world is governed (*Consol.*, I, 6).

The therapy will be incremental, and poetry will be used to make the process bearable. But the power must stay under Philosophy's control, because poetry can not only bring pleasure but also make falsehood taste sweet in the mouth, though it will turn bitter in the stomach. "Let us bring to bear the persuasive powers of sweet-tongued rhetoric, powers which soon go astray from the true path unless they follow my instructions. And let us have as well music, the maidservant of my house, to sing us melodies of varying mood" (*Consol.*, II, 1).

Not all will be sweetness: the guiding image in the *Consolation* is that of Fortune, her wheel turning "with the domineering hand," ruthless, trustless, hearing no cry, heeding no tears (*Consol.*, II, m1). This is nothing new to Boethius, for he has heard Homer's tales of the two jars standing in God's house – one full of evil and one full of good, an image of God Socrates did not like (*Consol.*, II, 2; Homer, *Iliad*, 24.527). Boethius had much from the jar of good. But if a person is convinced that he or she needs more, no matter how much they have, they are not rich (*Consol.*, II, m2). Truth brings some relief to Boethius, but the relief endures only as long as the words are being spoken. Not to worry, Philosophy says, "for none of this is meant to be a cure for your condition, but simply a kind of application to help soothe a grief still resistant to treatment" (*Consol.*, II, 3). The deep cure is yet to come, at which point the sweetness of poetry will dim and be replaced by the real treatment for which he is being prepared. Philosophy insists that the astounding thing is not that Boethius finds himself in a grievous situation but rather that, up to this point, fortune has been so friendly to him. In his groaning and moaning he is acting as though he was a stranger to this world where nothing stays the same for long and where only a fool trusts in luck and mortal wealth.

Boethius agrees. He rapidly grew wealthy, and this memory is part of his grief. "In all adversity of Fortune, the most wretched kind is once to have been happy" (*Consol.*, II, 4). But it is not the change in events that makes Boethius unhappy – that is to be expected in the world of change and chance. Rather, Philosophy says, the source of unhappiness is his misguided belief. By placing the source of happiness outside himself, Boethius ensures that happiness will be vulnerable to change. "If happiness is the highest good of rational nature, and anything that can be taken away is not the highest good – since it is surpassed by what cannot be taken away – Fortune by her very mutability cannot hope to lead to happiness" (*Consol.*, II, 4). Hoarding riches is a poor and barren approach to life that leads to poverty in others and sickness in the one who hoards. It is absurd to marvel over the beauty of a jewel and fail to see the beauty of your own rational nature, which is far higher and should not be sacrificed to gain the lesser. Nature teaches this – we err in asking for excess. "Nature is content with few and little: if you try to press superfluous additions upon what is sufficient for nature, your bounty will become sickening if not harmful" (*Consol.*, II, 5).

Boethius understands power as little as he understands wealth. It is the wise person with inner goodness that exercises true power rather than the tyrant who, in rage and lust and insatiable greed, is not master even of himself. If a mouse stood up in a community of mice and began to vie for power over the other mice, we would laugh. Philosophy asks, Are people any less frail and feeble than mice? One bite from the wrong fly and Nero is dead. The tyrant might steal one's possessions or inflict harm on one's body, but "you cannot impose anything on a free mind, and you cannot move from its state of inner tranquility a mind at peace with itself and firmly founded on reason" (*Consol.*, II, 6). Philosophy concludes that riches and power, far from making a person happy, actually reveal unworthiness. Fortune does not associate with good people and does not have a good effect on those with whom she associates. In the first Nero poem, Philosophy asks, "Could this high power stretched east and west / check Nero's frenzied lunacy" (*Consol.*, II, m6)?

As with wealth and power, so with fame. It is absurd to strive after fame as though it is something of value. Consider the arena in which one is to become famous, and then compare that domain with the vastness of the heavens against which all the earth amounts to a single point. Take that little point and remove the seas and deserts, and you are left with almost no regions in which people can live and you can grow your fame. The absurdity is to sacrifice the higher – your tranquillity, your life – for something like what is renowned, "as if glory constricted within such tight and narrow confines could have any breadth or splendor" (*Consol.*, II, 7). In fact, not only is so-called good fortune – powers, riches, fame – not good, but bad fortune is actually better than good fortune because it is truthful: adversity reveals the most precious wealth of all, "friends who are true friends" (*Consol.*, II, 8). Where fortune is fickle, Love is the bond that suffuses and sustains the universe, creating harmony among elements prone to clash. Without Love, the unity and fabric of nature would dissolve. Without Love, neither treaties between nations nor marriage vows between individuals would be sustained. This is not yet the personal Love of the Christian, but closer to the Stoic notion of Love. Nonetheless, this cosmic power that binds a cohesive universe provides a more stable background for a deeper discussion of happiness: "O happy race of men / if Love who rules the sky / could rule your hearts as well" (*Consol.*, II, m8).

This is progress. Philosophy offers respite in the form of poetry that stays with him. "She had stopped singing, but the enchantment of her song left me spellbound" (*Consol.*, III, 1). Poetry has a bewitching effect, which can be refreshing, and when used well and in love, it can prepare one such as Boethius for the later remedies, which are "of such a kind that they taste bitter to the tongue, but grow sweet when they are absorbed" (*Consol.*, III, 1). It was precisely the power of poetry to draw in and delight that made it important in the beginning to dismiss the poetry sluts who were hovering around, drawing him toward the rocks. Boethius is coming along, but he is still in danger of missing true happiness. He is in the cave, and his "sight is clouded by shadows of happiness and cannot see reality" (*Consol.*, III, 1). He has seen what a false good looks like. Now it is time to learn about the nature of true happiness, the true good.

The supreme good for a person is happiness, and all agree on this, although many take false paths in their attempts to reach it. True happiness does not depend on riches, power, respect, honor, or bodily pleasure, the presence of which "is full of anxiety and its fulfillment full of remorse ... [as] is known to everyone who cares to recall his own excesses" (*Consol.*, III, 7). So what is true happiness? To see the answer requires conversion. Philosophy counsels Boethius. He has seen false happiness: "Now turn your mind's eye in the opposite direction and you will immediately see the true happiness that I have promised" (*Consol.*, III, 9). Following Plato in the *Timaeus*, Boethius and Philosophy "pray to the Father of all things" for guidance, and Philosophy embarks on a poem asking for freedom from earth's weight so that they can see the true good. In this hymn the cosmic bond that has been cast as the nonpersonal force of Stoic Love becomes the personal force of God, a "Thou" in whose mind resides the highest beauty and the archetype of the world, and to whom one might pray: "For Thou art rest and peace / to those who worship Thee; to see Thee is our end, / who art our source and maker, Lord and path and goal" (*Consol.*, III, m9).

As soon as love is made a Thou, Philosophy strengthens the argument for the Plotinian conviction that supreme happiness is identified with supreme Divinity: though only God is divine by nature, "as many as you like may become so by participation" (*Consol.*, III, 10). Each of the lesser things we seek is sought because we believe it to be a good – power, fame, riches, leisure. The chief reason for seeking something is goodness. So nothing is more desirable than the good itself. But when we desire, we desire for the sake of happiness. So happiness and the good are identical. As God and happiness are the same, and happiness and the good are identical, philosophy concludes that "God is to be found in goodness and nowhere else." All other lesser goods veil the truth that the end of all things is the good. As in the *Meno* and the *Phaedo*, here Philosophy offers in poetry a reminder that the way to deeper truth is to allow our thoughts to circle around, to turn our gaze inward and see that the treasure we frantically pursue in outward things like power, fame, and riches is in fact within us. This is what Boethius learns as he sits in prison, separated from all external "goods" that made up the life he has lost: "And if the muse of Plato speaks the truth / man but recalls what once he knew and lost" (*Consol.*, III, m11; Plato, *Rep.*, 548b).

The happy person is the one who sees the good. The blessed person is the one who turns to higher things without looking back to the lower. To clarify and strengthen this point for Boethius, Philosophy says, "You have learnt on the authority of Plato that we must use language akin to the subject matter of our discourse," and she proceeds to offer the Orpheus poem in which the story of Orpheus and Eurydice is adapted to Platonic ideas – especially that of the cave and the prison motif from the *Phaedo*. This story in Boethius's hands becomes a story of failed ascent from the cave into the light. In grief, Orpheus pursued Eurydice down to Hades, and drawing on the power of the Muses, Orpheus sings, asking lords of the underworld – the Furies, Ixion, Tantalus – to give him back his wife. Overcome by this power of song (a power we see Philosophy use to her own purposes throughout the *Consolation*), the lords yield and let him take her on the condition that he not look back at her until they are out of Hades and back in the light. But he does look back and by doing so loses her forever (*Consol.*, III, m12).

So how does one ascend? Philosophy offers the only worthwhile ascent, which is the philosophical ascent of the philosophical mind:

"I will give your mind wings on which to lift itself," she says, and again, "I have swift and speedy wings / with which to mount the lofty skies" (*Consol.*, IV, 1 and IV, m1). In response to this poem, Boethius "cried out in wonder at the magnitude of her promises" (*Consol.*, IV, 2). She has awakened him to possibility, and now he cannot wait for fulfillment of the promise. Fundamental to realizing the promise is seeing that the good are always strong and the wicked are always powerless. Both the good and the wicked pursue what they consider to be good, but the pursuit of the true good leads to further goodness, whereas pursuit of the false good stops pursuit of the common goal of all things – true goodness – and by abandoning true goodness, which is the good of existence, such men "thereby cease to exist themselves" (*Consol.*, IV, 2). Thus, the tyrant's rise to power leads to the tyrant's destruction, whereas the rise of the philosophical mind leads to true happiness. But even in scarcity the philosophical mind can rise. When we abandon goodness, which is the proper good of a person, we cease to be human, which means that by refusing to rise to a divine condition as is fitting and right, we sink below the human to the level of the animals, as Philosophy teaches in the metamorphosis poem: Circe turns the external form of Odysseus's companions into a boar, a lion, a tiger, and a wolf, though they retain the heart of a human, whereas there is a stronger poison that does not change the human form of the body but rather penetrates the heart and "cruelly wounds the mind" (*Consol.*, IV, m3). Boethius is encouraged by Philosophy to see rightly and to "love the good, show pity for the bad" (*Consol.*, IV, m4).

The ruling power of the universe is God. Humans, if they are to remain truly human, must become more than human (divine) or risk becoming less than human. A question remains for Boethius, who has observed that God seems sometimes to be pleasant to the good and unpleasant to the bad, and also sometimes pleasant to the bad and unpleasant to the good: "What grounds are there for distinguishing between God and the haphazards of chance" (*Consol.*, IV, 5)?

This, Philosophy answers, is the greatest of all questions, and one never comes to the end of it. "The subject is of such a kind that when one doubt has been removed, countless others spring up in its place, like the Hydra's heads. The only way to check them is with a really lively intellectual fire" (*Consol.*, IV, 6). And as difficult as this knowledge is, it is part of Boethius's cure. She warns him, though, that these most difficult matters require careful argument, not the refreshing drafts of poetry, so he will have to do without enchantment for a while. Boethius agrees, at which point Philosophy embarks on the longest prose piece in the consolation.

What is the relationship of divine providence and fate? Providence is the divine reason of God containing all at once, in a unified whole, the universal plan, whereas fate is that plan unfolded over time. From that divine simplicity come the unchanging causes governing a mutable world that would otherwise be random in its fluctuations. If only we were in a position to contemplate the whole order, we would see that everything is in its place and directed toward the good. But we are in the middle of it all, and so it looks confusing. We will not be able to fully comprehend divine providence, Philosophy says, and she quotes the *Iliad* for support, "'Tis hard for me to speak as though a god" (*Consol.*, IV, 6; Homer, *Iliad*, 12.176). The ways of God will not fit into language. What we are given – and for this we should be grateful – is a vision of God, "the author of all natures [who] orders all things and directs them toward goodness" (*Consol.*, IV, 6).

Seeing that Boethius is worn out by the weight of the question and the strain of reasoning about it, Philosophy gives him a break and refreshes him with a poem: "If you desire to see and understand / in purity of mind the laws of God / your sight must on the highest point of Heaven rest / where through the lawful covenant of things / the wandering stars preserve their ancient peace" (*Consol.*, IV, m6). As Augustine portrayed the beauty of poetry and the beauty of the world as following up on the antithesis and the juxtaposition of contraries, so Philosophy sings to Boethius of the ordered succession of opposites – wet and dry, cold and hot, birth and death – partaking in love, moving toward the good, guided and governed by God. The conclusion of all this rightly astounds Boethius: "All fortune is certainly good" (*Consol.*, IV, 7).

This conclusion leads Boethius to ask the question that opens the fifth and final book of the *Consolation*, a question of some interest to a man who will soon be bludgeoned to death: is there such a thing as chance, and if so, what is it? Chance is not randomness, for such a concept is not compatible with the pervasive order proceeding from God's providence. Rather, it is something that appears to us when there is an unintended consequence to an action done for some other purpose (*Consol.*, V, 1). But if the order of providence is so pervasive as to exclude any random event and to subsume even chance, is there room for free will? There must be, for rational nature requires freedom, and this freedom is increased as the human soul progresses in contemplation of God (*Consol.*, V, 2). But if we are actually free, does that not eliminate the possibility of God's foreknowledge? Whether God knows things because they will come to pass, or things must happen in the future because God has foreknown them, in either case foreknowing something seems to imply a necessity that is not compatible with freely choosing. The consequences are far-reaching: not only is there no freedom, but our own wickedness must come from the Author of all good, and our two means of communication with God – hope and prayer – are rendered pointless if the future is absolutely bound by necessity. Boethius ends his conundrum by reciting back to Philosophy a poem of his own, which begins with twenty-one lines of questions and ends with the Platonic observation that we neither fully know nor have we fully forgotten the truth of things – but we must continue to recollect and add to this part we know (*Consol.*, V, m3). Boethius is close to the end of the book, and close to the blood and flesh reality of being bludgeoned to death. To break out into a poem of questions and partial ignorance suggests that real consolation is still elusive. If consolation is going to occur, it better occur soon.

Philosophy's answer? "This is an old complaint about Providence" (*Consol.*, V, 4). The problem has not been adequately examined to this point, and the immediacy of divine foreknowledge has not yet been grasped. Foreknowledge does not predestine acts of the will. The key to seeing this is to understand the nature of knowledge and the fact that there are two kinds of necessity. When something is known, it is not comprehended according to its nature but according to the ability of the knower to know. Even within myself, my capacity to know grows as I move from childhood, in which all is sense and imagination, to adulthood, where I may grow in my capacity to reason and in my ability to grasp intelligible reality. Thus, the child and the adult may look at the "same" object but know it in distinctly different ways, though the higher way of knowing on the part of the adult includes the child's way of knowing. These degrees of knowing – sense, imagination, reason, intelligence – are expressed in the penultimate poem of the *Consolation* (V, m4). Reason belongs to humanity, intelligence belongs to divinity (*Consol.*, V, 5). Humanity, in its humanity, must strive to become divine, or else risk becoming mere animal: "Let us, then, if we can, raise ourselves up to the heights of the supreme intelligence." This is the final sprint toward consolation, and in the last poem Philosophy encourages the prisoner who began in contemplation of the lowly dust to celebrate human capacity, for humanity alone is capable of winging toward divine intelligence. "You who raise your eyes to heaven with thrusting face, raise up your thoughts as well" (*Consol.*, V, m5).

The *Consolation* began in poetry with a poem of lamentation. It ends in prose with a recovery of human freedom that is both compatible with divine providence – so that we are not merely bobbing in a sea of chance happenings – and capable of opening to us the higher life of the Divine, not tangled in time but caught up in an eternity that "is the complete, simultaneous and perfect possession of everlasting life" (*Consol.*, V, 6). All of this is made possible and consistent when Philosophy reveals to Boethius that, as we see things in present time without that seeing determining the free acts of others, so God sees all things in the eternal present. God's knowing does not disturb the nature of the thing known. If an act is truly chosen, God's seeing of the act does not change the freedom with which the act is chosen. Nonetheless, it is true that God's seeing of a future event makes it such that the event cannot but come about, which means it is necessary – which seems still incompatible with freedom. The answer to this, following Aristotle, is that there are two kinds of necessity, simple and conditional. Simple necessity is such that necessity is in the nature of the thing (Boethius's example is the fact that it is necessary that humans are mortal) (*Consol.*, V, 6). Taken in this way, necessity is not compatible with freedom. Conditional necessity, on the other hand, does not exist in virtue of its own nature. If I choose to walk across the room, walking is necessary for walking. But that is not simple necessity: I still chose to walk, though I can only walk by walking. And if you watch me walk, your watching does not affect the freedom with which I choose to walk. So when God sees my freely chosen actions, God may see two actions, one necessary by its nature (a billiard ball hits another ball resulting in the second ball's motion) and one not necessary by nature (I choose to hit the first billiard ball with my cue stick). Though both actions are seen by God, only one has simple necessity. To God, all things are eternally present. Unlike humans, who experience fate as providence played out in time, God is not conditioned by time. And so, when God sees what to us is future, to God it is present, and the seeing of a free act (which to us is future) in no way constitutes anything other than the seeing of a free act.

Neither fate, nor determinism, nor time removes the weight of our freedom. "Man's freedom of will remains inviolate and the law does not impose reward and punishment unfairly, because the will is free from all necessity" (*Consol.*, V, 6). Therefore, our two means of being with God – hope and prayer – are restored, not obviated by some providence that leaves no room for freedom. The tyrant pursuing fame, power, riches, and pleasure will forever be compelled by these things outside

the soul and susceptible to the nonfree determinations of fate. And so
the soul is submitted to the lower. But for a man in prison, about to be
executed and so interested in the true nature of freedom, the consolation lies precisely in the restoration of this freedom in the mind of one
who began benighted with grief and was lured by false poetry away from
the hard road Philosophy offered as the only means for truly seeing this
pearl of great value.

There is only one way to keep this freedom: the paradox (a joyful
paradox) is that to be truly free it is *necessary* that we be good. It is a
freedom drawn by and measured by the good, who is God, judge of
all things and equivalent to and inseparable from happiness. No wonder, then, that this prisoner who would soon die beneath a bludgeon
concludes this great consolation with these words as relevant to one in
prison or outside: "Avoid vice, therefore, and cultivate virtue; and lift
up your mind to the right kind of hope, and put forth humble prayers
on High" (*Consol.*, V, 6).

The poets are hedged in at this point – exiled from the Republic,
accused of serving demons by Augustine, limited to the philosopher's
Muse by Boethius: and so through the Middle Ages the voice deliv-
ering divine wisdom will have to be a voice other than the poet's. As
Augustine suggested, these voices will be found in the camp of the
prophets. Interpretation will still be needed along with discernment
distinguishing the true prophet from the false, but the one taken by
a god and made to speak will no longer be a theological poet. There
is something worth reaching toward, for which discursive reasoning is
inadequate, and yet the utterances of a seer are potentially dangerous
and undisciplined.

In the Middle Ages, it was Thomas Aquinas who brought Aristotle
firmly into the arena of Christian philosophy and theology. But second
only to Aristotle for number of times quoted by Aquinas was Pseudo-
Dionysius, a Neo-Platonist mystic probably from Syria through whom
the pagan Proclus came to have profound impact on Christian doctrine.
Proclus took the divine ideas of Plotinus and made them into gods that
can not only be known (as in Plotinus) but can also know. Dionysius
makes them into angels. Thus it is that the Forms of Plato become the
Angels of Christendom.

Pseudo-Dionysius was a forger writing around A.D. 500. It was a fortunate fraud that left us these works of contemplation that brought the
quarrel (as it encountered Christianity) a profound and valuable dimension. What was the fraud? Chapter 17 of Acts, verses 16 to 34, records

an experience had by Paul the apostle in Athens. Wandering through Athens Paul saw many idols to many gods. The Athenians, we are told, spent all their time telling or hearing about something new. So they brought Paul to the Areopagus to listen to him talk about this new divinity of his. Paul knew that the Athenian philosophers liked to debate and so he began, "Athenians, I see how extremely religious you are in every way. For as I went through the city and looked carefully at the objects of your worship, I found among them an altar with the inscription, 'to an unknown God.' What therefore you worship as unknown, this I proclaim to you." In his argument Paul quoted the Greek poets, pointing out that "even some of your own poets have said, 'for we too are his offspring.' Since we are God's offspring we ought not to think that the deity is like gold, or silver, or stone, an image formed by the art and imagination of mortals." Some scoffed at Paul, but some converted, including Dionysius. It was under this name, Dionysius the Areopagite, that the unknown author wrote *On the Divine Names*, *The Mystical Theology*, *The Celestial Hierarchies*, and *The Ecclesiastical Hierarchies*. It was "the way of unknowing" that he described, the *via negativa*.

In *The Mystical Theology*, Dionysius says that the names that are explored – Life, Wisdom, Power, Good, Existent, and so forth – are necessarily metaphors, inspired imagery of allegoric symbolism.[2] It is poetry, as all language must be when naming the unnamable, speaking of the unspeakable. The *via negativa* is the way of the quarrel which, at its center, is finally silent, but silent only after climbing up the alternating rungs of scriptural utterance and exegesis, intuition, and discursive reasoning. Not all words are equal, however, and the only truly acceptable starting points are the words of Holy Scripture.[3] But even Scripture must be interpreted, and its literal meaning must be transcended because all words, including those of Scripture, cannot finally contain the whole reality of God. The way of unknowing surpasses discourse, intuition, and being. We speak and we shape our language, but we do not mistake that which is contained in language for the truth about God – "The Good which is beyond utterance surpasses the reach of words" (*DN*, I, 2). The Godhead – "It," as Dionysius refers to God – has lovingly revealed in Scripture the truth that Its depths cannot be plumbed. But this does not mean that It is incommunicable, for in love It draws creatures toward

---

[2] Dionysius, *Mystical Theology*, trans. C. E. Rolt (Whitefish: Kessinger Publishing, 2007), III, hereafter cited in text as *MT*.

[3] Dionysius, *The Divine Names*, trans. C. E. Rolt (Whitefish: Kessinger Publishing, 2007), I, 1, hereafter cited in text as *DN*.

Itself according to creatures' powers, "and then draws upwards holy minds into such contemplation, participation and resemblance of Itself as they can attain."

This upward movement leads to divine praises, a poetry that is a "Sacred hymnody," and our praise conforms ever more to the truth of It through holy illumination. Scripture gives us the divine names, each of which reveals It in some way – Wise, Fair, Benevolent. This is what is available to us at the start – symbols of the Divine. Boethius was taught by Lady Philosophy that human nature is such that it properly aspires to divinity, and if it refuses that call, it becomes less than human by becoming animal-like in greed, lust, and rage. Likewise, Dionysius follows Scripture in saying that we are properly destined to become equal with the angels, children of God. We start with our poetic language of symbolism and metaphor, then pass on to contemplation in which we behold truth in simple unity, and thence to the highest contemplation, which is the *via negativa* – transcendent, beyond knowledge, beyond being (*DN*, I, 4).

This is an experiment in language that has a great deal of subtlety. In saying, for example, "Being," there is something in that word that touches upon It, that is a product of Its illumination through words (especially of Scripture) to our minds. And yet when I say Being, I know that It cannot be contained in language. Therefore, at the very least when I say It is beyond Being, I mean that It is beyond whatever I might mean by Being. In the first stage I "comprehend" by symbol, by saying. Then discursive reasoning makes me test the limits of my saying, even if the saying itself began in intuition or through the direct illumination of the sacred writers. To say is necessary, but the moment one says, It is revealed as being beyond what is said, and this principle eventually trains the seeker to understand It as beyond what can be said, beyond the limits of reference, beyond pointing, beyond comprehension, beyond knowing.[1] We start where we must, and the tension between intuitive and discursive reasoning keeps us from idolizing our images or growing static in our philosophical demonstrations. Our longing to know the Godhead is the real force that propels us on and is the life of the quarrel, for "the sacred writers celebrate It by every name while yet they call It nameless" (*DN*, I, 5).

---

[1] Aquinas will refine this insight, showing God to be the most knowable of all, even if God cannot ever be comprehended: one is always in the act of knowing God, moving in further but never coming to an end, never summing up, never concluding. There is no QED in the knowledge of God.

The Divine cannot be expressed in language or known by even the highest angel's mind. Not even the incarnation and birth of Jesus, the plainest instance of divine revelation, can be comprehended (*DN*, II, 9). And yet in the incarnation, the Godhead descended through all layers of nature and again returned to the highest, exalting humanity (*DN*, II, 10). In this exaltation, then, how do we approach that which cannot be comprehended?

We begin in prayer. In prayer our own minds rise to the primal goodness and prepare for union with God. In prayer we reach toward the rope of light hanging down from heaven so that we might start toward the unnamable (*DN*, III, 1). This is only a start, and at the beginning, in comparison with people such as Dionysius's master Hierotheus, who was "rapt of God and endued with utterance divine," the beginner always falls short (*DN*, III, 2). However, the very fact that such people have had extraordinary experiences should encourage the seeker: "Such knowledge of divine truth as is possible must not be disregarded" (*DN*, III, 3). We are compelled both by our natural longing and by Divine ordinance to learn all things within our reach and, in courage, to search for whatever measure of divine truth is accessible. The beginning involves naming what is within our reach through metaphor and poetic expression. But such naming in the world of things is not without an important connection to the highest reality because the Good "extends Its goodness by the very fact of Its existence unto all things" (*DN*, IV, 1). In proportion to our receptive powers, we can perceive this goodness, and likewise (as with the angels above us) we can be perceived. The whole of Being is grounded in the Good simply because the Good is, and yet we quickly see that this quality of Being that we (angels, people, animals, vegetables, matter) enjoy cannot apply to the Good, for all Being flows from the Good. So we can move from our own naming of Being to the statement that the Good is beyond Being – that the Good, through an *excess* of Being, *is* Not-Being (*DN*, IV, 3). This is how language opens the way of unknowing. Likewise, as we enjoy life, It is lifeless; as we enjoy Wisdom, It is mindless, but mindless through an excess of wisdom. So all our language must proceed, "and all the attributes of the Good we express in a transcendent manner by negative images." The truest poet, then, will be the poet of the negative image, but when great art is "beautiful," it is so because *It* is Beautiful. It is the cause of all beauty, causing "the harmonies and sympathies and communities of all things" (*DN*, IV, 7). From the Beautiful all things possess their existence, and each existing thing is beautiful in its own manner. The Beautiful and the

Good are the same, and everything in the world has a share in the Good and the Beautiful, which transforms the world and the way we contemplate the world. The whole intercommunicates, with the lower converted by the higher – people influenced by angels, lower angels by higher angels. The whole universe is thus harmonized and coordinated.

Longing for the Beautiful and the Good moves all things (especially angels and humans) to every outward work and every act of the will (*DN*, IV, 10). Even the Creator has a divine yearning from which, in the abundance of Its goodness and power, the universe was created. The mind begins with the things of sense, especially things seen distinctly and said with the clearest words. From there the mind is stirred toward spiritual contemplation (*DN*, IV, 11). The sacred writers equate this yearning with love, which is the "faculty of unifying and conjoining and of producing a special comingling together in the Beautiful and the Good: a faculty which pre-exists for the sake of the Beautiful and the Good, and is diffused from this origin and to this end, and holds together things of the same order by a mutual connection, and moves the highest to take thought for those below and fixes the inferior in a state which seeks the higher" (*DN*, IV, 12). This preexistent faculty identified with love and longing, leading us to seek the Beautiful and the Good, drives the back-and-forth between the work of poetry and that of philosophy, between intuition and discursive reason, drawing us further up and further in. Far from the "enthusiasm" of divine possession that was regarded with suspicion when Socrates encountered the poets, here the Creator "in His Beautiful and Good Yearning toward the universe...is drawn from His transcendent throne above all things, to dwell within the heart of all things, through a super-essential and ecstatic power whereby he yet stays within Himself" (*DN*, IV, 13). The same is affirmed within the *Hymns of Yearning* by Dionysius's master Hierotheus (*DN*, IV, 15).

Given this fundamental yearning for the Good and the Beautiful, how is it that evil comes about? How does any being not desire the Beautiful and the Good but rather choose the lower matter? "How is it that the Devils, having been produced wholly out of the Good, are not good in disposition?" (*DN*, IV, 18). The Good can produce only things that are good. Everything that is, is because it is from the Good. So, says Pseudo-Dionysius, evil is nonexistent, not in the manner of the Good's "nonexistence" resulting from Its infinite surpassing of limitations inherent in "existence," but nonexistent in an absolute sense. It is difficult to speak without the language of being, and evil in its nothingness "is" only as a deprivation of a thing that *is*, and which, insofar as it *is*, is good. Evil is utter deprivation of the Good, and thus, insofar as such a thing is evil, it has neither goodness nor being (*DN*, IV, 20). Dionysius goes on a rather long tirade about all this, suggesting that perhaps he also had difficulty getting his meaning straight. He does attribute to evil an accidental kind of existence (*DN*, IV, 32). However, this is not self-originating: "Evil is, then, a lack, a deficiency, a weakness, a disproportion, an error, purposeless, unlovely, lifeless, unwise, unreasonable, imperfect, unreal, causeless, indeterminate, sterile, powerless, disordered, incongruous, indefinite, dark, insubstantial, and never in itself possessed of any existence whatsoever.... Evil is nowhere qua evil" (*DN*, IV, 34). Even Satan derives his existence from the Good, and the mere existence of the devils is good. We have heard similar ideas from Boethius, for whom much evil results from pursuing lesser goods rather than higher goods, and Augustine, who, though he grants no positive existence to evil, does find illuminating contemplation of the role of shadows and dark lines in a painting, as well as the role of contraries and antitheses in constructing a beautiful poem.

Having said all of this, we still can never know the unutterable Godhead but can only "celebrate the Emanation of the Absolute Divine Essence into the universe of things" (*DN*, V, 1). The path of affirmation applies only to the world that emanates from the Good. But the ultimate Godhead can be approached only through the negative way, the way of unknowing. One approaches this infinitely bountiful God through perception, then reason, and then beyond reason, as in accord with our finite powers we participate in the Good and the Beautiful, driven by our yearning. Thomas will refine this, saying that God is the most knowable, though we never come to an end of knowing precisely because God is infinitely knowable.

Philosophy depends on reason, critique, and judgment of ideas and concepts. But, as Socrates taught us, philosophy is not wisdom, but is rather an *activity* of love, the love of wisdom, and it is always on the way, testing, getting to the truth of things, whatever the truth of things may be. This is where the human seeker, in coming upon the ineffable, the incomprehensible, must pause before a path that looks like foolishness. Philosophy sent away the Muses of the poets because they were sirens luring Boethius toward the rocks. She gave her own poems along the way, but *The Consolation* began with a poem of grief and ended with prose, as poetry became a source of refreshment more than a well from which unique truths might be drawn. Dionysius draws us to the edge where philosophy may not be comfortable. But we will never move up if we hang on to our human standards. We need something much more like the possession of the poets who are inspired when they speak: we should "consider that while the human intellect hath a faculty of intelligence, whereby it perceives intellectual truths, yet the act whereby the intellect communes with the things that are beyond it transcends its intellectual nature. This transcendent sense, therefore, must be given to our language about God, and not our human sense. We must be transported wholly out of ourselves and given unto God" (*DN*, VII, 1). This is a "foolish wisdom," which has neither reason nor intelligence and yet is the cause of Reason, Intelligence, Wisdom, and Understanding. If the language of the poets carried the ideas of the pagan gods, it will be the voice of the prophets who do so in Christianity, as will be clearer in Thomas's consideration of rapture and prophecy.

So our language must be of a very special kind and follows well only upon a complete yielding to God. Our truest guide to metaphors about God is Scripture, where metaphors are revealed and images used to lead us toward God (*DN*, IX, 1). Even the images in Scripture can seem on the surface to be contradictory, and we must understand them for what they are – "we must have a care, lest in expanding these different forms and figures we unwittingly confound the incorporeal meaning of the divine names with the terms of the sensible symbols" (*DN*, IX, 5). That He is different from all things is attested to by Scripture.[5] Dionysius says, "The same things are both like unto God and unlike Him: like Him in so far as they can imitate Him that is beyond imitation, unlike Him in so far as the effects fall short of the cause and are infinitely and incomparably inferior" (*DN*, IX, 7).[6] Sacred theophanies and mystical visions tend to yield the metaphors, such as God being Ancient or Young (*DN*, X, 2). But these, too, open fields of thought about time and eternity.

Ultimately, though, we must move beyond all of these divine names, toward an act of contemplation that brings us to an unutterable peace – contemplation of "that one and simple nature of the Peaceful Unity which unites all things to Itself, to themselves and to each other, and preserves all things distinct and yet interpenetrating in a universal cohesion without confusion." We come to see this beginning with reasoning about the various names of God as giving a glimmer of one aspect or

---

[5] This idea is important for Aquinas in his comparison of analogy and metaphor, the former being neither equivocal nor univocal but still a species of literal knowledge.

[6] Dionysius tends to apply this without distinguishing between the metaphorical (sitting, standing) and the analogical (good, loving), but as with so many things, Aquinas will clear up that problem.

another of that which cannot be fully articulated. But we must move beyond knowledge if we are ever to come in contact with truths that transcend the mind. "Thus it is that souls, unifying their manifold reasoning powers and concentrating them in one pure spiritual act, advance by their own ordered path through an immaterial and indivisible act of spiritual intuition" (*DN*, XI, 2).

When we understand that the fullness of truth is far beyond us, the negative way can guide us through the names of that God who transcends all name, reason, and knowledge. The Intelligible Names – Good, Light, Beauty, Desire, Ecstasy, Jealousy, Existence, Life, Wisdom, Mind, Reason, Truth, Power, Righteousness, Great, Small, Same, Different, Like, Unlike, Standing, Motion, Omnipotent, Ancient, Peace, Being, Holy, Perfect, One – bring us to the threshold of a unified intuition. It is God who grants "first the faculty of speech and then the power to use it well." Where our use of language leads us astray, the same God can be prayed to "in thy loving kindness to correct my unwilling ignorance, to satisfy with *argument* my desire for knowledge" (*DN*, XIII, 4; emphasis added). Speak the name, test, question, climb these rungs toward that which is higher than metaphor or reason but which is approached through the back-and-forth of the quarrel until both are transcended.

Dionysius goes even further in the few pages of *The Mystical Theology*. He calls upon the mystic oracles to open the mysteries of heaven that lie in silence. He asks to be "led upwards to the Ray of that Divine Darkness which exceedeth all Existence" (*MT*, I). Only the seers, the oracles, can point us in the right direction, as opposed to the philosophers and unmystical theologians, "who cling to the objects of human thought, and imagine there is no super-essential reality beyond, and fancy that they know by human understanding Him that has made Darkness His Secret Place" (*MT*, I). There are stages, and we do indeed begin with what is human and accessible to human modes of thought – anthropomorphism. We move from this to a metaphysical stage that breaks free of the limits of metaphorical personality ascriptions, but this is still dependent on a reason that is not capacious enough to more fully encounter God. Finally, there is the stage that passes beyond oppositions and distinctions of philosophical analysis, so we leave behind "all divine enlightenment and voices and heavenly utterances and plunge into the Darkness where truly dwells, as saith the Scripture, that One which is beyond all things." Even the highest things accessible to mind are still symbolic language, the highest poetry, but one that resides at the threshold necessarily. From this highest poetic opening, the next rung is not philosophy, not further questioning, not further testing, but rather a renouncing of all our understanding as the "true initiate" is plunged into "the Darkness of Unknowing" and, like the man in the parable who sold all in exchange for the pearl of great value, "by a rejection of all knowledge he possesses a knowledge that exceeds his understanding" (*MT*, I). It is not terribly surprising that such a one would be thought mad. But here the elements of joy in response to happiness function as a sign that the seeker has indeed found the object of deepest human desire.

Having emptied ourselves of sight and knowledge, and thus having come to a truer sight and knowledge, we can offer a "transcendent hymnody" that is a new poetry of praise grown from the *via negativa* (*MT*, II). *The Divine Names* is an explication of inspired imagery and allegoric symbolism. This is a holy poetry that is offered in Scripture and drawn from the world of sense, from mental and material images that reveal important truths on the way to higher experience. What we learn as we move past popular theology (which is anthropomorphic) and philosophical theology (which is metaphysics) is that the higher we soar, the more our language becomes restricted to intellectual concepts. As we are plunged into the holy Darkness, our speech becomes more brief until finally there are no terms of thought, "and when the whole ascent is passed it will be totally dumb, being at last wholly united with Him whom words cannot describe" (*MT*, III).

If we speak, we say only what It is not: It is not soul, or mind, or imagination, or reason, or understanding, or number, or order, or motion, or life. "Nor is It Godhead or Goodness; nor is it Spirit, as we understand the term, since it is not Sonship or Fatherhood" (*MT*, V). This is a truly radical relinquishing of the sayable and the knowable. This is relinquished only when thought itself is transcended and It is seen as greater than any form of positive existence, simpler than any thought abstracted from particulars, "free from every limitation and beyond them all." Up to this point poetry, philosophy, and the third way that is the quarrel have had important roles, though for Dionysius their material is best limited to Holy Scripture. After the way of unknowing, however, all speech is diminishment, except insofar as it is offered in love to lead the next seeker. One of the greatest of these seekers was Thomas Aquinas, who took the road of speech farther than nearly anyone, and who also discovered at the end of his life a benevolent silence so wonderful that it made all his writing seem to him like so much hay and stubble.

# 5

# Thomas and Some Thomists

Writing about Thomas Aquinas, G. K. Chesterton says, "He very specially possessed the philosophy that inspires poetry, as he did so largely inspire Dante's poetry."[1] Aquinas was a trained poet. In Naples he studied the art, rules, and methods of rhythmic composition. He wrote *Office of the Blessed Sacrament*, which is counted among the finest pieces of medieval literature. Thomas thoroughly understood what the poets were doing, thought the role of speaking for God was important, and allowed in several places that the pagans had been used to speak for the Divine. He also thought revelation had advanced beyond the pagans, and for him the division of labor was clear. Words from God come through revelation, through the prophets who experience something beyond their own capacity, at times even through "rapture," a concept very close to the *theia mania* of the poets in the *Phaedrus* but trustworthy because of reasons Aquinas gives us in his treatises on prophecy, rapture, and contemplation. It is the Christian thinker (philosopher/theologian) who can judge the pagans and listen for God's voice. In the case of the prophets of God, the philosopher is bound to listen to the *whole* as delivered by God and, as it were, make sense. Among the pagans, however, the philosopher can dismiss more inconvenient statements that complicate the effort to "make sense."

Aquinas was not one to put great stock in flashes of insight. What Aquinas wanted was not flash, beauty, or surprise. He did not want comfort, or rest in simple platitudes, or ease in opacity. He wanted the truth. When he addressed the nature of language and poetry, his view was close to that of Aristotle, a vision of poetry as a thing made according to rules.

[1] G. K. Chesterton, *Saint Thomas Aquinas: The Dumb Ox* (New York: Doubleday, 1956), 126.

Though he acknowledged that sometimes the pagan poets seemed to hit upon prophetic utterances, Aquinas took the physical universe from the hands of the metaphor generators, making it not a universe of signs but rather a secular and natural thing. His work, however, unleashed the prophetic aspects of poetry as never before – most especially in the poetry of Dante.

To understand poetry, one must understand the nature of beauty. Form is central to Aquinas's understanding of beauty. We contemplate the form of a thing and so, he says, "The beautiful is that through which the appetites come to rest in true contemplation or knowledge."[2] Aquinas's understanding of form is close to Aristotle's concept of the structured principle in things (entelechy) that combines with matter to bring about the object. This is the substantial form that makes things "be," makes them stand out from nothing. Art of all sorts lacks the substantial element. Art is always made from things that already are, whereas nature is from God's essence, made from nothing. This is why everything that exists, "material or spiritual, perfect or wretched, and in fact, whether good or evil – everything that has existence, confronts us in the most direct way with the primal reality of God."[3]

Contemplation is the means by which we most fully apprehend this formal reality. It is through contemplation that the material apparent to us and our five senses reveals that God must be intimately present in anything that exists. And precisely because these forms emerging from nothing came to be through the design of an unfathomable creator, we cannot reach the bottom of created things. Thomas tells us that we have not reached full knowledge even of a single fly. Not one fly. It was true in the thirteenth century, and it is true now. But what a wonderful endeavor it is to describe the fly in all its glory, to get at the function of its parts, and the parts of those parts. The meaning of the fly, however, cannot come through natural description only but rather requires Christian philosophy to grasp, to urge us toward that contemplation and understanding of contemplation that opens up the form of a fly as a window onto some aspect of God simply because, apart from God, form does not emerge from nothing.

You could never move from the form of a fly, down, to discover God. You could not describe the way in which the fly changes in response to

---

[2] Thomas Aquinas, *Summa Theologica* (New York: Benziger Brothers, 1948), I-II, 27, 1ad3, hereafter cited in text as *ST*.

[3] Joseph Pieper, *Guide to Thomas Aquinas* (San Francisco: Ignatius Press, 1991), 142.

its environment and get to an understanding of God. The enumeration of parts in itself, the elaboration of relationships between parts of things and between whole things, creates lists, lists that do not signify – that is, the lists of data are not signs about the meaning of God. But the lists are redeemed when we see that we can know these things only because they were creatively thought. The Thomist philosopher Joseph Pieper writes, "Things have their intelligibility, their inner clarity and lucidity, and the power to reveal themselves, because God has creatively thought them."[4] We are made for such knowledge. Aquinas says, "The very reality of the thing is also its inner light."[5] The soul is structured to put itself in relation with, and to encounter, all being.[6] It is this that Joseph Pieper sees as the basis for the way in which we encounter the world both as poets and as philosophers: "To find the truly unusual and extraordinary, the real *mirandum*, within the usual and the ordinary, is the beginning of philosophy. And here is where, according to Aristotle and Aquinas, the philosophical act is related to the poetical: both the philosopher and the poet are concerned with 'astonishment,' with what causes it and advances it."[7] When we respond contemplatively to the essence of things, this is made possible because the things themselves are created, thought by God. However, because things come from this Divine Logos, though they are knowable, their infinite source renders them inscrutable. They are not unknowable, and yet they cannot be fully grasped: "If in our groping after the essences of things we find ourselves in an unfathomable abyss, it is an abyss of light."[8] Pieper points out that this major premise – things have an essential nature only insofar as they are fashioned by thought – is a premise shared by Thomas and Jean-Paul Sartre.[9] But for Sartre, because he begins with the nonexistence of a God who might creatively think the nature of humanity, there is no human nature, and we are free to create ourselves as we wish.

The fountain pen with which I write is a made thing, a thing fashioned from thought, and insofar as it is fashioned from thought it is knowable. So with poetry. For Aquinas, poetry is indeed a kind of knowing, but it is also a kind of labor, a kind of making, and insofar as it is both knowing

---

[1]  Joseph Pieper, *The Silence of St. Thomas* (South Bend: St. Augustine's Press, 1999), 55.

[5]  Aquinas, *In Librum de Causis Exposition*, 6; quoted in Pieper, *Silence*, 56.

[6]  Pieper, *Silence*, 15, drawing on Aquinas, *Questiones Disputatae de Veritate*, I, 1.

[7]  Joseph Pieper, *Leisure, the Basis of Culture* (South Bend: St. Augustine's Press, 1998), 102.

[8]  Pieper, *Silence*, 96.

[9]  Ibid., 52.

and labor, it is inferior to pure thinking.[10] All human making and all human art are limited and constrained by what is already in the created world. We bring nothing from nothing, in contrast to the absolute creativity of God. When we create poetry, we are creating fiction to give pleasure: "Poetry employs metaphors for the sake of representations, in which we are born to take delight" (*ST*, I-I, 9ad1). The poet presents things that, as fictions, are unreal, and so graspable only through the use of similitude, analogy, and metaphor. Aquinas's primary interest in discussion of poetic metaphor and analogy is explication of how these function uniquely in Scripture. The objects in nonscriptural poetry are imagined or invented, and the poet must borrow from reality to present the poetic world of fiction: "Human reason fails to grasp the import of poetical utterance on account of its deficiency of truth" (*ST*, I-II, 101, 2ad2). This deficiency in poetry suggests that analogy as it functions in poetry must, somehow, be different from analogy as it functions in Scripture. Divine mysteries exceed human reason, but biblical analogy allows these mysteries to be cast in familiar forms and so to bring the mind of the seeker to the threshold of truth (*ST*, I, I, 9c; I, I, 10).[11] The medievals, under the tutelage of John Scotus Eriugena, viewed the universe as a universe of signs and symbols, whole networks of mystical correspondences. Not so Aquinas. Only in relation to sacred history does he allow universal allegory. The remainder of history and nature concerns facts rather than signs.[12] When the poets speak about nature, borrowing from the real, created universe, they know exactly what they are doing, and exactly what they are saying, which is to say they speak "literally." Even when they use rhetorical figures, poets speak literally, for "words can signify something properly and something figuratively, [and] in the latter case the literal sense is not the figure of speech itself, but the object it figures" (*ST*, I, I, 10ad3).[13] On the other hand, scriptural poets in their use of figure, analogy, and metaphor write under divine inspiration without having a full grasp of what they are saying because their metaphors and analogies refer to the unplumbable depths of God's reality.

Aquinas as a well-trained poet knew that the poet's job is to say things well. This "deflated" sense of what the poets are up to cannot last long

---

[10] Umberto Eco, *The Aesthetics of Thomas Aquinas*, trans. Hugh Bredin (Cambridge, Mass.: Harvard University Press, 1988), 148.

[11] Eco, *Aesthetics*, 150.

[12] Ibid., 152.

[13] Ibid., 153.

in the world Aquinas leaves behind, and the prophetic sense will reappear powerfully in Dante. But in the work of Aquinas, this *theia mania* appears among the prophets where it belongs and is more reliable as coming from divine inspiration. To understand Thomas's view of poetry, we must understand something of his view of language as such. Pieper quotes, "Nominibus utendum est ut plures utonur" – we must use names as they are generally used (*Questiones Disputatae de Veritate*, 4, 2).[14] That is, the *use* of language rather than Heideggerian etymologies or even definitions guides him in his search for the meaning of things, and in this he follows Aristotle, who also said that "in the naming of things one must go with the crowd" (Aristotle, *Topics*, 2.2.110a).[15] This means that, as we have no means for fully knowing the essence of things that are created from nothing by God ("Created things are darkness in so far as they proceed from nothing"),[16] we cannot name things in such a way as to convey their true being, and so we derive names from conventional circumstances. But poetry, like philosophy, is still a response to something that is "in the way," and far from being taken for granted (except in the deepest sense of, mirabile dictu, having a grantor) or used merely for the advancement of practical tasks in a practical day, such encounters hurl us into the realm of wonder. The calculus is this: happiness is having the desired object and, in the ascent, finally knowing God in contemplation; joy is a *response* to this happiness; the source of joy and the source of wonder are the same thing.[17] Here the poet and the philosopher attend to the same thing as they confront the *mirandum*, wonder.[18] In this also, we find the contrast that Aquinas dwells on between the active and the contemplative life. Wonder has a way of disturbing by taking our attention away from the practical tasks of daily life. This is not to say that the wonder holding the philosopher and the poet distances either from the world. On the contrary, wonder powerfully opens the everyday world to us. But this joyful disturbance of wonder is a different thing from the working world, so different as to cast the philosophical question and true poetry as incommensurable with the terms on which the workaday world proceeds. "In such a disturbance (for the philosophical act, genuine poetry, musical experience in general and

---

[14] Pieper, *Guide*, 114.
[15] Ibid., 113.
[16] Pieper, *Silence*, 67, drawing on Aquinas, *Questiones Disputatae de Veritate*, 18, 2ad5.
[17] *ST*, I-II, q32, a8; cf. Aristotle, *Rhetoric*, 1.2.
[18] Joseph Pieper, *In Defense of Philosophy* (San Francisco: Ignatius Press, 1992); Aquinas, *In Duodecimo Libros*, 1, 3, no. 55.

prayer as well – all these depend on some kind of disturbance) in such
an experience, man senses the non-ultimate nature of this daily, worri-
some world: he transcends it; he takes a step outside it."[19]

Aquinas will not, however, be taken by poetry or art in the way he is
taken by nature. Albertino Mussato (a contemporary of Aquinas, who
was known, among other things, as a poet and defender of poetry)
thought of the poetic imagination and poetry as a form of knowledge,
a gift from heaven that might inspire wonder, taking us to the threshold of truth. Aquinas did not agree. Imagination was, for him, a kind
of storehouse of forms received by sense (*ST*, I, 78, 4c). This is a storehouse of real form. "Art is deficient when compared with the operation
of nature. For nature bestows substantial form, which art cannot do.
Rather, all artificial forms are accidental" (*ST*, III, 66, 4c). And again,
"The material for art products comes from nature, while that of natural products comes through creation, by God."[20] The arts were divided
into the servile and the liberal, with the former (such as sculpture and
painting) requiring physical labor and the latter (such as music) not
(*ST*, I-II, 9, 57, a3, ad3). The artist was an artisan. "The blessed humility
in which the artist was situated exalted his strength and his freedom,"
Maritain observes.[21] As the Middle Ages come to a close yielding to the
Renaissance, he goes on to say, the artist was driven mad and made miserable "by revealing to him his own grandeur and letting loose upon
him the wild beast Beauty which Faith kept enchanted...obedient, with
the gossamer thread for a leash."

Following Aquinas's clear vision of poetry, Maritain makes the distinction between poetry and metaphysics that gets to the heart of the
quieted quarrel in Aquinas – quieted because of sobriety on both sides,
held together by the power of faith. "Divination of the spiritual in the
things of sense, which also will express itself in the things of sense, is
what we properly call poetry. Metaphysics also pursues the spiritual, but
in a very different way, and with a very different formal object. Whereas
it keeps to the line of knowledge and the contemplation of truth, poetry
keeps to the line of making and the delight procured by beauty."[22] And
so in its images drawn from the created world, poetry captures and

---

[19] Pieper, *Leisure*, 68.
[20] Thomas Aquinas, *Summa Contra Gentiles*, trans. Fathers of the English Dominican
Province (New York: Benziger Bros., 1948), III, 65, 6.
[21] Jacques Maritain, *Art and Scholasticism*, trans. J. F. Scanlan (Whitefish: Kessinger
Publishing, 1923), 18.
[22] Ibid., 75.

delights in glimpses that are clues and hints of the order beyond order, while metaphysics, also seeking a super-reality, pursues essences and definitions. Metaphysics "isolates mystery in order to know it," whereas poetry, "through the harmonies it constructs, handles and makes use of mystery like an unknown force." As a created thing, in making use of mystery as an unknown force, poetry does well to be led by faith rather than thinking itself capable of pursuing spiritual liberty without the discipline of metaphysical inquiry, in seeking not to give glimmers but to know. The danger comes when poetry loses its humility, and this danger is answered by Thomas's view of poetry as delight, as amusement, but amusement in the middle of a world mysterious for being and for being created. Before science rose to the stature, not of being powerful, but having its methods embraced as the only way to real knowledge, the romantic poets were losing their souls to the applause of many because their power had been unchained from the discipline of faith. What Thomas can teach us is that poetry is best made when responsive to the world as created. Responding to the world as created is a way to make sense of poetry, because it is a way to make sense of sense. If poetry can respond to and use mystery as an unknown force, its ability to so respond before and apart from "knowing" is the clue to a faculty that makes this possible, the answer to why, upon seeing a cloud, a mountain, a tree, the ocean, and so forth, humanity has produced poetry. One of the most useful expositions on Thomistic poetics is a book by Father John Duffy called *A Philosophy of Poetry Based on Thomistic Principles* and his arguments are worth reviewing briefly.[23]

A thing is beautiful to the extent that it exists. This is ontological beauty. But persons are the ones who actually experience beauty, and not all things are equally experienced as beautiful. Therefore there is a gap between ontological beauty and the experience of beauty. Beauty is beyond mundane experience and is rather "a meeting of person and some splendid being [which] affords a fuller view of being to the mind, and is therefore a deeper penetration into the mysterious core of reality" (Duffy, 7).

When someone makes an artifact of any kind (a statue, a poem, a piece of useful furniture, a motorcycle), the unity of the artifact is imposed on it by its maker. As noted earlier in the comparison of Thomas with Sartre, apart from a maker (or creator) there is no unifying essence to

---

[23] John Duffy, *A Philosophy of Poetry: Based on Thomistic Principles* (Washington, D.C.: Catholic University of America Press, 1945), hereafter cited in text as Duffy.

be known. The unity of a poem does differ from, say, that of a piece of furniture or a statue in that the elements of a poem (ideas and images) are accidents which belong to the poet, but the poem is wrought within the poet, rather than in stone or wood (Duffy, 14).

Logical truth is agreement of intellect and thing, and so ideas, far from being barriers to what is real, actually bind the mind to what is real: "They put a mind in union with its object" (Duffy, 19). Form is what makes this possible (form in reality and form in the mind as meeting reality), and splendor of form is related to the intelligibility of the thing. Between this ontological beauty and a person's experience of beauty is relational beauty connoting the relation of a thing to the soul and the soul to a thing (Duffy, 28).[24] The thing is both beautiful and good insofar as it attains its end, and in the case of the beauty of an artifact such as a poem, its end "is attained completely and perfectly in the very fact of its existence" (Duffy, 27; II *Ethic*, lect. 4). Now, the entire universe is the creation of God and is intelligible but not comprehensible, and so, in its incomprehensibility, it is a source of wonder. For there to be an experience of beauty, the splendor of the thing must be proportionate to the individual intellect. Splendor arises from the ordered perfection of an actual object, and as it is proportioned to an apprehending mind, it founds relational beauty which makes possible an individual's experience of beauty.

In the experience of beauty, "the mind is first flooded with the light of knowledge, apprehending being as individual and delightfully knowable; and upon this may follow an inquiry into the foundation of the objective and mental splendor" (Duffy, 48). This is the priority, first, of *topos* (a starting place) and, second, of philosophical questioning and probing. The experience of the beautiful involves "a sudden and complete grasp of the sensibility and intelligibility of the thing," and so this experience is distinguished by a relatively perfect knowledge of the object possessed in contemplation. The object and the act of contemplation as determined by the object's form – these are the elements of the experience of beauty.

In Thomas's view of any human knowledge (with the possible exception of the knowledge of one's own soul), all comprehension of the beautiful comes through intention and judgment. For Thomas there

---

[24] Regarding proportion, Duffy draws on a number of passages: *In Davidum*, ps.44; *De Div. Nom.*, c.4, lect. 4, 5, 6, 8; IV *Ethics*, lect. 8; I *Sent*, d31, q2, a1. Also from the *Summa Theologica*: I, q5, a4; I, q39, a8; I-II, q27, a1; II-II, q145, a2; II-II, q180, a2.

is no purely "intuitive" knowledge, except perhaps the Beatific Vision in the next life. The importance of this for the experience of the beautiful is that it is "a species of full knowledge about an individual being in which senses have rich knowledge (after their own manner) of the thing, and the intellect uses these apprehensions of the sensible individual to improve its own comprehension of the thing as a striking singular of its class: but that this knowledge by intellect is through concepts and judgments. It is, as we say, delightful knowledge on the sensible and spiritual planes together" (Duffy, 65). In this kind of experience, habit is very important, helping one to experience, say, a sonnet or a sonata as beautiful without labor, analysis, or commentary.

So with ontological beauty. The limitation of the experience of ontological beauty is not the beauty attributable to all things in their capacity as things that are – and so which are capable of being experienced as beautiful. Rather, it lies in the fact that we are not capable of experiencing reality as a whole and so cannot experience the beauty of all reality. What then determines whether we experience a thing as beautiful? Thomas offers harmony, integrity, and brilliance as candidates, but this seems only to get at what makes for an experience of ontological beauty as such, while our deep experience of beauty is somehow an unusual knowledge. I can experience as beautiful only objects suited to my capacity for such, and I will experience as beautiful only the objects that match my capacity. And so, among us who differ in our experiences of beauty, and among those in different ages who experienced beauty in different ways, the variability must derive from variation in the habits of beauty appreciation, "so that what is beautiful for one person and not for another rests finally upon cultivated habits" (Duffy, 73).

Habit disposes the individual toward particular capacities and potential for experience. But knowledge *that* we are having certain wonderful experiences, *what* we are experiencing and, as far as we can grasp, *why*, become the basis for thought about our joy in the meeting of mind and thing that yields the experience of the beautiful. It brings us also to the threshold of a question: in the experience of the beautiful, is there a causal connection between an object and a mind that knows the object in contemplation? The answer is in two parts: yes; and we will probably never know why. Nonetheless, there is still something to say about our experience of art even if the nature of the connection is inexhaustible.

For Aquinas, art is an intellectual habit rather than a skill (*ST*, I-II, q57, a3). It belongs to the practical intellect because it is directed toward making something. Following Aristotle, Aquinas distinguishes several other habits: practical habits of the intellect (art and prudence), and speculative habits of the intellect (science, intellection, and wisdom) (*ST*, I-II, q57, a1–4). What is the difference between the two habits identified as practical – art and prudence? Briefly, in the case of art the aim is to produce a certain artifact, a particular contingent thing according to a rule existing in universal reason – according to a proper plan. Prudence does likewise, not to produce an artifact, but rather to arrive at the right way of thinking in a particular situation, doing good and avoiding evil (*ST*, I-II, q57, a4). The proper plan through which to make a thing (art) or to arrive at the way of acting (prudence) is the fruit of habit. Thus, the artist encounters a beautiful object in the world or recollected that suggests itself as a starting point for an artistic creation, judges that this good end is desirable, and decides through practical intellect strengthened by habit how best to bring about this artifact (Duffy, 105–6; *ST*, I-II, q17, a1).

Aquinas says, "Those in whom the imagination, memory, and the cognitive power are better disposed, are better disposed for intellectual activity" (*ST*, I, q85, a7). Memory is distinct from imagination (*ST*, I, q79, a4). Memory recognizes an image of a past event *as* past. The imagination can retain and reproduce past perceptions, but does not recognize them as past. In addition, in cooperation with the intellect the imagination can produce images of things either perceived or previously experienced (Duffy, 113). Art as the habit of practical intellect uses extramental objects perceived, things recollected, and things produced from the imagination to make works. Universal reason (whose rules are formed under the habit of art) provides the general framework and source of general guidelines for the artist's craft, while particular reason addresses aspects of particular works that are unique to that work. As the work proceeds, the universal rules guide the artist in accepting or rejecting aspects of a particular work – a word, a musical phrase, a brushstroke, a hit of the chisel against a fragment of stone. Using memory and imagination, the artist, apprehending beauty and proceeding by the universal rules of the craft following upon habit, shapes the artifact and so passes on – in the poem, painting, sculpture, or bicycle (as a mechanical artifact with a useful end) – the beauty discerned.

The artist's work, the artifact that results, proceeds from efficient causality, meaning the impression of a form on external matter. The artist's intentional form is accidental in relation to the stone that already exists and exists fully prior to the sculptor's work, but when one considers the artifact qua artifact, the intentional form of the artist is perfecting precisely because it is the intentional form that gives the artifact being as an artifact (Duffy, 128). The form exists potentially in the stone, for if it did not, the stone would not have the potential to receive the form. And the material itself limits the potential for forms: within a stone exist many potential forms of sculpture, but no potential forms of Bach cantatas. When the material has expressed upon it a form, if the artifact perfectly contains the intentional form, even if the intentional form is ugly, the artifact is beautiful: "An image is said to be beautiful, if it perfectly represents a thing, although it be an ugly thing" (*ST*, I, q39, a8).

A poem (unlike other artistic productions, with the exception, in some ways, of music) exists in the mind. Certainly it can be written down, as music, with its notation, can be written down, but the point stands – external words communicate the poem, but are not the poem, and the poem can exist fully in the mind with no pen or paper, no book, no voice. The object of the poem is the content of the poem, and this object can be sensible (as with the harmonious perfection of an object in nature) or spiritual (with the twofold beauty, intellectual and moral, the former being the beauty of thought proceeding toward truth, and the latter being the beauty of the will moving toward goodness) (Duffy, 146). Aquinas says that the act of contemplation turned toward infinite truth possesses beauty essentially (*ST*, II-II, q180, a2). When the poet's mind is so turned, the object of the poem becomes this beauty. Aquinas followed Richard of St. Victor (*De Gratia Contemplationis*, lib. I, c.6) in identifying six kinds of contemplation to which the mind ascends from creature to contemplation of the Trinity (*ST*, II-II, q180, a4, obj3). Duffy uses these six kinds to deepen our understanding of the genesis of the climb from the perspective of poetic principles:

1.  Contemplation according to the imagination alone in which there is free attention to the appearances of sensible things in their diversity, sweetness, and so forth, but without reason's investigation, a type of contemplation pertaining to poetic creation only, perhaps, in some experimental poems with patternless streams of images

2.  Contemplation in the imagination, according to reason where the consideration of the order of sensible things leads to a kind of sensuous poetry

3.  Contemplation in reason, according to the imagination in which we are lifted from viewing visible things to contemplation of invisible things, founding the most common kind of poetry that

expresses the invisible realities of the universe such as love, beauty, moral goodness, and so forth through the visible realities in the content of the poem

4. Contemplation in reason, according to reason in which the mind contemplates invisible realities of which the imagination is ignorant, such as the intellect, will, and the soul itself, realities that nonetheless (as in the fifth and sixth types of contemplation) must still draw on the repository of the imagination if they are to be communicated through the poem to others

5. Suprarational contemplation in which divine revelation teaches things that can be received, though not fully comprehended, by human reason

6. Contemplation that is both suprarational and praeterrational in which, by divine illumination, we know things such as the mystery of the Trinity that can even seem repugnant to human reason

Different types of poets will make use of contemplation in different ways. The objective poet, without personal reference, contemplates the universe as beautiful and worth knowing and expressing, whereas the subjective poet contemplates the inward realities of the soul's thoughts and appetites. Still others combine these approaches to poetic contemplation, considering the universe, the soul, and the relation between the two. In any case, regarding each type of poet, "it can be said that each is absorbed in the fact, the wonder, reality, strangeness of his particular object" (Duffy, 152).[25]

The poet's concern is with disinterested beauty rather than with persuasion or arguments about the truth. When Aquinas speaks of logic as an art (in his commentary on Aristotle's *Posterior Analytics*), he discusses degrees of knowledge (analytic, dialectic, rhetoric, and poetic), and he places poetry last because, rather than leading to certainty, opinion, or suspicion, it merely provides a delineation in the mind of one represented aspect of a thing (Duffy, 153; *I Post. Anal.*, lect. 1; *ST*, I, q1, a9, obj1). A poem can certainly spring from contemplation of highest reality and engender intense contemplation, but the point and sum of poetry are the delightful contemplation of the beautiful thing qua beautiful

---

[25] Duffy also points out in a footnote that by wonder here he does not mean the wonder shared by poets and philosophers, noted by Pieper, referring to the early Greek philosophers who were poets – though a poet can view an object in the light of the oversplendoring of the first cause of beauty – but rather contemplation of the reality, existence, and essence of things.

thing rather than some logical proof legitimizing the content of the poem. Whatever the content of the poem, proof of its truth must come from elsewhere besides the poem – and philosophy, of course, has a long history of responding thus. The poem can start one along the way, can spark a love of beauty, and even open the eyes to realities worthy of higher forms of contemplation. In such presentations of beauty, and with no further argument, poetry is justified. That said, the old danger still lurks when the poet considers the poem sufficient unto truth without the rational testing that belongs to other arts concerned with knowledge rather than beauty as such.

The work of the poet, then, "is a construction primarily of ideas, to carry out in singular expression the deep meaning of the contemplated experience" (Duffy, 163). This requires the imagination (even for poetry expressing the higher forms of contemplation) as the poet seeks for words, images, and ideas in the imagination that can be used to embody this deep meaning. This is one fundamental mystery of poetry, that the exultation of the mind and soul breaks forth into poetry, as Aquinas said of Canticles (Duffy, 170; *In David, Proemium*).

The matter of a poem not merely is the individual external words that are signs of the cognitive acts of the soul (though the words are part of the matter) but is every word and *group* of words, understanding that the grouping of words has a formal element (Duffy, 185). The form, however, goes beyond that present in a single group of words and binds the whole – all simple words and groups of words. Still, the meanings of the words are a limit for the artifact known as a poem, as the matter of a stone is the limit of the statue – the sculptor might do many things with stone, but he or she cannot do anything and everything with a stone. Words are signs of the "passions of the soul," meaning the actions or changes of the soul, and are established by human institutions and are thus arbitrary and instrumental signs of thought (Duffy, 189; *I Periherm*, lect. 2). Aquinas says there are three ways to use the term "word" – the word as signifying a concept, the word as imagined, and the external or vocal word (*ST*, I, q34, a1). The operative "word" of a poem is distinct from a "concept" and is that in which the object is expressed and actually known (*ST*, I, q27, a1). It is called "word" by analogy to a spoken word. "The uttering of this word is a kind of self communication, the person speaking to himself in silence about the object known" (Duffy, 192). This word implies actual knowledge, which, as we know things presently, requires recourse to the imagination. Ideas, images, and external words are distinct expressions made by distinct faculties in the human soul, but each expression is about the same object (Duffy, 196). Consequently, although a particular word is used of a particular object by arbitrary human convention, for one acquainted with the word it will, as assigned, give the object to the mind. Poetry aims at the beautiful presentation of the things (including ugly things). This is accomplished through verbal images, which, when well formed, give the content of the poet's mind to another (Duffy, 199). This leads to the question how poetry differs from prose, and this distinction is difficult to make clear, though the process of attempting to make the distinction is useful for one thinking about poetry and philosophy. Duffy makes the distinction this way: "Poetry is the perfect verbal expression of an apprehended object, whose execution is normally capable of principling delight in the mere contemplation of this perfect expression, while prose – to put it negatively – is any other form of verbal expression" (Duffy, 198). The poem is an artifact wrought in a poet, constituted of multiple expressions to convey the intentional content of the ideas and images of the object toward which the mind is directed. Though the power is ultimately transcribed in external words, this transcription is of verbal images in the poet's mind. The poem means, and is a poem, apart from its physical sound (Duffy, 209). This view following from Thomistic principles implies that rhythm and harmony, while artistically valuable, nonetheless add only an accidental – not essential – beauty to the poem. Fundamentally, a poem is a verbal artifact that yields pleasurable contemplation of an object through words. It is the emphasis on *content* given through verbal images that leads to the placement of harmony and rhythm as accidental to the real poem.[26]

Beauty is splendor according to the form of the thing, and art aims to make a beautiful thing by perfectly representing its exemplar – in the case of poetry, representing the perfection of meaning, of the real order of intentional existence. Ideas and images are part of the matter of a poem, but not insofar as they are themselves real entities. Rather, as signs relating to each other and to the poetic object of the poem, ideas and images are part of the matter of the poem and, when arranged as part of a whole oriented toward the poem's poetic object, they possess meaning. This is poetic meaning. The matter of the poem is produced by the poet, which lends a uniqueness to the products of the poetic arts.

---

[26] Following this emphasis, Duffy is consistent. He affirms that according to these definitions, works of art such as novels, essays, and any other form of verbal making whose immediate end is in the category of a relatively rich or perfect giving of a content, for the simple sake of this expression are poetic artifacts.

The poet impresses form upon this matter (which the poet likewise produces), and this is the source of the unity of the poem. The unity, the
oneness of the poem following from form perfects the harmony of the
ideas and images as they are oriented toward the poetic object, and this
harmony yields splendor, a splendor of meaning.

This splendor of meaning is most deeply accessible to the poet as
cause of the poem, having operative knowledge of the poem in a manner analogous to God's operative knowledge of all creation (Duffy, 266;
*I Sent.*, Prol. S. Thomae). The poem is recited or read. The poetic object
is then present within the mind, not as the extramental thing on the
page or in the reality of the reciting voice, but as poetic object with its
full being in the mind. When this occurs – irrespective of the recipient's
understanding of the source of the richness of meaning experienced –
the recipient "need only know that he is in the imaginative presence of
an individual thing, whose sensibility and intelligibility give him delight
and contemplation" (Duffy, 232). One can turn from this contemplative
delight to an analysis of the rational foundation of the delight, and this
effort may even deepen subsequent experiences of the poem, but it is
a thing different from the delighted contemplative experience of the
poem. This delight in the exercise of the imagination to achieve such
representation is not susceptible to further justification beyond the fact
of its delightfulness.

Aquinas says this delight in representation is natural, so we can be
grateful for poetry. But what does one do with the poets who claim
more, those who claim to see by divine inspiration? For Thomas, the
short answer is they do not: poets know exactly what they are doing and
what they are saying, and it is this capacity that allows them to produce
a poetic artifact most perfectly representing the exemplar, the poetic
object. But the actual mind of God is not, for Aquinas, a candidate for
poetic object – the poets do not speak for God. And yet this claim to
speak for God, this mysterious aspect of the poetic oracle so characteristic of the quarrel from its beginnings, will persist past the Middle
Ages. Where does such a power appear in Aquinas and what does he
do with it?

For Aquinas, the power appears among the prophets. Prophecy primarily consists in knowledge, but the things prophets know are different
from usual human knowledge, and such things appear to them from
afar (*ST*, II-II, q171, a1). These are the people identified as soothsayers
in heathen nations, Aquinas points out, citing Isidore. Speech is second-
ary for a prophet, after knowledge, and functions so that the prophet

can instruct others. Prophets know from afar things of God that surpass human reason and so cannot be confirmed through reason. The prophet's knowledge can, however, be confirmed by accompanying miracles.

Prophecy requires an intellectual light surpassing natural reason, and so, unlike an intellectual form that is at our disposal, prophecy is not done at will by the prophet. It is a transient event, and the prophet is ever in need of new revelations because such supernatural revelation cannot remain as an abiding form in the intellect (*ST*, II-II, q171, a2). The unity present in prophecy derives from the unity of divine light (*ST*, II-II, q171, a3).

When God gives an express revelation to a prophet, the prophet has the most certainty about the prophetic utterance. But there is also a kind of instruction from God to the prophetic mind by means of a mysterious instinct that the human mind may not be certain of, and in these cases it can be difficult for a prophet to know whether the thoughts come from God or from the prophet's own spirit. In cases where they speak in error from the human spirit, the Holy Spirit soon corrects the prophets, who then reproach themselves (*ST*, II-II, q171, a5).

The prophets do not see the divine essence, which is the state of beatitude had by those in heaven. Rather, the things the prophets see are given in images illuminated by divine light. Following Dionysius, who said that "the wise theologian calls that vision Divine which is effected by images of things lacking a bodily form being wrapped in divine things,"[27] Aquinas argues that the nature of these images is more like that of a mirror, and the prophet's mind is a "mirror of eternity" with God's knowledge – not the divine essence – represented there. In teaching, a person can represent things to a disciple through speech, but in prophecy God enlightens from within. The enlightenment is not merely a matter of being presented with images, for prophecy requires images along with enlightenment for the purpose of judgment. Yet prophets do not always know the things about which they prophesy.[28] The Holy

---

[27] Dionysius, *Celestial Hierarchy*, iv, quoted by Aquinas in *ST* II-II, q173, a1.

[28] There is also the large question how we know when a true prophet speaks in error versus when a false prophet speaks. All things are eternally present to the divine intellect and so all "future" things are "foreknown." When a prophet utters prophecy regarding such future things it must be from divine revelation, and it is therefore infallible, whereas "knowledge" of the future based on causes is natural and fallible because it is dependent upon the clarity of our own understanding and the perfection of our imagination. Angels – who according to Dionysius are between us and God in the divine order – convey divine enlightenment to us. Prophecy does not require that the prophet have a natural disposition for divine inspiration nor does it require that a prophet lead

Spirit moves the minds of the prophets, and sometimes they are moved in such a way that they understand the words they speak, and other times they are moved to utterances which they do not understand. It is best when a prophet knows that the Holy Spirit is inspiring an utterance. But the prophet's mind is a defective instrument, and so the prophets will not always know what the Spirit is leading them to see, say, or do (*ST*, II-II, q173, a1–4). This is in stark contrast to the work of the poet, who generates the poem as an expression of the exemplar, the poetic object, and who is a better or worse poet for the degree of success in this making.

The object of prophecy is something that is known by God but which surpasses the faculty of humanity, whereas the poetic object is something known by the mind of a person, limited therefore by the human mind and the dependence on imagination. Prophecy aims to manifest truths that surpass human comprehension. The more the prophet sees the supernatural truth by intellectual vision without images of corporeal things in the imagination's vision, the loftier and more excellent is the prophecy. But there is a limit: "In the present life the enlightenment by the divine ray is not altogether without any veil of phantasm, because according to his present state of life it is unnatural to man to understand without a phantasm. Sometimes, however, it is sufficient to have phantasms abstracted in the usual way from the senses without any imaginary vision divinely vouchsafed, and this prophetic vision is said to be without imaginary vision" (*ST*, II-II, q174, a2, obj4). The loftiest prophetic vision is approached asymptotically. Degrees of prophecies are distinguished by the expressions of the imaginary signs conveying the intelligible truth. Because words best express intelligible truth, prophecy expressed in words is higher than that expressed through signifying images such as corn, beasts, and ladders. All degrees of prophecy are surpassed by prophecy through which an intelligible supernatural truth is shown without any imaginary vision, but again this goes beyond what is possible in this life, "and consequently the degrees of prophecy are properly distinguished according to imaginary vision" (*ST*, II-II, q174, a3).

a good life in terms of charity. However, evil and worldly work can hinder prophecy by hindering the mind's ability to be raised to the high levels of contemplation of spiritual things through the distractions of passion and pursuit of external things. Indeed, in a certain restricted sense, demons can give revelation to prophets, but these are the "false prophets" identified in Scripture and by Augustine. When the false prophets say true things, it is with the aim of gaining credit for other lies.

Another kind of event called rapture is identified as "violent" by Aquinas because it is outside a person and occurs contrary to a person's inclination. This state gives one access to blessed visions not accessible to prophecy in which one sees not corporeal images and mirrored representations but the very essence of God, and this vision is beyond words and not granted to humanity to speak. It requires that a person be withdrawn from his senses because the whole mind is summoned to the vision. In natural form, the intellect always turns, to some extent, to phantasm, to the imagination for understanding. But in rapture alone, so that the intellect can actually be taken to what transcends all images, the intellect must be withdrawn from all phantasm. It may even be that in rapture withdrawal from the body occurs (*ST*, II-II, q176, a1–6).

In sum, the poets know what they are doing, and in what they are doing, they make a poetic artifact that, insofar as it resembles its exemplar, is beautiful. The poem is unique in that the matter of the poem comes from the poet, and the poem is held in the mind, unlike the statue or the painting that exists outside. The poetic artifact is not the written thing, but the written thing can produce the poem in the mind of the reader, though the poet's penetration into the poem's meaning can surpass that of the recipient because the poet (in approximation to the divine act of creation) formed the poem within. The delight we experience in the poem is a natural delight, for humans naturally delight in representation. Unlike the poet, the prophet speaks the words of God (or displays actions signifying a message from God) and may or may not know the meaning of the prophecy. There are degrees of prophetic knowledge, and the higher forms are more removed from imagination and reliance on images, though in our current state we cannot completely escape reliance on the imagination for understanding. How one tells the true prophet from a false prophet can be more difficult. Accompanying miracles help. But because even a prophet may not be certain when the word is from God and when it has more natural sources, it seems that, though the truly prophetic word may be infallible as coming from God, we may not be infallible in recognizing that word. Both poetry and prophecy depend on the imagination for images used for representation. The exception to this necessity in our natural state is rapture in which one is taken from one's senses and may see the essence of God, an experience otherwise reserved for the beatific vision in heaven. All of this the philosopher must consider, and consider it Thomas does. When doing so, Thomas is not engaged in poetry, prophecy, or rapture. His consideration is in the form of the *Summa Contra*

*Gentiles*, the *Summa Theologica*, voluminous commentaries on the major works of Aristotle, the Gospel of John, and the epistles of Saint Paul, as well as polemic pamphlets and the *Quaestiones Disputatae* on the virtues among other things.

Joseph Pieper points out a saying common among Thomists: Thomas feared logic as little as he feared mystery.[29] Only by the use of reason do we find those boundaries beyond which reason fails. Aquinas followed reason in his works all the way to this boundary. But an interesting event occurred toward the end of his life that interrupted this activity. As G. K. Chesterton tells the story, on the feast of Saint Nicholas in 1273, after Holy Mass, Thomas stopped writing – he stopped in the middle of the treatise on the Sacrament of Penance in the *Summa Theologica*. His friend Reginald asked him how he could just stop such a great work. Thomas's answer: "I can write no more." Later on Reginald asked him again, and Thomas repeated, "Reginald, I can write no more. All that I have hitherto written seems to me nothing but straw." A third time Reginald asked him why he would not write. And after a long silence he said, "All that I have written seems to me nothing but straw... compared to what I have seen and what has been revealed to me."[30] Not long after, he died on the way to Lyons while he was traveling at the behest of the pope. When he fell ill on the trip, he was taken to a monastery at Fossanuova. He asked that the Song of Solomon be read to him in full, and then he made confession and took the Eucharist. When the great man died after giving confession, the confessor ran out of the room in fear. His comrades asked him what had so affected him. His answer was that Thomas's confession had been that of a child of five.[31]

We may not always know what to do with oracular utterances, and Thomas would have us test all with reason if only to find the limits of reason, for without this knowledge we risk being benighted though surrounded by light. But the life, work, and conclusion we find in Aquinas remind us that even when up against mysteries beyond what we can reach by reason, even when we are at risk of error, we need not fret because in the darkness and reality of mystery, there is a love that possesses us but exceeds our capacity to possess, and in this we can rest.

[29] Pieper, *Silence*.
[30] Ibid., 39–40.
[31] Chesterton, *Dumb Ox*, 117.

# 6

## Vico's *New Science*

In his *New Science*, Giambattista Vico offers a very different perspective on the quarrel between poetry and philosophy, in which he reconsiders who the poets are, what their role has been, and what philosophy is to do with them. He offers a view that exiles neither poetry nor philosophy from the domain of wisdom, and he resists artificial boundaries set up between disciplines. Vico was born in the same city as Aquinas, Naples, in 1668. He attained a professorship of rhetoric in 1699 at the University of Naples and held this position until his retirement. In his first inaugural oration ushering in the academic year, he insisted that all branches of knowledge, the entire "universe of learning," should be the aim of the human mind, an aim that cultivates a kind of diversity in the mind. The key to all accumulated knowledge is that we rightly know ourselves: the truth of the whole and knowledge of the self are always related for Vico.[1] In the range and type of idea that he is willing to entertain, he has a kind of daring that rests in a notion of providence that allows us not to worry too much about "getting it right," for providence is robust enough to avoid being foiled by our own limitations: "Intensely ambitious as we are to attain truth, let us engage upon its quest. If we fail in the quest, our very longing will lead us as by the hand toward the Supreme Being, who alone is the Truth and the Path and Guide to it."[2]

Vico calls his project *The New Science*.[3] This new science considers the whole, rather than attending to some part and calling it a whole – an error

---

[1] Giambattista Vico, *On Humanistic Education (Six Inaugural Orations, 1699–1707)*, trans. Giorgio A. Vinton and Arthur W. Shippee (Ithaca: Cornell University Press, 1993), 50.

[2] Giambattista Vico, *On the Study Methods of Our Time*, trans. Elio Gianturco (Ithaca: Cornell University Press, 1990), 24.

[3] Giambattista Vico, *The New Science*, trans. Thomas Goddard Bergin and Max Harold Fisch (Ithaca: Cornell University Press, 1984), hereafter cited in text as *NS*.

that prevented others from conceiving the science. In the course of the work, he offers several points that readers should keep in mind if they are going to understand him. The first is the fundamental methodological postulate of his new science: "Doctrines must take their beginning from that of the matters of which they treat" (*NS*, 314). The beginning of nature rests with God; the beginning of nations and civil institutions rest with humanity. So the understanding of nature in the deep sense will be reserved for God, whereas the principles of that which originates with humanity are available to us in a different way because people made these things. This distinction guides the path-breaking horizons of the new science. Second, when Vico speaks of human civil institutions, he refers to Gentile nations as distinct from the Hebrew-Christian tradition and institutions that have a unique relationship to the providence of God. This point is especially important for understanding his notion of providence, and for understanding the stable point of reference that allows the moving development of Gentile nations. Third, and most important, is an insight that Vico claims cost him twenty years of his life to discover, and which is the key to his system. In honor of twenty years of work, the insight deserves full quotation:

> We find that the principle of these origins both of the languages and letters lies in the fact that the first gentile peoples, by a demonstrated necessity of nature, were poets who spoke in poetic characters. This discovery, which is the master key of the science, has cost us the persistent research of almost all our literary life, because with our civilized natures we cannot at all imagine and can understand only by great toil the poetic nature of these first men. The [poetic] characters of which we speak were certain imaginative genera (images for the most part of animate substances, gods or heroes, formed by their imagination) to which they reduced all the species or all the particulars appertaining to each genus; exactly as the fables of human times, such as those of late comedy, are intelligible genera reasoned out by moral philosophy, from which the comic poets form imaginative genera (for the best ideas of the various human types are nothing but that) that are the persons of these comedies. These divine or heroic characters were true fables or myths, and their allegories are found to contain meanings not analogical but univocal, not philosophical but historical, of the peoples of Greece of those times. (*NS*, 34)

In many ways, *The New Science* retells the tale of Augustine's *City of God* and in some respects is an answer to that earlier great book. But it tells the story of history, myth, fable, poetry, and the Gentile nations from a very different perspective and in a different cultural atmosphere entirely, one in which, as Vico says, the minds of the freethinking youth in Europe had been pried off the ways and assumptions of scholasticism by the philosopher René Descartes. Descartes was at the center of a fundamental shift away from recognition of authoritative texts and toward the thinking self as the source of insight into the truth. For Scholastic philosophers such as Aquinas, one properly began with authoritative texts, and from these, rational questioning and deliberation proceeded. Descartes in his *Discourse on Method* begins rather with truths that present themselves as clear and distinct, ideas so clear and distinct that they can be rejected only on pain of falling into absurdity. The most famous such idea is expressed in the phrase *cogito, ergo sum,* "I think, therefore I am." That is to say, doubting itself is a form of thinking, so if I try to doubt that I am thinking, that itself is an example of thinking, and thinking requires a thinker, myself. So I cannot doubt that I am a thinking thing or that I must exist in order to think. From such indubitable starting points, the thinker proceeds deductively so that at the end of the day, the conclusions one reaches are unassailable given the firmness of the starting points and the manner of proceeding from them. However, this leads to a problem: if one defines the value of knowledge by these criteria, there is no room, for example, for history, myth, fable, and poetry. Descartes agreed and responded, saying, so much the worse for history, poetry, and its ilk. These things might provide pleasant conversation, but they should not be mistaken for knowledge. Vico agreed that this followed from Descartes' approach, but his response was to reject Cartesianism in the arena of the human disciplines and to offer his own rejoinder: *The New Science.*

As might be expected, therefore, Vico's method will be very different from Descartes'. To subsume the human disciplines under a Cartesian banner is to abandon humanity: we need the knowledge that comes through our history, poetry, religion and institutions. Both the poets and the philosophers draw on memory and the imagination that, because of its power, can be either a distraction from the truth or the means by which a certain kind of truth is expressed. In the book's first two sentences, Vico marshals both imagination and memory as aides for the task at hand: "As Cebes the Theban made a table of moral institutions, we offer here one of civil institutions. We hope it may serve to give the reader some conception of this work before he reads it, and, with such aid as imagination may afford, to call it back to mind after he has read it" (*NS*, 1). This frontispiece is a memory device with parts representing God's providence, metaphysics contemplating both God and the world of human minds, hieroglyphs representing human institutions, a Globe, the belt of zodiac, and other signs that can serve to help us recollect the whole science Vico offers. It is indeed a picture of the whole where all can be seen together, which is a very different approach than tearing things down to their smallest parts and examining those, as Descartes recommended. It is the wholeness of the thing that is thus emphasized in the frontispiece and its explication.

The civil world that Vico addresses with his new science is a world of human spirit, of human minds. This world *is* the metaphysical world, he tells us, in which God's providence works (*NS*, 2). The domain of metaphysics is a peculiarly human world. Inquiry into the physical world is significant to metaphysics primarily because of the human sense of longing that motivates it. Descartes would replace this domain with his method. For Vico, the great error is not so much that of mistakenly offering metaphysics as a foundation for the sciences but of offering the sciences as a substitute for metaphysics. Discovery in the physical sciences leads to manipulation of the physical world. But without understanding our origins and our meaning, our purpose and our relation to providence, nothing in the sciences can tell us which manipulations are fitting with wisdom, appropriate to humanity.

The beginning of human thinking at the start of the Gentile nations was in the crude, stupid minds of the founders, "all robust sense and vast imagination." Here is where poetry started, what Vico called "poetic wisdom." He said, "This poetic wisdom, the knowledge of the theological poets, was unquestionably the first wisdom of the world for the Gentiles" (*NS*, 6). These theological poets took all necessary and useful institutions to be gods from which came their fables. The poetic principles in the new science provide the means for understanding the rational chronology of the history of the gods and so to understand the nature of human institutions – marriage, burial, religion.

This pursuit of origins among institutions arising in and through the minds of humanity is not to be undertaken lightly. In the Table of Cebes, pilgrims are warned that, should they persist in their questioning and yet fail to understand the answers, they will live in wretchedness. The pursuit of origins is likewise a perilous undertaking, Vico says. If the pursuit is started with an eye to the discovery of meaning, only wretchedness awaits the searcher should the journey's yield be no more than an explanation. Descartes' approach is dangerous insofar as it claims to be the whole truth. Whatever the tools used to penetrate the surface of things – the anatomist's scalpel, the biologist's electron microscope, Descartes' deductive movement from clear and distinct ideas – what is revealed is not the meaning of the thing, the inner truth of the thing that metaphysics properly pursues, but rather another surface. We need not carry out every possible experiment to know what we will find when the last experiment is complete, and the last, most impenetrable surface is pulled away. What we will find is precisely this: nothing. In the study of the physical world, we shall always, in a sense, be outside of it no matter how far we go, whereas the world of nations and human institutions can be approached from inside. As we pursue the physical sciences, analysis becomes enormously complex to be sure, and we can spend a lifetime so enthralled by the complexity of the explanation that the most important questions are never asked. Longing drives us in such pursuits, but if we do not see rightly, at the end of the day when every technique is exhausted, the question will remain, What does it mean?

It is tempting to think that, if we analyze sufficiently and add up explanations, the sum will eventually equal wisdom, a vision of truth as the whole. But Vico says the calculus of wisdom does not fit the calculus of physics, not because there is anything wrong with physics properly conceived, but because wisdom is a different kind of thing, and the tools of the new science open up for us insights into the origins, into poetic wisdom. Meaning is the difference between everything and the whole. The key to understanding the whole is to understand the relationship of providence to the world of human minds and institutions. This requires some measure of storytelling, for it is in the stories of the poets that human culture is recorded.

After the universal flood, Vico tells us, the world was divided into two groups – the Hebrews and the Gentiles. The Hebrews are those people following from Noah who continued in their father's religion, following the true God (*NS*, 167). The Gentiles descended from Ham, Japheth, and Shem, who renounced their father's religion and went wandering through the forests of the earth (*NS*, 369). Divine reason was shown to both, but in ways that provided the distinctness of the two groups. To the Hebrews, and to the Christians who followed them, divine reason was *revealed* both through internal speech to their minds and through an external speech expressed by the prophets and through Christ (*NS*, 948). The history of this revelation is a sacred history with which the new science does not directly deal. The Gentile history – the history of that city which stands in contrast to Augustine's City of God – is the object, and it is within Gentile history that the quarrel between the poets and the philosophers first evolves. But the revelation from God to the Hebrews and the Christians opens a way to understand more fully the struggle between poetry and philosophy, without eliminating either or reducing one to the other. The category of revelation is distinct from the metaphysical pursuit of the world of nations and human institutions, and it completes wisdom.

The first wisdom in the Gentile world was poetic and comprised the knowledge of the theological poets. From the beginning, when the human mind first encountered wisdom, it has been associated with the thought of God. And, from the beginning, the flavor of wisdom has been theological. In Vico's metaphysics, as he studied the common nature of nations in the light of divine providence, he found the divine and human institutions proceeding through three ages – the age of gods (Gentiles believed that they lived under divine government and were commanded by oracles), the age of heroes (Gentiles reigned over plebs in the aristocratic commonwealth), and the age of men (Gentiles recognized all people as equal in human nature and so formed the human governments of the popular commonwealth and the monarchies) (*NS*, 31). In the movement from the age of gods and the age of heroes to the age of men, language had a movement of its own, from a language of signs with a natural relation to the ideas expressed, through the language of metaphor and image, to the language of humanity in which choice played more of a role, a language ruled by human consciousness. This is the movement from the earliest and most torpid theological poets, through Homer and Hesiod to the free self-consciousness of Socrates, who moves beyond words toward wisdom. This is the movement that enables consciousness to be freed from the first language in which it grew, and so to move among languages – a capacity that engenders philosophical consciousness. Understanding the difference in the relationship between the mind and language from the first age to the third is a key to understanding the difference between poetic wisdom and philosophy. Likewise, there are three types of jurisprudence corresponding to the three ages and the three languages: that of mystic theology (in which Gentiles are commanded by the gods through the oracles of the theological poets delivered in verse and fable), that of heroic jurisprudence (manifested best by Ulysses, heroes not yet capable of universals, but assuming a natural right to deliver particular laws), and that of natural equity (in which the people of free commonwealths are led to a command of universal laws, each for their own particular good, but without understanding that it is the same for all) (*NS*, 27–9).

The Gentiles, given neither revelation nor the direction of a transcendent providence as was provided the Hebrews, nonetheless had minds with a natural disposition that made them capable of being guided by what Vico calls "immanent providence." Such a mind's natural tendency is toward meaning. Because God made the natural world, the human mind can never have full knowledge of it in the way the mind can know the world made by humans. But in ignorance our minds are stirred to wonder, and through the work of poetry the natural world is first given sense. Where meaning is not found, it will be made. This disposition is an important clue: even where the mind discovers past errors, the longing itself serves to bring us to the Supreme Being and so is deeply valuable.

Vico offers 114 axioms, both philosophical and philological, which function to order the material of *The New Science*. In axiom 39, Vico says, "Curiosity – that inborn property of man, daughter of ignorance and mother of knowledge – when wonder awakens our minds, has the habit, wherever it sees some extraordinary phenomenon of nature, a comet for example, a sundog, or a midday star, of asking straight away what it means" (*NS*, 189). We have a disposition toward meaning. An attempt to explain the physical elements of a comet at midnight does not satisfy the need to know its meaning. When the behavior of the comet is predictable according to laws of inertia, mass, and gravity, when the composition of the comet is demonstrable – a big, cold rock with x percent iron and y percent nickel, toppled by the sun's gravitational field – we might stop there, short-circuiting a sense of what *this* comet, on *this* night, might portend. The physical predictability and describability of phenomena might lead us to conclude that they signified nothing further. They do not *mean*; they just *are*.

Why, then, does the question of meaning ever arise? Vico says it arises under the influence of providence because this is fundamentally who we are – creatures who seek after the meaning of things. As divine providence moves, the first gestures toward meaning establish the material on which philosophical minds will later work and test. The primary myth is the myth of god, and that arises because this is how we, in our origins, are disposed. Like Augustine, Vico enlists Varro, who collected thirty thousand names of God, and he observes in axiom 13 that every Gentile nation has its Jove (*NS*, 193). The name of god is the beginning of poetry. Poetry marks the beginning of human institutions. Institutions grow under the influence of an immanent divine providence, providing the content of human wisdom.

None of this refers to the real structure of nature made at the hand of God. It refers rather to civil society, to what has been made by humanity – to what can therefore be known by humanity. While many philosophers after Descartes were interested in prying natural science off of metaphysics in order to save natural science, Vico pried the natural sciences and metaphysics apart in order to save metaphysics by demonstrating its proper domains: "Whoever reflects on this cannot but marvel that the philosophers should have lent all their energies to the study of the world of nature, which, since God made it, He alone knows: and that they should have neglected the study of the world of nations, or civil world, which, since men had made it, men could come to know" (*NS*, 331). Metaphysics is not something to be undone or set aside as not meeting the mark of a Cartesian valuation of knowledge, but is rather the very means by which we explore the poetic world of meaning.

Wisdom began among the Gentiles with the Muse, "defined by Homer in a golden passage of the Odyssey as 'knowledge of good and evil,' and later called divination" (*NS*, 365). Later wisdom was attributed to the people who governed the Commonwealths well, and still later wisdom came to mean metaphysics. Metaphysics, preserved by a belief in divine providence, works for the good of the human race. Ultimately wisdom came to be understood among the Hebrews and Christians as "the science of eternal things revealed by God" (*NS*, 365). From this, following the way of Augustine in *The City of God*, Vico distinguishes "more truly than Varro did" the kind of theology that comprehends poetry, that which comprehends metaphysics, and a third kind of thinking that combines the two and is beyond both. These three are united in the contemplation of divine providence: poetic theology (that of the theological poets in the Gentile nations), natural theology (that of the metaphysicians), and Christian theology (which combines the two with "the loftiest revealed theology") (*NS*, 366).

The clue to the world of metaphysics is our pervasive disposition to think of God whenever we think of meaning. When something above the natural world is sought, that something is God. Vico acknowledges that this often does not occur until the natural world begins to dissolve. Death prompts us to ask what lies beyond because we are made for this question. Death prompts the answer "God" because we are made for this answer. For Vico, "something superior to nature is God, and this is the light that God has shed on all men. Confirmation may be found in a common human custom: that libertines grown old, feeling their natural forces fail, turn naturally to religion" (*NS*, 339). When the vulgar man sees a comet, that it is a comet is not disputed. But, as Vico says, there is always the further question what it means. Likewise, *that* every nation begins with the poets who speak the name of god leaves us still with the question what this fact means, and the key to answering *that* question is divine providence. God is the meaning of the mythopoeic disposition.

How did all this begin? Vico says in his axioms that in the beginning there was ignorance, the mother of wonder. For one ignorant of everything, everything is a source of wonder. The Gentile giants are ignorant and incapable of the abstraction of rational metaphysics, and so their metaphysics derives from a corporeal imagination that ranges over physical phenomena, taking these as elements of their imaginative world. The physical phenomenon first in rank is thunder. When this great burst of sound came upon the first men, the giants were frightened by it and did not understand it. These were the giants who descended from Ham, Japheth, and Shem, the children who renounced the true religion of their father Noah and ended up living like beasts, wallowing in filth and thereby absorbing additional nitrous salts, which led to their brawn and giant stature. They were tremendously robust men, inclined to shout because of their violent passions (*NS*, 369). As the human mind in ignorance attributes even its own nature to poorly understood origins, "they pictured the sky to themselves as a great animated body, which in that aspect they called Jove, the first god of the so-called greater *gentes*, who meant to tell them something by the hiss of his bolts and the clap of his thunder" (*NS*, 372). Such a mind is completely corporeal, buried inside the body and determined not by abstractions but by passion and sense. Such conclusions are reached by Vico despite his acknowledgment under the influence of Cartesian dualism that bodies cannot be minds. Poetry, likewise, began with a credible impossibility – that the thundering sky was Jove. Jove was born within poetry as an imaginative universal. How passingly strange that the mind would tend in this direction, but "all this is to be explained by a hidden sense the nations have of the omnipotence of God" (*NS*, 383).

Aquinas said that even when one is explaining spiritual things, one must have recourse to the imagination. Vico agrees with this, saying that we must form human images when we speak of our understanding of spiritual realities. However, the theological poets were not yet able to make use of understanding, and so they "did the opposite and more sublime thing: they attributed sense and passion ... to bodies as vast as the sky, sea and earth" (*NS*, 402). As imagination shrank and the power of abstraction grew, personifications were reduced to diminutive signs. This beginning in poetry could not yield the abstract universals used by the philosophers, but did yield imaginative universals that became the starting points for the work of the philosophers. Imagination precedes philosophy by necessity of human nature, not by accident. In the same way, poetry precedes prose. The development of prose accompanies the development of reason, "just as by the same necessity, the fables, or imaginative universals, arose before the rational or philosophic universals, which were formed through the medium of prose speech" (*NS*, 460).

Each people has its Jove, each has its poetry. Poetry arises within a single nation, within a single language, and with the first word, Jove. Not until nations meet do they realize the law given by divine providence is common to them all, an idea of great importance to subsequent thinkers such as Herder, Hegel, and the philosopher of novelistic consciousness with which this study concludes, Mikhail Bakhtin. When nations meet, the power of abstraction flourishes, and minds are prodded to leave the sequestered realm of their own language. Abstraction thus begun, the philosopher's consciousness is no longer bound by a language, a nation, or a particular fable. Rather, the truth common to them all could be abstracted from the particulars of poetry and myth, though "the philosophers later found all these fables convenient for the mediation and exposition of their moral and metaphysical doctrines" (*NS*, 720). Their ideas were born in poetry and myth, so poetry and myth were natural wells from which to draw for language.

This prompts an interesting question. Once the language of the poets from which philosophical doctrines are abstracted is shown to be fable, what weight will the abstracted doctrine have when all fables are shown to be equally that – fables? The mythic mind does not see myth as a myth, but rather as Jove. With the arrival of the philosophers, what new purpose is wrought, and what new dangers?

According to Vico's chronology a universal flood occurred in the year of the world 1656. More than fifteen hundred years later, after the poetic world had been wrought and the gods named, the philosophers arrived on the scene. In many ways the philosophers complete the world by bringing with them the device of the question. Here again is the power of dialectic, using the question to pry the mind away from a single language, the nest of poetic language within which it grew, allowing it to wander among the thoughts of other nations, other languages, and so to move beyond the particularities of a nation's myth to the general truths of philosophy.

There are four poetic tropes that are formed as little fables. The most luminous and common is metaphor. The second is metonymy, which, along with the third trope, synecdoche, arose because the first poets had to use the most particular and sensible ideas to give names to things. With the first trope we get such contributions as "the lip of the cup" and "the tongue of a shoe." With this second we have "sad old age" and "pale death." Using the third we are able to call a person a "head," as in "head count." But the fourth poetic trope – irony – did not begin until the age of reflection, and it was perfected by the philosophers.

The first poets in their simplicity could not say falsehoods. They had simple minds and could say only what they saw as true. It is for this reason that Vico describes their fables as true narratives (*NS*, 408). The "true narration" of these simple-minded poets makes for an interesting contrast with the philosophers whose arrival, Vico says, was brought about through "deceptions" permitted by divine providence, enabling the philosophers to use the opportunity afforded by religious devotion and the felicitous expressions left to them by the poets in order to express their sublime meditations (*NS*, 362). One important kind of "deception" was the ability to say one thing while meaning another, to use irony in speech and so to show one important way in which the mind is not determined by language but rather is able to express *through* language ideas that do not correspond to any particular set of words. The histories of the Gentile nations have fabulous beginnings grounded upon the first metaphysics, which was a felt and imagined metaphysics following from a terror of Jove who wielded the thunderbolt (*NS*, 375). These poets' fables provided the occasion for the subsequent metaphysics of the philosophers, which, "by means of the idea of God, fulfills its first task, that of clarifying the human mind, which needs logic so that with clear and distinct ideas it may shape its reasonings, and descend therewith to cleanse the heart of man with morality" (*NS*, 502). Why did providence permit these "deceptions" that gave rise to the philosophers?

Vico says that providence allowed the deception so that the philosophers might carry out the task of understanding divine wisdom as an attribute of the true God. Where imagination and memory had been the powers of the Gentiles for fifteen hundred years, the philosophers bring with them something that is neither imagination nor memory – understanding (*NS*, 662). The first people, the children of the human race, founded the arts. But it was the later people, the elders, the philosophers, who founded the sciences: the mind of the philosopher completes humanity. Before their arrival the people had the necessities of life as well as plenty of luxuries and things that are useful and bring comfort. It is reasonable to ask what the philosophers could bring that would "complete" this, and the answer is criticism, the foundation of science. In the fables of the nations, the sciences had a kind of beginning, because the poets were responding to the whole world as experienced. But the philosophers, through reason and generalization advancing the mind toward abstract universals, clarified what was started there. These "starting points" Vico calls *topics* (from the Greek, *topos*, meaning "place"). "Providence gave good guidance to human affairs when it aroused human minds first to topics rather than to criticism, for acquaintance with things must come before judgment of them. Topics has the function of making minds inventive, as criticism has of making them exact" (*NS*, 498). Topics is the art of first things, the primary operation of a mind that takes note of "the commonplaces that must be run over in order to know all there is in a thing that one desires to know well; that is, completely" (*NS*, 497). When the philosophers arrived, they began to question and test these starting places. But philosophy was not, of course, born in full maturity – it too grew from rather crude beginnings, using *autopsia*, the evidence of the senses. This evolved into a kind of vulgar morality (such as that of Aesop) and then into the use of dialectic, introduced by Socrates. Aristotle introduced syllogism, and Zeno introduced the sorites (which, like the methods of modern philosophers, "makes the mind subtle but not sharp") (*NS*, 499). And so as induction, synthesis, dialectic, and syllogism were born, the philosopher's toolbox began to fill up. Vico sums up the second book of *The New Science* by telling us that "the theological poets were the sense and the philosophers the intellect of human wisdom" (*NS*, 774).

The movement from the poets to the philosophers, from the imaginative universal to the intelligible universal, can tempt one to see this "progress" as a step toward no longer needing the art of topics, contact with origins. This is a part of the grave error made by the Cartesians that Vico is addressing and correcting. If the philosophers arrived to complete humanity rather than to replace it, if philosophy is to remain part of this completed humanity, it must retain its connection to the origins – the origins of thought, faith, society, wonder, and especially the origins of the languages of the nations.

When speaking of languages, Vico says that those are more beautiful which retain a connection with original and metaphorical meanings because they are more expressive and thus truer. Words that have no connection to their origins tend to be obscure and confused and therefore prone to lead astray (*NS*, 445). This can be illustrated by attending to Socrates, who translated fabulous history into philosophy. Watching the

Athenian citizens form legal ideas of equal utility to them all, he "began to adumbrate genera or abstract universals by indirection" (*NS*, 1040). He asks, "What is justice?" In his question, justice becomes an intelligible universal. He begins in the middle of a thinking culture grown from a fabulous history yielding the institutions of Athens, and, via the question, translates that fabulous history into philosophy. But a translation is always a translation of some original, and the intelligible universal does not itself divorce philosophical discourse from its origin in the imaginative universals of the poets. The true love of wisdom, if it is to be in any sense a completion of humanity where play and change are guided by providence, must be conceived not as a discipline directed by intelligible universals sequestered from their origins, or as a pale recapitulation of those imaginative universals plunged in sense, but rather as a fluid and peculiar consciousness born of a movement between the two.

Getting to the minds of the original poets without assuming they were like our own is no easy task. We are so familiar with the power of abstraction that we can forget the origins and history of ideas that deepen our grasp of humanity. The world of the theological poets was whole. Jove loomed large, but the whole world was small, with boundaries that could be pointed to – the top of the mountain where the god lived, for example. "Because of the indefinite nature of the human mind," Vico says in his first axiom, "wherever it is lost in ignorance man makes himself the measure of all things" (*NS*, 120). There is no questioning of the myth from within the myth because the myth *is* the experience of the world and the poetic mind – that of the theological poets, brutes that they were, but also the mind of the people. And the people, living in the cyclic stage of sense and imagination experienced the sky as Jove. They move in the palpable texture of divine (and often frightening) power – a power that could demand discipline to the point of sacrificing a child to appease it.

Among vulgar poets such as these, "poetic truth is metaphysical truth, and physical truth which is not in conformity with it should be considered false" (*NS*, 205). Myth is impervious to the question, even in the face of apparent physical contradiction. It is a great discipline indeed that permits such a complete and (often by brutal force) unquestionable world. In such a barbaric world, even when challenging a myth is a credible possibility, to question is to risk not only one's own survival but the survival of a whole people. Against such a background, the radical nature of the philosopher must be measured. The philosopher's ability to question and even to laugh in the process must be born of an entirely new capacity – the capacity to form a speech of falsehood, an ironical speech (*NS*, 408). But the "falseness" of the speech is a characteristic defined against the completeness of the mythic world. This capacity is qualitatively new and different: something has been gained in the formation of this quality, and humanity has been made complete. But whenever something is gained, one does well to ask whether something has also been lost. The mythic mind is incapable of comprehending irony. Neither can irony gain direct access to myth in the Gentile world. But if the idea has not been severed completely from its origin, a philosopher might recognize the mythic narration as the foundation of the world being questioned, of the philosopher's identity, and of the very language the philosopher is using. The ability to question finds its ground and possibility here. But as knower, the philosopher stands against the known.[1] It is this enormous step out of the mythic mind that enables the generation of an intelligible universal. The distance between the topic (the starting place grown in the minds of the theological poets) and the judgment of topics is forged by irony, the trope of the philosopher. Irony is the breath with which the philosophical question can be asked. And, given the relationship between survival of the people in the age of gods and heroes and the discipline forged by the wholeness of the mythic world, the gift of irony is a dangerous gift indeed, and the philosopher's work is dangerous work.

In axiom 53, Vico says that at first people felt without perceiving, then perceived with an agitated spirit, then reflected with a clear mind. "This axiom is the principle of poetic sentences which are formed by feelings of passion and emotion, whereas philosophic sentences are formed by reflection and reasoning. The more the latter rise toward universals, the closer they approach the truth. The more the former descend to particulars, the more certain they become" (*NS*, 219). This is the fundamental distinction between the true (*verum*) and the certain (*factum*). But once it is clear that there is a distinction between the poetic sentence arising from feeling and the philosophic sentence arising from reason, a problem arises for the philosopher. Irony did not come about until the period of reflection later in the history of the Gentile nations. The philosophers were born through a deception permitted by a divine providence. It is appropriate, then, that irony is the trope of the philosophers because irony is "fashioned of falsehood by dint of a reflection

---

[1] Donald Phillip Verene, "Poetic Wisdom," Symposium in Honor of Hazard Adams, University of Washington, Seattle, 1997 (typescript).

which wears the mask of truth" (*NS*, 408). The deception inheres in the philosopher's use of the fables – which were the true narratives of the theological poets – to express their own philosophical meditations. But now the fables, taken as true narration by the mythic mind, are used for a different purpose and so, in an important sense, are false. The swirl of the philosophic consciousness is initially grounded in the metaphorical origins of topics – *topos*, or place. But the ironical mind, which first made possible the move from Jove to the myth of Jove, can next turn upon the value of the myth of Jove as myth, and finally upon the value of knowing origins at all. Vico describes the diminution of Jove, which was brought about through metonymy until Jove, who was at first as large as all the sky, "becomes so small and light that he is flown about by an eagle."

The first poets experienced Jove, not the myth of Jove. Vico says that all nations have religion, but explaining myth as myth is not religion: by the time Jove becomes the myth of Jove – a transformation wrought by the philosophers – *Jove* is no longer telling us anything by the hiss of his lightning bolts and the clap of his thunder. With this distinction between Jove and the myth of Jove, Jove is diminished and philosophy takes on a new relationship to poetry. Given that humanity could not arrive at the intelligible universal without the imaginative universal being in place, the next question is this: Can something that required for its start the experience of Jove *as* Jove be sustained when all that remains is the *memory* of the myth of Jove? Does philosophy, when it comes into the fullness of self-knowledge, at that moment see the beginning of its own end?

This is the point at which the tension between Vico's theism and his humanistic historicism becomes important. For Vico, it was immensely important that Gentile history unfolded under the direction of providence. If God is the force in question, then the fate of philosophy (and poetry) is very different from what it would be if, as Isaiah Berlin and others have argued, the "finger of God" is no more than an argument that the forces at work in history are not wholly made by humans, and that human institutions are not wholly a result of conscious human intentions. Berlin says, "An atheist is left free to assume that the co-author of men's lives is an impersonal, and indeed purposeless and inanimate, nature, the laws of which are wholly discoverable by material science. Vico would doubtless have rejected this."[5] Vico's argument that there is this force is more conclusive than his contention that the force is God,

5 Isaiah Berlin, *Vico and Herder: Two Studies in the History of Ideas* (London: Hogarth Press, 1976), 81.

and necessarily so because the understanding of this providence as God requires that one introduce articles of faith – specifically it requires the history of the Jewish and the Christian people. A choice between philosophy pursued under the rubric of faith in a non-God power working beyond the conscious intention of humanity and that pursued under the faith in a God who works through history presents a fundamental fork in the road for philosophy. The differences between the outcomes of the two approaches are enormous.

Might the philosophical mind leaven humanity with falseness so that the moment of completion becomes no more than an apex, on the other side of which is a tumble down back into incompleteness, now on the side of abstracted intellect detached from its origins? Philosophy is in danger of devolving into a state in which purpose and meaning are themselves the new fables, in which the new myths used by philosophers to express their "meditations" are increasingly squeezed of content until finally the supreme ironist is left with little to stay the conclusion that there are only atoms in the void, with few resources to ground an argument that matter can really matter. The only solution to such a threat is a true myth, a myth that is also part of the real, which is not a product of human choice – a *factum* that is also a *verum*.

To get at the root of why Vico thinks this is so important, we must ask why we should care about origins? However language, thought, and meaning came about, they are here. However we acquired the capacity to generate intelligible universals, we have it. If we can no longer think in imaginative universals as the brutish first poets did, why should we care that they did? Understanding this question is to understand the question of what philosophy is and what it ought to be. In turn, for Vico this is a question of what humanity is and what humanity ought to be (*NS*, 131). When we detach ourselves from our own origins and substitute method for wisdom grounded in knowledge of who we are, what we are, and why we are, the philosopher's trope of irony balloons unchecked, and we risk becoming extreme ironists. But Vico resists this, saying that there is a common sense to the human race. At first, of course, we may not see it in others, with their strange languages, the barbarians. But this is where the philosophers can work well to show a people living inside the poetic world that in fact there is this common sense to the human race, judgment without reflection shared by peoples, nations, and indeed the entire human race, which is taught by divine providence and which determines the course of human institutions past, present, and future (*NS*, 248). This sets the balance of human reason and keeps the human mind from spinning into the emptiness of extreme irony. Vico warns that the ubiquitous principles founding common sense (divine providence, marriage that aims at moderation of the passions, burial as a sign of human immortality) are critical to the *right* role of philosophy. To those who are tempted to ignore the boundaries of human reason that derive from our connection to our origins and contribute to our knowledge of ourselves, Vico delivers a warning: "Let him who would transgress them beware lest he transgress all humanity" (*NS*, 360). Written in small letters, such a transgression leads to a lack of self-knowledge. Written in large letters, such transgression leads to fragmentation of human society and the eruption of what he calls "the barbarism of reflection."

One might still reasonably ask whether we have a say in this business of retaining a connection to our origins. Once irony is introduced, once the philosopher no longer apprehends Jove *as* Jove but rather as the confused attribution of divinity to a thunderbolt, do the "origins" actually retain enough power to halt the spiraling force of the ironic consciousness? We can certainly tell the story – or, in contemporary terms, the "narrative" – of the Giants who, when the earth was dry enough, experienced Jove in the thunderbolt, ran into caves, and formed families, yielding religion, marriage, and burial. But if we – with the gift of irony, of distance, of the question – see that all of this was founded on a mistake such as attribution of divinity to a thunderbolt, however innocent of guile and falsity, are we really left with enough to hold together the human mind and to ask questions of meaning, expecting answers?

Given only this much, Vico would likely say no, and I for one would join him. However much philosophy trades on language, the ironic posture toward the origins and stories ends up with a world in which aestheticizing the old game of ideas becomes the substance of the thinker's activity. This is a temporary antidote to boredom. Socrates distinguished between wisdom and philosophy. Philosophy is a kind of love. Insofar as desire is a part of love, love is a sign that what is desired is not yet completely possessed. Extreme irony leaves humanity with a philosophy as desire, but not desire for the ineffable, not for the Thomistic abyss of light, not for that which, as beyond comprehension, is the secret to understanding the pervasive and complex longing for eternal life. No, it is a desire for something that does not exist, and so it is a desire that cannot be satisfied. Because it cannot be satisfied, it must rather be cured. But we had better make sure that we are not "curing" something that is *the* clue to the meaning of human life.

Without some other ingredient, there is no power to discipline the philosophy of the abstract idea, no power that enables a meaningful response to the Delphic inscription, "Know thyself." But Vico has a clear response. The crucial ingredient on which any sustained Vichian notion of self-knowledge or civil wisdom will stand is divine providence. Vico's science is a rational civil theology of divine providence that began with the theological poets and was completed by the philosophers. Vico therefore needs a powerful notion of divine providence. The providence active in Gentile history must refer in some way to more than a Hegelian "cunning of history": it must refer to the *true* God. For his new science to be sustainable, this true God must not be accountable as number 30,001 in Varro's list of the names of God. What begins in the minds of the first poets, and what is completed in the minds of the philosophers, must finally be related to a transcendent divinity or else the whole of history is thrown into a new and desperately barbaric age.

Poetry is the first speech. Philosophy follows with the question. And when philosophy speaks, first constrained to use the images of the poets, a paradox occurs: the continued search for wisdom through the medium of language leads to a kind of falsehood that itself is necessary if language is not to become an idol, a substitute for wisdom. Poetry (complete with its depiction of unstable gods, heroes comforting themselves by getting drunk, and vulgar fables of wrath, violence, and bitterness) and philosophy (which comes to understand poetic characters as imaginative universals and, from there, comes to understand the reality of human acting in the world with a new and conscious self-awareness) are, in their quarrelsome relationship, the Gentile approximation of revelation. Poetry, philosophy, and the quarrel between the two are guided by an immanent providence springing from the same God who is the transcendent providence of the Jews and the Christians. However, we can see this only through the revelation to the Jews and the Christians. So, for the Gentiles the arrival of the philosophers was a good thing.

That said, the possibilities afforded by the introduction of the philosophical question brought also the possibility of lopsided thought, the barbarism of reflection – a monologic dominance of the philosopher's gift of analysis and critique that, by its exclusion of other valuable human realities, undermines its own value. It was only a matter of time before someone climbed the ladder of philosophic consciousness, ascending from imaginative universals to intelligible universals, and then kicked away the ladder, leaving the human mind stranded in the regions of abstraction, cut off from the mythopoeic origins that are part of the account of human thinking, heads severed from the bodies in which the first poets' metaphysics were felt. This is what began with Descartes. Vico saw the consequences as Naples was overrun with Cartesians.

Of course, if the "mythopoeic origins" were nothing more than a mistaken attribution of divinity to physical phenomena, the so-called ascent to abstraction is likewise folly if it is taken as some fortunate access to "truth." It is rather recognition of our unfortunate state regarding our longing for "truth." It is a recognition that we can never let down the skeptical guard and plunge into that for which we long. If that for which we long is truly an illusion, this is a courageous position. But if that for which we long requires a certain risk in inquiry that is obviated by such skepticism, the cost is high. Vico argues that there is something beyond the debunked particulars of Jove that is missed when the Cartesian project is carried to its conclusion, and this, Vico says, is divine providence. Divine providence is glue that holds together *The New Science* and the possibility of civil wisdom and self-knowledge. There is no essence, fixed and eternal, stable through the flux of history, but rather it is in flux that humanity is made and institutions are created. This flux is not, however, merely one thing after another. Divine providence keeps this science from the chaos of mere flux, on the one hand, and the sterility of mere causality, on the other. Humanity is weak and fallen, but even in weakness it retains sufficient power of choice to freely make virtues of its passions, given the natural aid of divine providence and the supernatural aid of God's divine grace (*NS*, 136). Divine providence is what saves humanity from the contrary tyrannies of a determinism that eliminates freedom, and an uninformed chaos that makes freedom meaningless, choice for the sake of choice. Maintaining the philosophers' proper place requires humility before God, and the propriety of such humility depends on how the world is structured. From the beginning, among the vanquished poets who came to fear God, there arose "the eternal property that minds, to make good use of the knowledge of God, must humble themselves, just as on the other hand arrogance will lead them to atheism" (*NS*, 502).

Once again, religion requires the experience of Jove, not the experience of the myth of Jove: the distinction is critical when one considers a Vichian perspective on the sustainability of humanity. Each of the gods in Varro's list of thirty thousand names may have been experienced as the *giganti* first experienced Jove. Each will eventually be seen as a myth, a fable – a "true narration" because the poets are incapable of falsehood, but a mistaken attribution of divinity nonetheless. With enough testing, the philosophers will eventually see that, however important religion is to humanity, the move from the clap of a thunderbolt to the presence of Jove as Jove is a move that will not finally stand up to critical questioning. On the other hand, "to be useful to the human race, philosophy must raise and direct weak and fallen man, not rend his nature or abandon him in his corruption" (*NS*, 129). How are these to be reconciled?

One solution is for philosophers to lie, quietly accepting the utilitarian value of religion in society while knowing that religion is false. The philosopher knows that Jove is a myth, that humans need religion, and that no religion can survive if the deity is nothing more than a mistaken (though sincere) attribution of divinity to the event of a loud and frightening thunderbolt. So the philosopher respectfully nods to the mass of passing theists without rending their nature through forthrightness. Or the philosopher may, as Santayana does, speak his beliefs, confident that his work will come into the right hands and not be destructive. This is not Vico's solution.

A second solution is to say that divine providence just *is* the pattern of ideal eternal history. This approach says that the natural law that arises within and among the nations exhausts anything we might mean by divine providence and puts aside any notion of a transcendent divinity, revelation, and the peculiar claims of the Jews and Christians. Vico says that this is the error made by Grotius, Selden, and Pufendorf, who advocated for this single concept of natural law (*NS*, 313). The primary weakness of their systems follows from a failure to distinguish between the natural law of the Gentiles; the natural law of the philosophers, who came two thousand years after the rise of the Gentile nations; and the law of the Hebrews. But a failure to make such a distinction is colossal.

The third solution, which Vico embraces, is to say that the whole, the poetic made complete by the philosophic, is preserved by the transcendent deity, by the fact that there is something outside the history of the Gentiles that both shapes that history and is not a part of it – the true God of the Hebrews. What was revealed directly to the Hebrews, God revealed indirectly to the Gentiles through corporeal signs (*NS*, 948). Despite errors of fact in their attribution of divinity to the thunderbolts, the light that shone forth was that of the true God. The particular presence of Jove in the thunderbolt was a myth: the presence of God was not. Under the guidance of divine providence and in the flux of a violent history, human consciousness moved from atheism and fear of thunder not toward despair, nor toward continuation of fear as simple fear, but rather toward the myth of the Jove, a poetic leap toward knowledge of the true God.

The Hebrew history and the Gentile history have this clear distinction for Vico, but that does not mean there are not similarities and points of tangency. Indeed, though sacred history is expressly not the concern of *The New Science*, the vocation of Paul the apostle was to connect the Gentile world with Christianity, grafting the Gentiles onto the Judeo-Christian tree. As the two histories intertwined in Christian Europe, did sacred history become subsumed under the same "ideal eternal history" that is the core of the account of an immanent providence in Gentile history? Vico says no. Because the referent of the Christian religion is a transcendent divinity who is able to work in many ways, even to the point of becoming incarnate and moving among us, Christianity is able to accommodate even the most refined and learned philosophers of the Gentiles, cultivating not only Hebrew but Greek and Latin as well: "Thus, even for human ends, the Christian religion is the best in the world, because it unites the wisdom of [revealed] authority with that of reason, basing the latter on the choicest doctrine of the philosophers and the most cultivated erudition of the philologists" (*NS*, 1094). What about other lands besides Europe such as the Americas? These lands, Vico says, would have followed the pattern laid out in *The New Science* except for the fact that Europeans moved in (*NS*, 1095).

This, then, is a start to a Vichian response to the quarrel between poetry and philosophy. In the religion of the Hebrews and the Christians, God makes possible the unity of the wisdoms of revelation and reason. And it must be so if the philosopher is to continue without rending human nature. The answer to the quarrel between poetry and philosophy, between the theological poets' naming of Jove in their terror and the abstraction of truth by the philosophers, culminates in the event of the historically true myth, the incarnation of Christ.

That said, Vico's science is an earthly science – and robustly so – not a heavenly one. It is the science of a history that continues. In some ways, the coalescing of revelation and Gentile wisdom would seem to offer a commonwealth akin to Plato's, but even greater for including the language and origins not only of Greek, but of Latin and Hebrew as well – poetry, philosophy, jurisprudence, revelation. But such coalescing is a kind of eschaton, and an eschaton ceases to be an earthly story. Revelation does not deliver us from our own work on Earth, but it does carry the fullness of our earthly selves to an unearthly threshold that in turn illuminates the meaning of things on earth.

Vico is accounting for Gentile history, and history often corroborates Vico's science: states become corrupt, philosophers descend to skepticism, and false eloquence is used to defend opposed sides of the case without regard for which side is more worthy of defense (*NS*, 1102). In a chilling passage, Vico looks around him and says that "through long centuries of barbarism, rust will consume the misbegotten subtleties of malicious wits that have turned them into beasts made more inhuman by the barbarism of reflection than the first man had been made by the barbarism of sense" (*NS*, 424). The few who survive this disease that makes the *polis* rot will find their harsh remedy at the hand of providence and be brought back to piety, faith, and truth (*NS*, 424). Humanity is fallen and weak, but the true philosopher holds a complete wisdom that recognizes that imagination, meaning, and understanding are given with the left hand of the same God who gives revelation with the right. Yet the philosopher, insofar as he or she is free, can still wreck the soul on forgetfulness, which, for Vico, is atheism, leaving them stranded and unable to give a true account of the self, for "he who is not pious cannot truly be wise" (*NS*, 1112).

The philosopher's consolation does not reside in an earthly hope that complete wisdom will stave off the dissolution of humanity. Consolation resides rather in awareness of divine providence with its persistent presence in *The New Science*, larger than the poet and the philosopher, founding imagination, memory, and understanding. It is the idea that, whether through the prophets, the incarnation, or the harsh remedy delivered to an ill Gentile people, God continues to recall humanity. Certainly this element can be culled from *The New Science* and turned into an idea such as "the invisible hand" or "the cunning of history," but this is not Vico, and from a Vichian perspective it is not sustainable in argument or history. From Vico's ground of pervasive divine providence, questions of meaning can be asked and asked boldly: even errors need not make us afraid because our longing will itself continue to draw us toward the Supreme Being. The presence of divine providence allows the *poiesis* of human life to mean by actually guiding the shape of human consciousness. Human consciousness is not an essence residing eternally in some independent state but arises in the whirl and flux. This ride does not feel as secure as eternal essence, but it is the feeling of life, and for the tumble of poetry and philosophy it is redemptive.

Divine providence makes possible the move from the imaginative universal to the intelligible universal through the trope and gift of irony, not as an end in itself but as a capacity that yields up the question and the tendency to question, separating the knower from the known – a tremendous leap. That very gift carries the risk of becoming an end in itself, leading to the two distinct forms of harmful barbarism – that of the extreme skeptic and that of the endless fact finder, seeking explanation without value, analysis without meaning, first this happened, then this, then this. This is a form of bad infinity that will be addressed by Hegel. But irony used well, wisely, and with humility allows the mind to move among the nations, among the names of God, among the poetries, and to see the way to a new kind of thought that is dynamic but is neither poetry nor philosophy. Though Vico's genius outstripped his capacity to express it, and much must be tolerated in reading *The New Science*, the power of his ideas grows clearer as similar insights are hit upon by others such as Kant, Herder, and Hamann.

# 7

## Kant and His Students on the Genius of Nature

Before winning his final post in philosophy at the University of Königsberg, Immanuel Kant was offered the position of professor of poetry in Berlin in 1764, which he turned down. Throughout his work, from his early observations on social habits and stories of ghosts to his final unfinished work full of notions about a priori matter, etymology, and recipes for the day, Kant always appears as a mind sorely tempted to go beyond what he viewed as "the boundaries of reason." He was unrelentingly disciplined in the face of this temptation, but the nature of his temptation was revealing. Regarding spirits, for example, he said, "I confess that I am much inclined to affirm the existence of immaterial natures in the world, and to place my own soul in the class of these beings."[1] But soon after this comment he tempered his inclination, saying clearly that "the appeal to immaterial principles is the refuge of a lazy philosophy" (*Dreams*, II, 331).

While he was establishing the firm boundaries of his island of truth, Kant knew the temptations and the dangers of sailing far from the shores and into the fog, and so he was at times scathing in his rejoinders. In his early book *Dreams of a Spirit Seer*, a book written to refute the spiritualist claims of Swedenborg, who said he could see action from a distance, in far away cities, for example, Kant said that "the realm of shades is the Paradise of visionaries" (*Dreams*, II, 317). Their materials are drawn from the bottomless well of "hypochondriacal vapors, wet nurse tales, and cloister miracles." Even if there were a so-called spiritual realm and power of the sort Swedenborg reported, the capacity to

---

[1] Immanuel Kant, *Dreams of a Spirit-Seer*, in *Kant on Swedenborg: Dreams of a Spirit-Seer and Other Writings*, trans. Gregory R. Johnson and Glenn Alexander Magee (West Chester, Pa.: Swedenborg Foundation Publishers, 2003), II, 32, hereafter cited in text as *Dreams*.

experience it would most likely be found in the kind of person in whom intensified images of the imagination tend to be confused with spiritual sensations such that truth cannot be distinguished from surrounding illusion (*Dreams*, II, 341). We have reviewed some of that long history, which says that those who speak for the spirit world – whether for the gods or demons – need to be "beside themselves" and out of their minds as a prerequisite for the task. Kant agrees. Whatever the advantages or disadvantages of contact with, insight into, or communication from the other world (if such a thing exists), the gift is "like that with which Juno honored Tiresias, making him blind so that she could impart to him the gift of prophecy." This is not the gift of healthy people, and it comes with a cost, for "intuitive knowledge of the other world can be obtained here only by one losing some of the understanding one needs for the present" (*Dreams*, II, 341). Although in some of his letters Kant is clearly drawn to the idea of this other world, when he takes a more public stand regarding people who claim discovery of this world, he cites the words of the coachman addressed to Tycho Brahe (who claimed he could travel the shortest way at night by the stars): "Good sir, you may well understand the heavens, but here on earth you are a fool."[2]

Readers who have felt the longing that comes through Kant's wonder at "the moral law within me and the starry sky above me" might wonder further at the extent to which he avoids being led by such longings for fear that they might lead to a "foolish" and "groundless" philosophy. His attacks on those who did not share his caution were often expressed with considerable humor. Speaking of that metaphysics airy and capacious enough to accommodate fevered brains in their search for mystery, he draws on the poet Samuel Butler, writing, "If a hypochondriacal wind should rage in the guts, what matters is the direction it takes: if downwards, then the result is a fart; if upwards, an apparition or a heavenly inspiration" (*Dreams*, II, 348; Samuel Butler, *Hudibras*, II, iii, 773–83).

Metaphysics is always in danger of degeneration in part because our reason is inclined to know where knowledge is not possible. Kant was familiar with that temptation, but he was sober in his assessment of the limits of metaphysics even before he staked out the boundaries of the island of truth in the *Critique of Pure Reason*. "Metaphysics, with which I have been fated to fall in love but from which I can boast of only a few favors, has two advantages" (*Dreams*, II, 367). He says that this mistress

---

[2] Though Kant quotes this in *Dreams of a Spirit-Seer* (in Johnson and Magee, *Kant on Swedenborg*, II, 27), he is the only known source.

allows one to spy out the hidden qualities of things using reason. At the same time, metaphysics, which opens up the possibility of seeing through reason, also reveals the limitations of human reason, especially by questioning whether an idea under consideration is related to *empirical* concepts that form the only proper basis for our judgments. This internal caution and safety net are meant to prevent reliance on what he jokingly called a *clinamen* – an unearned or ill-founded premise. The term comes from Epicurus, who required an uncaused and imperceptible swerve of one atom in the void to move from his image of atoms raining down in parallel to the world we see around us, with all of its complex collections of atoms in the forms of mountains, lemons, and beagles. One uncaused swerve – allow that, and everything else follows.

Kant emphatically will not allow this. Not once. Not a single *clinamen* is to be embraced. Of those like Swedenborg who would allow such entities, he says, following the poet Ludovico Ariosto, "His flask in the lunar world is completely full." For according to Ariosto in *Orlando Furioso*, when we lose reason in this world it migrates to the moon and is stored in a flask, so that there is an inverse relationship between our reason in this world and how full our lunar flask is (*Dreams*, II, 360). And even when such people hit upon something true, they have no means for sorting out the true from the false and are no longer philosophers but more like poets who "sometimes prophesize when they rave, as one believes, or at least so they say, when they now and then coincide with the truth" (*Dreams*, II, 359).

In *Dreams of a Spirit Seer*, one senses Kant's own attraction to Swedenborg [mystic] and to that "realm of shades" which is "the paradise of visionaries." At [early Intense] many points Kant seems ambiguous toward these ideas that have populated the works of poets, prophets, and oracles. But if there is any doubt in the book about the place Kant allows for poetic oracles in philosophy, any lingering suspicion that there is room for "the butterfly wings of metaphysics" to lift us up and enable us to converse with spirit forms, he brings it to a definite end that fully sets the stage for his encounter [empiricist] with the skepticism of David Hume, and the production of the first critique: "Now that the styptic power of self-knowledge has folded these silken wings, we see ourselves back on the low ground of experience and common sense, happy if we regard it as our assigned place from which we may never depart with impunity, and which contains everything that can satisfy us so long as we stay with what is useful" (*Dreams*, II, 368).

Kant says that these visionary sorts of minds are most common in hypochondriacs, a topic about which he knew a great deal because he was himself inclined toward it and had close friends who suffered from it. These minds are of several sorts, and not all are equally bad. The melancholic, for example, is a visionary about life's ills. Love leads to rapture, and those who are full of moral feeling rather than moral principle are labeled visionary by some. Indeed, he says that the semblance of vision and moral feeling that he labels fanaticism is a necessary ingredient for doing anything great in the world. These kinds of visionaries are quite different from "the enthusiast." "This person is genuinely deranged from an alleged immediate revelation and from a great familiarity with the powers of heaven. Human nature knows no more dangerous deception."[3] The danger of the enthusiasts is that their visions can simultaneously be beyond the power and discipline of critique and be attached to extreme action in the world that leads to the suffering of whole nations. Kant deplored the spinning of tales that filled so many volumes of "metaphysics" up to his age. He found it deplorable not because metaphysics is a trifling subject unworthy of so much attention but rather because it is vitally important, and the inspired ones, the enthusiasts, threatened that great endeavor by appearing to have insights without submitting to the test of philosophical criticism. "I am so far from regarding metaphysics itself, objectively considered, to be trivial or dispensable," Kant says in a letter to Moses Mendelssohn, "that I have been chiefly convinced for some time that I understand its nature and its proper place in human knowledge and that the true and lasting welfare of the human race depends on it, an appraisal that would seem fantastic and audacious to anyone but you."[4]

This is the background against which Kant approaches the questions of interest to both the philosopher and the poet. Kant addresses poetry (and finds it a proper home in the critical philosophy) most thoroughly in *The Critique of Judgment*, published in 1790. But that project, which approached the realities of the beautiful and the sublime, was Kant's second sustained visit to that world. The first work on the topic was published twenty-six years earlier, *Observations on the Feeling of the Beautiful and the Sublime*. Most striking in this early work is its lack of abstraction, its attention to the particular details of human life and experience.[5] The

---

[3] Immanuel Kant, "Essay on the Sicknesses of the Head," in Johnson and Magee, *Kant on Swedenborg*, II, 267.

[4] Immanuel Kant, "Letter to Moses Mendelssohn," in Johnson and Magee, *Kant on Swedenborg*, X, 70.

[5] Reading the two works side by side leaves the impression that the early work is an argument from concrete example and the later work is the map to the same country, now

sublime moves, while the beautiful charms. The site of a mountain with a snow-covered peak rising above the clouds is sublime, while the valleys with winding brooks and fields of grazing flocks are beautiful. Milton's portrayal of hell is sublime, Homer's portrayal of the Girdle of Venus is beautiful.[6]

He teases out categories of the sublime in that work like a biologist categorizing species of bacteria. So we have the noble sublime, the splendid sublime, and the terrifying sublime. This latter is associated with the experience of deep loneliness, and for this reason "far-reaching solitudes, like the colossal Komul Desert in Tartary, have always given us occasion for peopling them with fearsome spirits, goblins, and ghouls" (*Observations*, 48). He sorts out the distinction between the sublimity of a great height, which is accompanied by wonder, and that of a great depth, which is accompanied by a sensation of shuddering. A long duration is sublime. Understanding is sublime. Lonely shadows in a sacred grove are sublime. Flower beds, cow hedges, and wit are beautiful.

The sensation of the beautiful and the sublime can go wrong. The visionary errs in loving and believing the fantastic. When the feeling of the beautiful degenerates, Kant calls it trifling. A young man in whom this occurs is a fop, a middle-aged man is a dandy, and an elderly man is an old dandy, identified by Kant as "the most contemptible creature in nature, just as a young crank is the most offensive and intolerable" (*Observations*, 53). This characterization of the preternaturally responsive Immanuel Kant responding to the particulars of his Königsberg surroundings to yield conclusions about cranks, fops, and dandies in a book on the beautiful and sublime is not the image most readers are likely to have the first time they find themselves in the world of *The Critique of Pure Reason*. It is in the third critique, *The Critique of Judgment*, that we find poetry directly addressed as the highest ranking of the arts, originating almost entirely from a peculiar power Kant identifies as "genius." He made it clear in the works preceding the third critique that prophetic poets, spirit seers, the inspired, the enthusiastic, and all who claim to see heaven before actually getting there simply cannot have a place at philosophy's banquet table. In some cases, these are dismissed

---

processed through the critical mill, yielding categories that parallel the first critique (an issue with which Kant deals in a footnote, explaining the necessity and inevitability of this structure).

[6]  Immanuel Kant, *Observations on the Feeling of the Beautiful and the Sublime*, trans. John T. Goldthwait (Berkeley: University of California Press) 47, hereafter cited in text as *Observations*.

with argument in some cases with ridicule. But it is through the idea of genius in poetry that the old force finds its way in under a new guise.

As with other thinkers, a bit of background work is needed in order to understand the relationship of poetry to philosophy in Kant. The force operative in art is associated with the power that unifies our higher cognition, linking understanding and reason. This power is judgment.[7] In the first two critiques, two domains were explored – the domain of nature (the sensible) and the domain of freedom (the super-sensible). There is a chasm fixed between these two domains, that of a determined natural world and that of the moral world requiring freedom. And yet because we *do* live in a determined natural world and yet live as free, moral beings, there must be some basis unifying the two domains, and this is the power of judgment. We cannot reach cognition of this power theoretically or practically in the way we reach knowledge of nature and freedom. Judgment mediates the two domains but does not have a domain of its own (*Critique*, 176). It becomes apparent *only* through its activity: as we make judgments, the power of judgment makes itself known. Our judgments are of what either is or is not (theoretical), judgments of "ought" (practical), or aesthetic/teleological judgments. These last judgments are peculiar in that they do not involve a concept that is connected with an object but rather involve a feeling, such as the feeling of pleasure that leads to a judgment of taste in the case of a beautiful object, or an intellectual feeling in the case of the sublime (*Critique*, 191–2).

When we judge something as beautiful, because there is no *concept* associated with the judgment, there is no *rule* that can make a person acknowledge the beauty of the object (*Critique*, 215). Rules are what allow for universal applicability in science and in morality. In theoretical judgments, the universality of the *rule of nature* is present (X always causes Y in Z conditions), and in practical judgments the statement of "ought" is a *moral rule* applicable to everyone everywhere (willed to be a universal maxim). So in aesthetic judgments of taste, we *require* that everyone like the object, and yet in the absence of a rule, such judgments must be different from theoretical or moral judgments. "Beautiful is what, without a concept, is liked universally" (*Critique*, 219) The fact that *aesthetic* judgments are not associated with a concept gives us a unique window on the workings of the power of judgment. In scientific or moral judgments,

---

[7] Immanuel Kant, *The Critique of Judgment*, trans. Werner S. Pluhar (Indianapolis: Hackett, 1987), 177, hereafter cited in text as *Critique*.

Kant says, the judgment is "objective" in the obvious sense of referring to the object without reference to me as subject: the speed with which a stone dropped from a building falls or the wrongness of lying in no way depend on my feeling as a subject before an object or act. But an aesthetic judgment is *revealed* through feeling and is therefore fundamentally subjective. The relationship of the judgment to myself as subject, to *my feeling*, makes the universality of aesthetic judgments peculiar. Kant says that we feel the play of our natural faculties in such judgments, and this play reveals the workings of judgment in a unique way, being mine and given solely to me as subject (*Critique*, 228). Within ourselves, we can study the way in which judgment functions as we look at, say, a flower. A flower can be looked at scientifically or aesthetically. And as we stand before the flower considering it now one way, now the other, our exercise reveals the difference in these modes of judgment. "Hardly anyone apart from the botanist knows what sort of thing a flower is [meant] to be; and even he, while recognizing it as the reproductive organ of a plant, pays no attention to this natural purpose when he judges the flower by taste" (*Critique*, 229). The beauty, then, is not a purpose that can be pointed to as with the reproductive function of the flower but rather is the *form of purposiveness*, felt, but felt as necessary and something to which everyone *ought* to give assent (*Critique*, 236, 238, 240). The subjective principle that allows judgments of taste *felt* with universal validity Kant calls "common sense," not in the vulgar sense of "plain common sense" but rather as *sensus communis* in which my judgment is weighted with that of others, the "public sense." "We must take *sensus communis* to mean the idea of a sense shared [by all of us]" (*Critique*, 293).

Such is our experience of the beautiful. The sublime is similar to the beautiful in that we like it for its own sake, but there are some important differences. One difference is that, while we can correctly call many objects in nature beautiful, we err if we call objects in nature sublime. Rather, "sublime objects" are properly objects that provide the occasion for revealing a sublimity within the mind. In the experience of the sublime we are discovering things about ourselves rather than about the natural object that is the occasion for the experience (*Critique*, 245). Our imagination strives toward infinity, and we feel the tension between what can actually be an object of sense (which excludes the idea of infinity because one cannot experience infinite anything, as "sense" is necessarily bounded) and that toward which our mind strives. This is a feeling of the sublime, and it reveals a power in our mind that surpasses sense (*Critique*, 248). Reason demands "absolute totality as a real idea," but to think such a thing – the infinite as a whole – requires, and thus reveals, a supersensible power that is the "substrate" underlying this experience of the world. This experience of the infinite is an aesthetic experience that teaches us something about ourselves and so, Kant says, it functions as a kind of "respect for our own vocation" (*Critique*, 256). The imagination in its aesthetic judgment reveals our strength, uncovers our vocation, and, through the aesthetic experience of the sublime, shows the character of our minds as being beyond mundane interests such as tending our possessions, our bodies and our life, and indeed even being above nature (*Critique*, 262).

In the experience of the sublime, there is an element of mental agitation, but this agitation is not sufficient for the experience. The sublime always refers to our way of thinking, "to maxims directed to providing the intellectual [side in us] and our rational ideas with supremacy over sensibility" (*Critique*, 274). That is, imagination, because it is not bound by the sensible, can uniquely exhibit the infinite, which, though negative, "still expands the soul." This is contrasted with those impetuous agitations of the mind that do not expand the soul, and which Kant compares to the belief that one has been edified by a sermon with no "system of good maxims" or improved by attending a tragedy at the theater "when in fact they are merely glad at having succeeded in routing boredom" (*Critique*, 274).

When we ask how we are to approach genuine experiences of sublimity, Kant responds with one of his favorite examples – the starry sky. But when we say the sight of the starry sky is sublime, we must not base our judgment on something like the possibility of intelligent life on other planets – another of Kant's recurrent peripheral favorites. Rather, we must encounter it merely as we see it, "as a vast vault encompassing everything," and upon this do we exercise the aesthetic judgment yielding an experience of the sublime. So with the ocean, "We must be able to view the ocean as the poets do, merely in terms of what manifests itself to the eye" (*Critique*, 270). Thus, when it is calm, we see it as "a clear mirror of water bounded only by the sky," and when turbulent, as "an abyss threatening to engulf everything." The experience is negative, inscrutable, and simple: "*Simplicity* (artless purposiveness) is, as it were, nature's style in the sublime" (*Critique*, 275).

This sense that is shared by all, entitling us to require that everyone agree with our judgment, must be based on an a priori principle. What is this a priori principle, and how does one get to it? At the outset Kant is clear on one approach that will *not* get us to the principle: "We can never arrive at such a principle by scouting about for empirical laws about mental changes. For these reveal only how we *do* judge; they do not give us a command as to how we *ought* to judge, let alone an unconditional one" (*Critique*, 278). Empirical laws will not get us to the principle, but it is necessary nonetheless to begin with nature. An interest in the beauty found in art does not prove moral goodness, but it is the mark of a good soul to take a direct interest in the beauty of *nature*. If this interest is habitual, it leads to contemplation of nature, and such a contemplative disposition is itself associated with moral goodness. The key phrase is "direct interest." Beauty in nature appeals in a unique way, and in order for us to take this *direct interest* in beauty as such, that beauty must be in *nature*. Kant gives us an example to illustrate his point: "What do poets praise more highly than the nightingale's enchantingly beautiful song in a secluded thicket on a quiet summer evening by the soft light of the moon?" (*Critique*, 302). But if we are sitting out on the porch lost in poetic reverie as the nightingale sings, and we then discover that the sound is not an actual nightingale, but rather some clever boy with a gift for imitative whistling, we are no longer interested, and likely annoyed by the deception.

How then, in our pursuit of the a priori principle, do we get from this perspective on nature to the highest art, which is poetry? The answer is, through genius. "Genius is the talent (natural endowment) that gives the rule to art" (*Critique*, 307). But because the talent is innate to the artist and thus a part of nature, one might state the definition differently: "Genius is the innate mental disposition (*ingenium*) through which nature gives the rule to art." Genius is what makes possible a fine art that can appropriately be admired, but this is because genius is *nature*, is the means by which *nature* gives the rule, and so is not something about which the artist can give an account. Kant says that "if an author owes a product to his genius, he himself does not know how he came by the ideas for it" (*Critique*, 308). The genius cannot make such products at will, show a plan for such products, or communicate a procedure by which others might produce such works. Kant goes on to say that this is why the word "genius" derives from the Latin for the guardian spirit given to one at birth, which then inspires such ideas. It is not much of a stretch to hear in these ideas the return yet again of the poet as oracle, with the argument summed up in this way:

1. Poetry is the highest art.
2. Genius gives the rule to art.

3. Genius, as innate to the artist, belongs to nature. Therefore:
4. Genius is the means by which nature gives the rule to art.
5. We can only admire that beauty that is in and of nature. Therefore:
6. Only genius, as nature, makes possible admirable fine art.
7. But the poet does not control genius and cannot give an account of the products of genius, because it is nature giving the rule. Therefore:
8. Nature is now the "possessor" for which the poet is the oracle.

Kant would no doubt avoid the language of the oracle. But the point remains: we apparently hear something in the poetry of the genius that merits our direct interest because of its relation to nature, and nature as that which is most real, in a way the roguish boy whistling like a nightingale behind the bush to fool us does not.

Kant goes much farther. Comparing the poet to the scientist, he says that however excellent the mind required to make the discoveries of Newton, nonetheless one can learn everything Newton set forth in his scientific works. By contrast, no matter how fine the models, one cannot learn to write inspired poetry. "In scientific matters, therefore, the greatest discoverer differs from the most arduous imitator and apprentice only in degree, whereas he differs in kind from someone whom nature has endowed for fine art" (*Critique*, 308–9). But genius provides only the material. This genius must learn to give the raw material form through academic training, so that the products of genius can stand up to the power of judgment (*Critique*, 310). As to the models that might be used, not for teaching genius that cannot be taught, but for teaching form that allows tasteful expression of the product of genius, the best models are those "composed in language both dead and scholarly" (*Critique*, 232n). In this way, the models do not undergo the changes that occur in living languages, but rather stay fixed with their own inalterable rule. The first time one studies the four chambers of the heart, better that it not be beating, and for this one requires a corpse.

Even in a living language, a poem can be elegant but spiritless. That element, which Kant calls the spirit (*Geist*) of the poem, is the animating principle of the mind, that which quickens the soul. Here we reach the principle that enlivens and expands the soul, opening whole worlds in a kind of play that nonetheless demands our attention as arising from nature, giving a feeling of purposiveness and so functioning as a kind of awakening to the reality of the supersensible, of that which goes beyond the sensible world: "I maintain that this principle is nothing but the ability to exhibit aesthetic ideas" (*Critique*, 313). These ideas expand the soul in part because the imagination presents something that prompts thought, but to which no concept is adequate and no language sufficient to enable us to fully grasp it. Poets strive "to give sensible expression to rational ideas of invisible beings, the realm of the Blessed, the realm of hell, eternity, creation, and so on" (*Critique*, 314). Using imagination, the poet tries to give sensible expression to things beyond the limits of experience, with no precedent in nature except, of course, for that part of nature which gives rise to genius. This is, to some extent, true of all fine art. But it is "in the art of poetry that the power [i.e., the faculty] of aesthetic ideas can manifest itself to full extent." Poetry is a kind of play, a special kind of play in the imagination, but a play with ideas so that it *acts* as if its tasks were those of the understanding. The poetic imagination *plays* with ideas, but in playing, "[the poet] provides food for the understanding and gives life to its concepts by means of his imagination" (*Critique*, 321). The purposive form we experience in fine art attunes the spirit to ideas, and this refinement is only *sustainable* if the fine arts are connected in some way with moral ideas – otherwise the arts devolve into mere enjoyment, which ultimately dulls the spirit (*Critique*, 326). The core of moral ideas is bound up with freedom, and freedom stands in contrast with the determinism we find everywhere in the sensible world of nature. Our minds strain past the limits of the sensible world, and Kant's entire project is to understand, <u>first</u>, the world as given to us in sense; <u>second</u>, the character and meaning of our inevitable inclination to strain past this world and the clues to be drawn from our moral life; and, <u>third</u>, once the limits are fully understood, to ask what else might be learned by the striving of the mind beyond the determined world.

The beautiful is symbolic of the morally good, and it is because of the reference of the beautiful to the morally good that one can claim everyone's assent to our liking for an instance of the beautiful (*Critique*, 353). That which underlies and makes possible the purposiveness of the product of genius (art, the beautiful) is that supersensible substrate inaccessible to any concept of the understanding but nonetheless responsible for harmonizing all of our cognitive powers (*Critique*, 344). And as we refer the beautiful to the morally good, moral goodness is the intelligible aspect of taste – and our responsiveness to the products of genius – with which our higher cognitive powers harmonize. Taste, Kant says, "is basically an ability to judge the [way in which] moral ideas are made sensible" (*Critique*, 356). Therefore, we cultivate our taste by cultivating our moral feelings and ideas.

Poetry, as the highest art, is the means by which we get at aspects of the phenomenal world beyond what nature itself can give. "Poetry fortifies the mind: for it lets the mind feel its ability – free, spontaneous, and independent of natural determinations – to contemplate and judge phenomenal nature as having aspects that nature does not on its own offer in experience either to sense or to the understanding, and hence poetry lets the mind feel its ability to use nature on behalf of and, as it were, as a schema of the supersensible" (*Critique*, 326). Poetry, properly conceived and behaving as it ought, always recognizes and embraces its character as play – "it does not seek to sneak up on the understanding and ensnare it by a sensible exhibition" (*Critique*, 327). One of Kant's great accomplishments is to attain a deep understanding of what it is we do in science, and to protect this project from the skepticism of Hume, but then to go on and ask about the remainder that is left over after the parts of nature accessible to science are divided up and accounted for. Here we find our longing for God, freedom and immortality, and the existence of fine art. The former are rational ideas and the latter aesthetic ideas. An aesthetic idea is a presentation of the imagination to which no concept is adequate, and a rational idea is its counterpart, a concept to which no presentation of the imagination can be adequate (*Critique*, 314). Summing up, Kant says, "I think we may call aesthetic ideas unexpoundable presentations of the imagination, and rational ideas indemonstrable concepts of reason (concepts of reason which are concepts of the supersensible)" (*Critique*, 342). Genius is the ability to exhibit aesthetic ideas.

The products of genius as arising from nature within the poet and of the beautiful as encountered in nature are judged by one who, in cultivating moral feeling, becomes capable of contemplating nature (including aesthetic ideas, arising through the genius of the poet). The centerpiece of this posture is the experience of purposiveness. In the first introduction to *The Critique of Judgment*, Kant says that we can approach appearances mechanically, "like an instrument, guided by the understanding of the senses," or we can deal with them artistically (*Critique*, 213). It is through the latter approach that we become aware of this *feeling* of purposiveness. This contrast between the mechanical and the artistic responses to nature, between the determined and the purposive, can be applied to all the world, though the two approaches are reconcilable only in a principle beyond both, that of the supersensible.

Kant's example shows how pervasive the effect of this habit of contemplation can be: "Consider a maggot," he says (*Critique*, 411). We can look at the maggot as a mere mechanism of matter. On the other hand, we can look at the maggot in terms of natural principles, in terms of a teleological principle that cannot be reconciled with the mere mechanical view. (Poetry tries to give sensible expression to invisible beings and so is always pointing beyond.) In this way, it serves to awaken the mind to the supersensible, which in turn reconciles the mechanical and the teleological.

Ultimately for Kant, this movement between the experience of the mechanical world and the awakening play of the imagination, as well as the movement between genius and judgment, opens up a world beyond that will finally lead to the idea of God via moral feeling, though there will be stages along the way that, in retrospect, seem dubious. The ancients, Kant says, cannot be blamed for thinking of their gods – including the chief god – in anthropomorphic terms. Later, the "physicists who wanted to be theologians" working under reason's desire for unity in nature progressed to the idea of a being in which all natural things inhere (*Critique*, 439). But, though fear gave rise to the first gods and the idea of a unifying being rose from reason's need for unity in nature, it was only through reason proceeding by means of moral principles that the idea of God fully dawned (*Critique*, 447). Here it is that the whole converges on these aspects of our contemplative life. Kant says toward the end of the third critique, "Consider a human being at those moments when his mind is attuned to moral feeling: it is surrounded by a beautiful nature, he finds himself calmly and serenely enjoying his existence, he will feel within him a need to be grateful to someone.... In a word, he has a need for a moral intelligence, because he exists for a purpose and needs a being that caused both himself and the world in conformity with that purpose" (*Critique*, 445). In the experience of the beauty of nature, we encounter this longing. Poetry, as a product of genius, which in turn is a part of nature, expands the soul, awakens us to this supersensible, and takes us to a threshold that philosophy brings into relation to all else the mind encounters and does.

In considering the reality of moral feeling, Kant sometimes wrote as though it was based on an internal law requiring us to view ourselves from an external point of view, with the agent as rational observer of himself or even as one split into nonrational actor and rational observer. This structure (which reveals, for Kant, his own moral life) is writ larger in the relationship of the genius's production of poetry by a means for which he cannot account, and the judge whose taste is shaped by moral ideas and moral feeling. This back-and-forth points beyond a determined world and is a hopeful enterprise. Always the play with purposiveness along with our deep need to look for purpose, even in the reality of a maggot, is a central and old theme in Kant, which started at the beginning of the critical philosophy. We cannot know what is beyond experience, but we can, and indeed must, think it. Within this compelling tension, poetry does its work, and philosophy delights in this revealing play.

Delight of the sort described in *The Critique of Judgment* is possible for Kant only so long as philosophy remains philosophy. Kant had a couple of students and friends at the University of Königsberg whose work stood as a critique of his own. One was Johann Georg Hamann, known as "The Magus of the North," the author of works that, though largely critical responses to the works of others rather than positive contributions, were nonetheless influential on both Hegel and Kierkegaard (the next two figures in this history).

In 1757 Hamann traveled to England to do some work for the firm that employed him. While in England, he not only failed in business but also became embroiled in a profligate group of men and found himself failing through dissipation as well until he ended up alone in a London attic with a Bible and no money. He read the Bible beginning to end and had a profound religious conversion to Christ. Like the prodigal son, he returned to Königsberg bringing not only his renewed faith but also a philosophy he found liberating – the skepticism of David Hume, which alone, Hamann thought, made room for faith in the otherwise suffocating air of Enlightenment ideas.

His friends, Kant among them, tried to undo his conversion and bring him back to the light of reason. He refused. Their world was simply not capacious enough for what he took to be true. Then it was that he translated a relatively short passage from Hume and published it in 1771 in the newspaper *Königsberger Zeitung* as an essay titled "Night Thoughts of a Skeptic" – the last chapter of book 1 of Hume's *Treatise on Human Nature*. Reading this translation led to Kant's awakening, which in turn led to the critical philosophy. The trajectory of Hamann's response to Hume's skepticism differed considerably from Kant's, and he became a severe critic of Kant's philosophy.

Hamann's critique of philosophy, expressed in his idiosyncratic stringing together of literary, historical, local, and especially scriptural allusion within a matrix of prose peppered with occasional vulgarities

and jabs of ridicule, was decisively a linguistic critique. Like Vico and
Herder, Hamann thought philosophy was most profitably pursued
alongside the study of language, and indeed he thought that whenever
the two are pursued independently, both are diminished. The modes of
thought that people use are, for Hamann, cobbled together from contemporary fashions and prejudices, and these have substantial influence
on people's language.[8] As languages grow, they come up against other
languages, as well as those processes of thought that work in tandem to
shape a language. The language grows in the tension between the two.
Hamann says, "It has been a real piece of luck for our language that the
craving for translation and for logical demonstration have kept each
other going; the latter would have become a rosary of enumerated neol-
ogisms, and the former would have been made into a net that captures
and takes the good and foul fish of every class."[9] Here is yet another
way to state the quarrel: A logic detached from the linguistic roots of
human thought is bloodless and empty, but the wholesale grab for language without logic becomes a murky swamp that is not of great use
for advancing human knowledge. "The wealth of human knowledge,"
Hamann says, "rests on the exchange of words."[10]

In *Aesthetica in Nuce*, he says that "poetry is the mother tongue of
the human race, as the garden is older than the plowed field."[11] But
nature presents itself in "jumbled verses.... To gather these together is
the scholar's modest part; to interpret them, the philosopher's; to imitate them – or bolder still – bring them into right order, the poet's"
(*Aesthetica*, 66). Speaking is translation from the angelic language of
thought into the human language of words. God speaks through creation (giving us select concepts) and through Scripture (revealing certain secret articles of faith). The two are unified by being the speech of
one author (*Aesthetica*, 75). When philosophy separates the two forms of
divine speech, the language of nature is no longer interpretable, and it
is here that he most starkly criticizes Kant. Hamann calls for the Muse to
come "like a refiner's fire, and like a fuller's soap – she will dare to purify
the natural use of the senses from the unnatural use of abstractions, by

---

[8] Johann Georg Hamann, "Essay on an Academic Question," in *Writings on Philosophy
and Language*, trans. Kenneth Haynes (Cambridge: Cambridge University Press,
2007), 15.
[9] Ibid.
[10] Johann Georg Hamann, "Word Order in the French Language," in *Writings*, 22.
[11] Johann Georg Hamann, "Aesthetica in Nuce," in *Writings*, 63, hereafter cited in text as
*Aesthetica*.

which our concepts of things are maimed as the name of the Creator is suppressed and blasphemed" (*Aesthetica*, 79). This effort, which Hamann calls "purism," is most fully the target of his attacks, the effort exemplified by his friend Kant to isolate reason from our lived experience and history and language. "Nature and scripture...are the materials of the beautiful, creative, and imitative spirit" (*Aesthetica*, 85). God has spoken through creation, prophets, poets, and seers, and ultimately, when God grew "short of breath" and wearied of these means, God spoke through Christ, the son of God (*Aesthetica*, 89).

In Hamann's perspective on the quarrel between the poets and philosophers, then, the poets fare rather better than the philosophers and are an important means by which God has spoken. Poetry is the mother tongue of humanity, and the origin of human language is divine.[12] The truth is found in this unified speech rooted in the divine, but "philosophers have always given truth a bill of divorcement by putting asunder what nature has joined together and vice versa."[13]

Some of his sharpest criticism and humor were directed not at philosophy as a whole (insofar as it isolates things that should not be isolated and which, when isolated, are not of the truth) but at Kant specifically. In his *Metacritique of the Purism of Reason*, he calls Kant to task for his misuse of language in his philosophically pretentious "solving" of problems that are unreal in the first place. "Pure reason" – this is what Hamann objects to and ridicules, a fiction that artificially separated reason from tradition, custom, everyday experience, and language grounded in tradition and usage, which is "the only, first, and last organon and criterion of reason."[14] In its effort to achieve "the apodictic certainty of mathematics," philosophical metaphysics misuses this language, which has been the currency of God's speech to us through the poets, prophets,

---

[12] Johann Georg Hamann, "The Last Will and Testament of the Knight of the Rose-Cross," in *Writings*, 100.

[13] Johann Georg Hamann, "Philological Ideas and Doubts," in *Writings*, 117. Hamann also argues that it is an error to abstract our moral life from the unity of the natural use of human reason and language as the "inner and outer band of all social life." This is the foundation of our "moral capacity to say Yes! or No!" and to sever reason from language as a human institution grown from divine origins leads to "lies and deceit, shame and vice...confirmed and stamped as means to Felicity" (Hamann, *Writings*, 175). In one of his more visual images, Hamann says, "Like worms through children, laws pass through sickly men of letters; laws are the golden emrods and the nymph Egeria of many a philosophical government" (Hamann, *Writings*, 172).

[14] Johann Georg Hamann, "Metacritique on the Purism of Reason," in *Writings*, 208, hereafter cited in text as *Metacritique*.

and the like, and which balances us in our social relationships, so that "through this learned troublemaking it works the honest decency of language into such a meaningless, rutting, unstable, indefinite something = x that nothing is left but a windy sough, a magic shadow play, at most, as the wise Helveticus says, the talisman and the rosary of a transcendental superstitious belief in *entia rationis*, their empty sacks and slogans" (*Metacritique*, 210). The crisis in Kant's philosophy, Hamann says, is one of language and a failure to recognize the priority of language with its roots in our history and tradition as a gift from God. Language, rising up from the beating of the heart and the rhythm of the breath, is the truest foundation of human knowledge and reason, and so Kant is wrong to think that reason is at variance with itself through nonempirical employment of reason: rather, as "the entire faculty of thought is founded on language...language is also the center point of reason's misunderstanding with itself" (*Metacritique*, 211).

Kant, in rejecting such mystery, has conjured mysteries of his own in the unplumbable "something = x" and "the synthetic mysteries of the forms a priori and a posteriori corresponding and contradicting themselves, together with the transubstantiation of subjective conditions and the subsumption into objective predicates and attributes through the copula of an authoritative or expletive word for cutting short dull wholes and filling out empty space in a periodic galimatias *per thesin et arsin*" (*Metacritique*, 214).

Hamann is an unusual responder, inclined toward humor and prone to deflate pretensions, arguing that God speaks, among other ways, through the poets and their kin, and poetry is the mother tongue. In the quarrel, Hamann embraces the priority of the poetic against the strain of philosophy that makes some of its fundamental errors early in language, and then he doggedly pursues the consequences of these misguided beginnings as though making discoveries of the highest importance. "Analysis is nothing more than the latest fashionable art, and synthesis nothing more than the artful seam of a professional leather- or cloth-cutter. And what philosophy metagrabolizes I have, for the sake of weak readers, transformed into a figure, the sacrament of language, the letters of its elements, the spirit of its institution, and I leave it to each one to unclench the closed fist into an open palm" (*Metacritique*, 217).

But Hamann does not want to get rid of philosophy. Rather, he would have the power of philosophy balanced by that of poetry. "The spirit of observation and the spirit of prophecy are the wings of human genius,"

Hamann says.[15] Philosophical genius abstracts, disrobing "actual objects into naked concepts." Poetic genius transfigures the domain of prophecy (to which belongs all that is absent – the past and the future) into present representations through its fictions. These two forces must be balanced, neither allowed to usurp the other. Whether the forces stayed balanced in Hamann's world is unclear. In any case, Kant did not see Hamann as one to whom he needed to make sustained response.

Herder was a different story. Johann Gottfried Herder was Kant's student in Königsberg, but he grew far from his teacher and became one whom Kant thought should be clearly refuted. However, Hamann was by no means sure that Kant fully understood Herder. When, in 1774, Herder published *On the Oldest Document of the Human Race*, Kant wrote to Hamann asking for an interpretation, but "if possible in language of human beings. For I, poor son of this earth, am not organized to understand the divine language of *intuitive reason*. What one spells out in common concepts and in accordance with logical rules I can indeed grasp."[16] Some of Kant's contemporaries thought the third critique was actually a sustained attack on Herder. In his biography of Kant, Manfred Kuehn argues that this is not true, and that in fact Kant tried to persuade his (complicated) friend Christian Jacob Kraus to refute Herder so that he could concentrate on writing the third critique instead of being distracted by such things.[17] Later he did briefly review Herder's most famous work *Ideas toward a Philosophy of History* in the *Allgemeine Literaturzeitung*, questioning whether the book's poetic spirit observed the work's philosophy and "whether frequently the tissue of daring metaphors, poetic images and mythological allusions does not serve to conceal the corpus of thought as under a farthingale instead of letting it glimmer forth agreeably as under a translucent veil."[18]

In any case Herder, who is fascinated with the mysteries of the creative process, had a revolutionary impact of his own on contemporaries and those who followed him. Though he likely did not read Vico's *New Science* until later in his life after his own positions had been formed and articulated, there is much agreement between Vico and Herder.[19]

[15] Johann Georg Hamann, "A Flying Letter to Nobody, the Well Known," in *Writings*, 221.

[16] Johann Georg Hamann, *Briefwechsel, III*, p. 82; quoted in Manfred Kuehn, *Kant: A Biography* (Cambridge: Cambridge University Press, 2001), 224.

[17] Kuehn, *Kant: A Biography*, 245.

[18] Lewis White Beck, *Historical Writings*, 45; quoted in Kuehn, *Kant: A Biography*, 297.

[19] Isaiah Berlin, *Vico and Herder* (London: Hogarth Press, 1992), 147, hereafter cited in text as Berlin.

Like Vico, Herder maintained that the heart and soul of the nation dwell in its language and that human thought and feeling are incorporated into symbolic forms such as poetry and ritual (Berlin, 165). Isaiah Berlin in his book *Vico and Herder* says that for Herder poetry was magical in character, a kind of pure activity that does not sit easily in the fixed form of the written word (indeed, poetry is threatened with becoming stagnant and dead through being written down), but which goads to action and lived experience (Berlin, 171). He is repelled by the efforts of philosophers such as Kant who try to isolate and classify "faculties" in contrast to lived experience (Berlin, 174). On the other hand, he embraced wholeheartedly Hamann's idea that our fundamental activity is to speak to God and each other and that the centerpiece of understanding and purposeful activity is language (Berlin, 167). As Berlin says, for Herder, "to create a language is to think, and to think is to use language" (Berlin, 168). Thus, he resists the idea that one culture can be a means to another, as almost all societies rich with their own language and tradition are good in themselves. Nor does he accept the idea of steady progress from some benighted past to some enlightened future – one of the great myths of the eighteenth century (Berlin, 189–90). What counts as true progress is for people and groups of people to ever more fully foster their peculiar growth within their own language, customs, craft, and form of life (Berlin, 191). In Herder's words, "To bind and interrogate this Proteus, which is usually called national character and which shows itself certainly not less in the writings than in the usages and actions of a nation – that is a high and beautiful philosophy. It is practiced most surely in poetry; for in the works of the imagination and feeling, the entire soul of nations reveals itself most freely."[20] Myths are not false stories invented by priests to deceive the people, and the poets do not exist merely to entertain the crowd or convey information. Rather, a whole vision of the world arises from such poetry, and in the process of grasping this poetic world contemplatively, we ourselves are able to flourish and grow within our own communities (Berlin, 194). We learn more fully who we are. In such engagement we can rejoice in the character and fullness of other groups and other nations.

Our stories and histories are most fully expressed in the art of the people and, above all, the poets: Herder says, "A poet is a creator of a people; he gives it a world to contemplate, and he holds its soul in his

---

[20] Herder, *Werke, XVIII*, 57–8; quoted by Berlin, 192.

hand."[21] Abstraction from this leaves us cut off from our divine origins and separated from the deeper truths of ourselves. "The savage who loves himself, his wife and his child...," Herder says, "[who] works for the good of the tribe as for his own...is in my view more genuine than the human ghost, the...citizen of the world, who, burning with love for his fellow ghosts, loves a chimera. The savage in his hut has room for any stranger... [while] the saturated heart of the idle cosmopolitan is a home for no one."[22] Thus, in resisting enlightenment myths and in valuing the integrity of each people on its own terms, with its own poetry, one culture giving way to the next without one being more or less valuable than another or defined by the terms of another, he is able to say that all wars are civil wars, "since men are brothers, and wars are a form of abominable fratricide."[23] There is a general purpose we are to achieve, which Herder calls *Humanitat* – a deliberately vague term Berlin describes as "connoting harmonious development of all immortal souls toward universally valid goals: reason, freedom, toleration, mutual love and respect between individuals and societies, as well as physical and spiritual help, finer perceptions, dominion over the earth, the harmonious realization of all that God has implanted in His noblest work and made in His own image" (Berlin, 193).[24] But there is no attempt to fit the stories of each nation rising from its poetry into some overarching story that makes all stories intelligible by showing where they reside in the larger pattern. This Herder resists. But soon after him, this idea of "the world spirit come to full self-consciousness of itself" would grow in the work of G. W. F. Hegel.

[21] Herder, *Werke, VIII*, 33; quoted in Berlin, 203.
[22] Herder, *Werke, XIII*, 339; quoted in Kuehn, *Kant: A Biography*, 300.
[23] Herder, *Werke, XVII*, 319; quoted in Berlin, 158.
[24] See also Herder, *Werke, XIII*, 154; reference noted in footnote in Berlin, 193.

# 8

# Hegel and the Owl of Minerva

The poet "out of his mind" is not trustworthy if our aim is wisdom. A philosopher cut off from the root and source of wisdom is no better. We want our souls to grow. We want our living consciousness of what is real and true to expand. Hegel is the philosopher of consciousness. Before he gave *The Phenomenology of Spirit* its final title, he had as his subtitle "Science of the Experience of Consciousness." Though consciousness ranges across all things, from sense experience to the objects of art and religion, philosophy is ultimately and uniquely about *our* being in the world, a kind of living consciousness that is the fullness of self-knowledge. In *The Philosophy of Right*, Hegel warns, "When philosophy paints its gray on gray, then has a form of life grown old, and with gray on gray it cannot be rejuvenated, but only known; the Owl of Minerva first takes flight with twilight closing in."[1] It is this "gray on gray" that is resisted by a philosophy that aims to grow the consciousness of seekers as they experience the world.

In much of the quarrel, the poets engage as prophetic figures used as the voice of the gods for better or worse, their words received and brought to fullness of understanding by the philosophers. At many points in this history, poetry has functioned as a means of gaining access to the "transcendent" in one form or another, moving past the mundane immanent world, however much such claims labor under suspicion. The role of the distinction between the transcendent and the immanent in Hegel evolves through the stages of the *Phenomenology* until the dictum "Know thyself" is fulfilled in absolute knowledge, and the distinction is no longer necessary. When this knowledge of truth as the whole is

[1] G. W. F. Hegel, *The Philosophy of Right*, trans. T. M. Knox (Oxford: Oxford University Press, 1967), 13.

achieved, the distinction between the immanent and the transcendent fails under the question, Transcendent to what? Transcendence is a relational term, and once one has arrived at the whole, it may not make sense to say that there is something else transcendent in relation to the whole. Such a claim may be nothing more than to say that what we thought was the whole is not. Through the stages of the *Phenomenology*, it is certainly true that, from the perspective of consciousness at certain stages, some things are transcendent, others not. But this way of construing transcendence does not refer to the relationship of material to nonmaterial entities, or to the created versus the noncreated. Rather, the meaning of transcendence in Hegel's system is always in relationship to consciousness, and exploring this relationship is the task of philosophy.

What about poetry? As was the case for many prior philosophers, Hegel views poetry as having a peculiar status because it uses the same medium as philosophy. Philosophy is not expressed in paint, stone, or musical notes. It is expressed in language. Philosophical ideas emerge in and through language, and these ideas are called concepts, notions. "Truth has only the notion as the element of its existence."[2] Hegel's formulation of the element of truth as the idea impacts his understanding of poetry, which appears in the drama of the *Phenomenology* as an artifact of one later stage of consciousness.

Hegel's most explicit discussion of poetry occurs in his lectures on fine art. Poetry is the art of speech. As such, its first principle is spirituality, meaning that it does not turn to matter to arrange it into an environment for inner life, as is done in architecture, nor does it cast natural form in matter as with sculpture. "On the contrary, it expresses directly for spirit's apprehension the spirit itself with all its imaginative and artistic conceptions but without setting these out visibly and bodily for contemplation from the outside."[3] Because this directness of expression is not mediated through matter, poetry is in a category distinct from other arts. The spirituality of poetry follows from the fact that the element with which poetry works is that of ideas. Poetry shapes spiritual forms as the sculptor shapes bronze and the musician, musical notes. Inward ideas constitute the material and the form of poetry (*Aesth.*, 964). Poetry uses language, but words are not themselves symbols of

[2] G. W. F. Hegel, *The Phenomenology of Spirit*, trans. A. V. Miller (Oxford: Oxford University Press, 1972), 4, hereafter cited in text as *Phen.*

[3] G. W. F. Hegel, *Hegel's Aesthetics: Lectures on Fine Art*, vols. 1 and 2, trans. T. M. Knox (Oxford: Clarendon Press, 1998), 961, hereafter cited in text as *Aesth.*

spiritual ideas: though they must be shaped by the poet to achieve the end of poetic contemplation in contradistinction to a prosaic use of words, words are merely signs. "Poetry is the art which can exhaust all the depths of the spirit's whole wealth," Hegel argues (*Aesth.*, 998). "The poet is able to penetrate all the depths of the contents of spirit and can bring out into the daylight of consciousness whatever lies concealed there" (*Aesth.*, 997).

Because of this characterization of poetry, it is important to consider how poetry is distinguished from philosophy in Hegel's work. The *Phenomenology* shows that, as the truth is the whole, philosophy excludes nothing. There is room for all things, including, most notably, opposites. Poetry is comparably capacious: "Any topic, all spiritual and natural things, events, histories, deeds, actions, subjective and objective situations, all these can be drawn into poetry and fashioned by it" (*Aesth.*, 965). How, then, is poetry distinguished from philosophy? Through form? Hegel does indeed have an idea of the poetically adequate form. And yet he says that "in the case of poetry proper it is a matter of indifference whether we read it or hear it read; it can even be translated into other languages without a central detriment to its value, and turned from poetry into prose, and in these cases it is related to quite different sounds from those of the original" (*Aesth.*, 965).

If form does not distinguish poetry from philosophy, what does? Poetry for Hegel is not scientific or speculative thinking. Whatever might finally be said about poetic form, for Hegel "it is not ideas as such but the artistic imagination which makes some material poetic" (*Aesth.*, 965). The first way to distinguish between poetry and philosophy, then, is to consider not only the products but the kind of mind in which the ideas are formed. Furthermore the content of poetry, as with any art, "must be an end in itself and, with a purely contemplative interest, fashion everything that it conceives into an inherently independent and closed world" (*Aesth.*, 965). The nature of poetry is to be finished, to be brought to a kind of closure. This kind of closure is a manner of approaching ideas that may be typical of a certain kind of consciousness, and perhaps of the poetic consciousness. Part of the threat of the poets for Plato derived from the shared content, media, and claims. Hegel does not view this as a threat, but he has a fair amount of history between him and the age when the poets presented the threat Plato identified. In Hegel the quarrel is not about kinds of text but about kinds of imagination.

As with other arts that occupy the domain of the beautiful, poetry "is bordered on one side by the prose of finitude and commonplace thinking, out of which art struggles on its way to the truth, and on the other side by the higher spheres of religion and philosophy where there is a transition to that apprehension of the Absolute which is still further removed from the sensuous sphere" (*Aesth.*, 968). Though poetry draws on the sensuous content of other arts, the first concern of poetry is the spiritual idea. Poetry is on the spiritual side of the transition from the material world and the world of sense to that of the absolute, and as such it tends toward the risk of losing its identity as art. Distinguishing the work of speculative philosophy from poetic tasks is not straightforward, and "to define the poetic as such or to give a description of what is poetic horrifies nearly all who have written about poetry" (*Aesth.*, 971).

Language, as the property of spirit, is best fitted to express the interests of the spirit and so "the subject matter really corresponding to poetry is the infinite wealth of the spirit....Accordingly, the chief task of poetry is to bring before our minds the powers governing spiritual life...the all-encompassing realm of human ideas, deeds, actions and fates, the bustle of life in this world, and the divine rule of the universe" (*Aesth.*, 972). Hegel says that poetry is the most universal teacher of the human race, and that humans, in order to conform to the law of their existence, must follow the old inscription on the temple at Delphi, which has appeared repeatedly in this history, "Know thyself," by which is meant, know who we are and know what powers and drives direct us: "It is such a knowledge that poetry provides in its original and substantive form" (*Aesth.*, 973).

Through the development of the prosaic mind, universal laws of nature became accessible to us, allowing us to abstract and classify, while poetry presents its complex subject matter "as a totality complete in itself." The understanding generalizes from the particular to yield a theory or else a way to achieve a practical end. Poetry lingers over the particular as whole itself, fully valuing the instance present at the moment rather than rushing off to many like instances in order to categorize *this* sort of thing as a class distinct from *that* sort of thing as a class (*Aesth.*, 981). Poetry and speculative philosophy both contain particulars that form a whole, a unity. Indeed, the unity of particulars allows both poetry and speculative philosophy to develop and achieve their full identities. Philosophy does this by demonstrating through logic that the particular is what it is only in the unity, and this dialectically supersedes the particular. Poetry is different: though the harmonizing unity is certainly fully present in poetry, it is implicit rather than explicit, "just as the soul is directly living in all the members of the organism but

without depriving them of their appearance of existing independently"
(*Aesth.*, 985).

In his lectures on aesthetics, Hegel approaches poetry and its relation to philosophy more directly than he does in the *Phenomenology*,
though in the latter work of philosophy the place of poetry in thought
is easier to see. The lectures on aesthetics, and especially the lectures
on poetry, provide an excellent preface to the work philosophy does in
the *Phenomenology*. Art puts us on different ground from what we find in
everyday life, religion, or philosophy, and its ability to do so in poetry
depends on poetry's peculiar use of poetic diction. Though it is difficult to delineate clearly the line between poetic and prosaic uses of
language, at the very least poetry must avoid "the philosophical forms
of judgment and syllogism, etc., because all these forms transport us at
once out of the province of imagination onto a different field" (*Aesth.*,
1007). In his discussion of lyric poetry as art, Hegel goes farther and
says that such poetry tears itself free of prosaic consciousness "and out
of an imagination now become subjectively independent creates a new
poetic world of subjective mediation and feeling whereby alone it generates in a living way the true contents of the inner life of the man and the
true way of expressing them" (*Aesth.*, 1127). This is not to say that poetry
is superior to all forms of the spirit, for there is one that "outsoars the
imagination of heart and vision because it can bring its content into free
self-consciousness in a more decisively universal way and in more necessary connectedness than any art at all. I mean philosophical thinking"
(*Aesth.*, 1128).

Philosophy, however, struggles against being diminished by excessive
abstraction, for the full expression of our inner life requires that the
content of the philosophical mind also be expressed concretely with
imagination and feeling. So the two modes of poetry and philosophy
contrast with, but also complement, each other. Where imagination
strains against its own boundaries in the soul's fight and struggle, and
where philosophy tends toward a severe and universal ideality shorn of
the particular, poetry can give to philosophy the elements of feeling,
illustration, and "the free play of particular aspects," while philosophy can offer "clearly grasped and systematically pursued thoughts"
(*Aesth.*, 1128).

As with Vico, Herder, and Hamann, Hegel agrees that poetry arises in
the nations when language is undeveloped. The astonishing thing about
the language of the first poets is that language made possible the revelation of what, before language, was concealed in the inner life: "This

new creation appears as a miracle wrought by a gift and a force not yet made familiar but, to men's amazement, freely unfolding for the first time what lay deeply enclosed within their own hearts" (*Aesth.*, 1009). If philosophy outsoars the imagination, it was poetry that made it possible "to open the lips of a nation, to bring ideas into words, and by this means to help the nation to have ideas" (*Aesth.*, 1009). Once the poets made it possible for the nations to have ideas, the prosaic speech of everyday life began to evolve as people grew in their ability to reflect and expand on the first ideas. Subsequently poetic diction itself evolved in its divergence from prosaic speech. In this development, however, the poetic imagination continued attending to the particular, which allowed particular ideas to be juxtaposed without being related in the way ideas are related in thought through its logical judgments, syllogisms, and so forth (*Aesth.*, 1035). Poetry excludes neither the sublime ideas of speculative philosophy nor the existence of nature, but it is distinguished by the artistic presentation of these things, the completeness of the world it presents relying on artistic unity rather than unity arrived at by abstraction.

There are three kinds of poetry – epic, lyric, and dramatic. Each kind presents a different aspect of that depth of spirit which is the subject matter of the poetic imagination. The epic poem contains and is driven by the spirit of an age or nation. Nations do not write poems; poets do. The spirit of the nation is distilled through the genius of the individual poet, "for poetry is a spiritual production, and the spirit exists only as an actual individual consciousness and self-consciousness" (*Aesth.*, 1049). But the poet does not invent the spirit of the nation, and in the epic poem, that epic world must seem self-made if it is to seem truly poetic rather than mere invention. Likewise, when the divine is introduced, directing and controlling events in a nation, "the poet himself must have a fresh and lively belief in the gods... [or else their effects are] degraded to an intentional and merely artificial creation of the poet" (*Aesth.*, 1087). Epic poetry presents an objective world, but it is an objective world seen from the vantage point of the poet's inner vision and feeling of it (*Aesth.*, 1111).

While epic poetry presents an independent, objective totality set over and against the subject, lyric poetry expresses the mind of the poet and apprehends the mind in that self-expression (*Aesth.*, 1113). Within this field fall human faith, ideas, knowledge, and "even philosophical thoughts so far as these are accommodated to the form of imagination and intuition and enabled to enter the sphere of feeling" (*Aesth.*, 1114).

Whereas epic derives its unity from objective reality as seen through the genius of the poet, the unity of lyric poetry is provided by the "inner movement" of the poet's soul (*Aesth.*, 1119). The complete world that is the poet's inner world is sufficient for lyric poetry (*Aesth.*, 1120). The sine qua non of lyric poetry is the artistic expression of the poet's mind as it absorbs and transforms not history but the world of the human heart populated with ideas, passions, and conflicts (*Aesth.*, 1126). It plays against the dense fabric of the prosaic world and so becomes art as it separates and creates "a new poetic world of subjective meditation and feeling" (*Aesth.*, 1127).

The highest stage of art is dramatic poetry, and within the category of dramatic poetry Hegel says that "of all the masterpieces of the classical and modern world – and I know nearly all of them and you should and can – the *Antigone* seems to me to be the most magnificent and satisfying work of art of this kind" (*Aesth.*, 1218). Here are combined the objectivity of epic and the subjectivity of lyric in the medium most suited to expression of spirit, namely, speech (*Aesth.*, 1158). In drama, spiritual, moral, and divine powers enter from opposing sides creating struggle and obstacles. The resolution of conflict assumes and requires some element besides and beyond either of the opposing forces, a working principle of composition at the heart of Hegel's own structuring of *The Phenomenology of Spirit*. "Therefore the drama, no matter in what way, must display to us the vital working of a necessity which, itself self-reposing, resolves every conflict and contradiction" (*Aesth.*, 1163). In order to achieve such a thing, the dramatic poet must have "a full insight into the inner and universal element lying at the root of the aims, struggles, and fates of human beings" (*Aesth.*, 1163). The breadth of human experience and concern that constitutes the proper domain of the philosopher populates the domain of the dramatic poet as well. The poet "must acquire the most profound insight into the essence of human action and Divine Providence, as well as clearly and vividly revealing this eternal substance of all human characters, passions, and fates.... He himself has no other duty but to follow the truth of his impelling genius which, if only it be of the right sort, cannot fail to be victorious in the last instance, as is always the case when truth is at issue" (*Aesth.*, 1179–80). In such poetry, as in the real world where everything is differentiated and subject to particularization, ethical powers that rest on the divine become particularized and motivate action against action.

Art always "aims at the identity, produced by the spirit, in which eternal things, God, and absolute truths are revealed in real appearance and shape to our contemplation, to our hearts and minds" (*Aesth.*, 1236). Because of the high purpose of art in its role of liberating the spirit from finitude, understanding the complex beauty and truth in the arts is "one of the worthiest tasks that philosophy is capable of completing" (*Aesth.*, 1236). This is high praise indeed. But the soaring thoughts of the philosopher still rank highest, and the starting points in art are finally woven into the fabric of truth by philosophy, and art finds its place in the larger world of philosophy. This is most clear when Hegel turns from direct consideration of poetry in his aesthetics to consideration of the truth of the whole in the *Phenomenology*.

In *The Phenomenology of Spirit*, Hegel begins with sense certainty, a mode of consciousness that is not able to accommodate a whole world because it resides entirely within the *now* where there is not room for simultaneous contraries such as day *and* night, hot *and* cold. In Hegel's account of consciousness moving toward absolute knowledge, toward that wisdom which knows that the truth is the whole, consciousness does not begin with a whole world. Consciousness will experience now hot, now cold, and only through one of many inversions does the mind progress from this toward absolute knowing. The move toward the absolute is the move toward philosophy, conceived as that form of thought winging higher than poetry. But there is more than one poetry at work in this idea. There is that poetry grown against a prosaic background (from which philosophy, existing simultaneously, distinguishes itself), and there is a kind of poetic existence from which the tools of poetry and philosophy both derive. This is the poetry that precedes the growth of conscious thought expressed in the *Phenomenology*. This is the world of myth, a whole world that exists prior to abstract thought of any sort, and which does not enter into the *Phenomenology*.

Vico said that the mythmakers worked through imaginative universals; Hegel says, "The peoples at the time when they composed their myths lived in purely poetical conditions and so brought their inmost and deepest convictions before their minds not in the form of thought but in shapes devised by imagination without separating the universal abstract ideas from the concrete pictures" (*Aesth.*, 311). The people, poets, and priests were not capable of the kind of thought that would allow them access to abstract universals. Rather, for prephilosophical cultures, universals were clothed in myth, a whole world was expressed in comprehensive myth, and, as affirmed by Vico, this world in its wholeness was not susceptible to questioning from within. The contrast between the wholeness of the mythic world and the progress of the *Phenomenology* (within which poetry goes on to find its place) is at the heart of how the quarrel manifests itself in Hegel's work.

Phenomenological investigation assumes from the very beginning a kind of consciousness, even if it is just the bare "I" confronting some particular content, "hot here now" – a kind of consciousness that can be scrutinized. Such scrutiny reveals that the immediacy that seemed present is not, in fact, so immediate: in the very first part of the *Phenomenology*'s journey, this most elemental form of consciousness is subjected to philosophical questioning that reveals the inherent conflict within sense certainty. This question has no place in the mythopoeic world. At the start of the *Phenomenology*, the question is already on the stage revealing the conflict in sense certainty, and the wholeness of the mythic world is fractured by a battle that began before page one. Indeed, if the mythic world were not already broken open, the *Phenomenology* could never begin. The *Phenomenology* must, as a portrayal of consciousness, begin in this way because consciousness is born of conflict.

Ernst Cassirer noted this characteristic in Hegel's philosophy and objected to this starting point, arguing that any complete philosophy *must* begin with a philosophy of myth. From inside myth, the feeling of unity is so strong that it even defies the fact of death.[4] Myth expresses itself in the world of the image. Cassirer says that as mythical consciousness advances, this manifestation in and through images is increasingly seen as residing outside the mythic consciousness, and so the mythic image becomes the basis for a conflict that finally splits the unity of the mythic consciousness.[5] There is then a scattering of symbolic domains or forms – language, science, art.

The danger of not beginning with myth and not acknowledging the persistent presence of myth in philosophical thought is not only that the true power of myth is diminished but that some deep threats thought to have been overcome through philosophy continue to lurk, more dangerous for being forgotten and ignored. We have heard the ideas of the mythic in poetry and philosophy, manifested repeatedly in versions of the ancient quarrel. Cassirer shows a second more sinister way in which myth can function, a way exemplified by the dangerous power of the political myth. This danger's presence becomes possible when

---

[4] Ernst Cassirer, *An Essay on Man* (New Haven: Yale University Press, 1944), 26.
[5] Ernst Cassirer, *The Philosophy of Symbolic Forms*, vol. 2: *Mythical Thought*, trans. Ralph Manheim (New Haven: Yale University Press, 1955), 13.

desperation is linked with new technical tools.[6] As a critical moment is reached within social life, "the rational forces that resist the rise of the old mythical conceptions are no longer sure of themselves. In these moments, the time for myth has come again" (*Myth*, 280). The Nazi state arises. Such political myths are as impervious to correction as any myth (*Myth*, 296). But unlike other myths, these do not freely rise from the imagination. Rather, they are deliberately wielded and manufactured "according to the same methods as any other modern weapon – as machine guns or airplanes. That is a new thing – and a thing of crucial importance" (*Myth*, 282). This is a monstrous invitation to chaos, irrationality, and the destruction of human culture. It is also evidence that the mythic is always lurking somewhere nearby. This power is subdued only through "superior forces…intellectual, ethical and artistic" (*Myth*, 298). On the one hand, myth is the origin both of meaning in human culture and of the language with which we discuss meaning. On the other hand, the power of myth is such that, untamed, it can undo human culture and introduce chaos. Cassirer notes that one distinction between myth as origin of culture and myth as destroyer of culture is that the former rises freely in the imagination and as a result of unconscious activity, whereas the latter is cunningly crafted. A second distinction can be seen in the results: the former grounds intellectual, scientific, and artistic domains, whereas the latter makes possible such things as the Nazi state.

Cassirer makes another point that is helpful in understanding Hegel's starting point and the role of the quarrel in his work. The attempt to subdue myth is not the same as the attempt to sever myth from experience. When conflict arises within the mythic consciousness, art and language are liberated, only to be unified at a higher level in poetry.[7] From its roots to its best production in that poetry, the connection to myth is maintained and recollected. Lyric poets such as Holderlin and Keats were "men in whom the mythic power of insight breaks forth again in its full intensity."[8] But the words and images were neither magic nor harnessed to literal reality. Instead, they become the expression of pure feeling. In this domain, we are neither denied access to the spiritual creativity of myth nor faced with the invulnerability of myth.

[6] Ernst Cassirer, *The Myth of the State* (New Haven: Yale University Press, 1946), 277–9, hereafter cited in text as *Myth*.

[7] Ernst Cassirer, *Language and Myth*, trans. Susanne Langer (New York: Dover, 1946), 98.

[8] Ibid., 99.

Hegel, of course, did not see the Nazi state. But the question remains why he began where he did. Hegel is the philosopher of awakening, and his domain is consciousness. Point for point, the true is present in the mythic mind, but a philosophy of myth can begin only by acknowledging that the one thing for which there is no room in the mythic mind is philosophy. Nevertheless, as consciousness is born, the entire mythic world is recapitulated, only now from the vantage point of consciousness. *The Phenomenology of Spirit* is a battle document giving an account of philosophy's step-by-step invasion into the mythopoeic world. The final chapter on absolute knowledge – the conscious proclamation that the truth is the whole – is a planting of the flag in the capital of the conquered land. In one sense, every landmark in the territory is the same. In another sense, everything is transformed by the new rule. Indeed, poetry itself is transformed into an artifact of consciousness. Poetry has an important place, but the fact that it has a place at all suggests the profundity of the change: a governing principle does not have a place but rather is the medium in which everything else finds its place. This medium was once myth, the first poetry. Now it is philosophy.

The quality of this change is determined in part by one central characteristic of philosophy, namely, that philosophy is bound up with mortality. This is why philosophy is not a discipline of the gods. It is a discipline that proceeds toward that most difficult kind of knowledge, self-knowledge, but there is uncertainty at every step. There is always the risk of error, and Hegel says that if the fear of falling into error sets up a mistrust of the pursuit of truth, we do well to turn the tables and ask whether this fear is itself the error: "What calls itself fear of error reveals itself as fear of the truth" (*Phen.*, 74). Philosophical timidity results in part from an instrumental image of reason that sets up a false idea of the gap between the knower and the known, and it restricts us to one side of this false dichotomy. Once we have dispatched this false image in which timidity resides, we can progress toward the real goal, which is to reach "the point where knowledge no longer needs to go beyond itself, where knowledge finds itself, where notion corresponds to object and object to notion" (*Phen.*, 80).

The *Phenomenology* records the education of the philosopher, and the enterprise is haunted by death. At the very beginning Hegel says, "Death...is of all things most dreadful, and to hold fast to what is dead requires the greatest strength.... the life of the Spirit is not the life that shrinks from death and keeps itself untouched by devastation, but rather the life that endures it and maintains itself in it.... Spirit is this power only by looking the negative in the face, and tarrying with it" (*Phen.*, 32). Death is not one among many considerations in the pursuit of philosophy but rather is at the center of philosophy. Death brings to a close and marks the point at which a life is seen in its totality, by others. This spirit maintains itself in the face of death, tarries with it. So conceived, the centrality of death in the act of philosophy is not some morbid preoccupation. It is rather something that, in maintaining itself, creates a tension with the totalizing power of death.

Death provides a peculiar kind of limit that leads the philosophic mind to a new kind of thought that is not extensive but, rather, intensive. Philosophy, because bound up with the limit imposed by death, becomes aware that infinity itself need not be conceived as extensive, but may be intensive, an infinity occurring within limits, as with the number of points on a line. This is Hegel's secret of self-knowledge. In the ostensible search for "self" and "self-identity," and the subsequent pronouncement that no self is to be found (many have followed Hume in this exercise), some philosophical seekers have failed to see that tarrying with death defines a limit, gives a boundary as profound as that given by our bodies, and yields a kind of unity. My death is an opportunity for others to recollect the totality that was me, but which could never be present to me. The tendency to elide the cohesive self is a symptom of our own forgetting of mortality and its meaning for us. When we forget our mortality, we live as gods, which is to say we live unphilosophically and unpoetically. To think, we must tarry with death. Tarrying with death is qualitatively different from simply being around the dead. During their training, physicians take apart the dead piece by piece to learn anatomy. Anatomy requires only a scalpel, not philosophy. As much as philosophy requires the presence of death, the ability to tarry with death requires philosophy.

Death will turn what I experience as subject, myself, into substance, a dead body. It is therefore death that most powerfully jars me into consciousness of myself as both subject and substance, the insight that is at the very center of Hegel's understanding of what it is to philosophize: "Everything turns on grasping and expressing the true, not only as substance, but equally as subject" (*Phen.*, 17). Philosophy is founded on this premise and conclusion: the true is the whole. The true is both substance and subject, and it is not enough for the philosopher to describe what is "out there." Substance alone cannot fill the philosopher's discourse, anymore than one looking for the meaning of death can approach the effort by prodding and dissecting the dead body.

The whole includes what remains when all that is "out there" has been described. The philosopher's inroad to this whole is the subject, and in the beginning, at least, the subject means me: I am not an abstraction that can be excluded from discourse on substance or Being in general. My consciousness is my unique way in.

Why does this point need to be made? Why would a philosopher ever want to discuss Being apart from the subject? Why would I want to discuss Being apart from myself? Part of the reason is that the consequences of doing otherwise are frightening. When the philosopher as subject grasps that the true is the whole, abstraction accessible to the understanding leads to the application of this realization to the subject at hand – namely, myself. This abstraction allows generalization, generalization allows application, and the negative enters thoughts as nonactuality – death – suddenly becomes personal, a threat to the subject, a threat to me.

There are several possible ways to respond to this striking realization. One can ignore the question entirely. One can retain the power of analysis without acknowledging the presence of the subject – which is myself – and so focus only on what is not the subject, but thereby miss the true, which is the whole. The second option is to acknowledge both the subject and the substance, to underscore the power of the understanding, but to move no farther than this dichotomy of being-in-itself and being-for-itself. Finally, one can tarry with death, confronting the negative directly but staying, acknowledging the two moments – substance and subject, being-in-itself and being-for-itself – while allowing that these two moments and the nothing that is between them constitute the whole. This is the response that overcomes the fear that produced Kant's phenomena-noumena dichotomy in the first place. This allows the birth of the speculative philosopher. Here, from this starting point of tarrying with death, of conceiving the negative with all of its implications and still staying, the thinker makes the crucial move toward one central idea: "Für-das-Bewusstsein-Sein des Ansich wird."

A. W. Miller in his translation of this phrase renders it as "a being-for-consciousness of the in-itself." Donald Verene has suggested that the meaning of the phrase is better retained by translating it as "a for consciousness being of the in-itself," the point of the alternate translation being that Hegel's two moments of consciousness related to the *Ansich*, the in-itself, are retained without synthesis: a consciousness of something (something that is not a product of consciousness is there in itself before consciousness); and a consciousness that this something is an object for consciousness (a consciousness of the consciousness of the object).[9] For the purposes of understanding the quarrel between poetry and philosophy, this is especially important because the two moments, kept as two moments, constitute the basis for the distinction between the mythic world and the philosophic world, the latter growing through introduction of this second moment of consciousness.

In the *Phaedo*, Socrates said that philosophy is practice for death. We all must die. Death makes philosophy necessary. The negative is neither substance nor subject. It is rather an absence of being, and from the perspective of the subject thinking of himself, it is the difference between being subject and being mere substance, which for the subject is death. The negative enables consciousness by separating the two moments, keeping them distinct but coincidental. Consciousness of life, which is my experience as subject, when examined via the philosophical question, becomes consciousness of death, which is the reality of my own dead body as substance. In the cauldron of the disturbing realization of this fullness of self-consciousness, the philosopher is made. It is not always a happy making.

The path toward a newly conscious philosophic mind emerging from the totalizing mythopoeic world begins with myself as a particular, though it certainly does not end there. This is to say that philosophical courage cannot begin with the general. Hegel warns of the treacherous waters toward which the *Phenomenology* can lead. I must take the effort personally: I cannot care about death as such unless I have considered my own death. Philosophy is distinguished from poetry in part because it is not limited to the particular but is able to find its way to the universal. At the same time, the progression of the *Phenomenology* as a work of philosophy is followed by individual readers. This is the only place real philosophy can begin.

Part of Hegel's task in the *Phenomenology* was pedagogical. In teaching us to be philosophers by demonstrating the progression of the philosophical mind, he makes good use of one of the novelist's most powerful tools, that of the tension created between two characters, each of whom holds part of the story, neither of whom can be reduced to the other, and he explores the way in which self-consciousness is engendered, the way in which, through the negative, the two moments of *Ansich* are maintained as two.

[9] Donald Philip Verene, *Hegel's Recollection: A Study of the Images in the Phenomenology of Spirit* (Albany: State University of New York Press, 1985), 16–18.

Poetry, absent the power of abstraction, is the original way truth is presented to the mind. Language that first arises as poetry is the property of spirit. Phenomenology, that history of consciousness, requires something beyond this, namely, consciousness of consciousness. Conceptually prior to the work of phenomenology, the whole world as a totality complete in itself is served up by this oldest poetic expression of spirit. This serving up is the first moment. To say again, "The chief task of poetry is to bring before our minds the powers governing spiritual life, and, in short, all that surges to and fro in human passion and feeling or passes quietly through our meditations – the all-encompassing realm of human ideas, deeds, actions, and fates; the battle of life in this world; and the divine rule of the universe. Thus, poetry has been and is still the most universal and widespread teacher of the human race" (*Aesth.*, 972). Poetry as serving up this totality to the conscious mind is the first moment, while phenomenology as consciousness of this consciousness is the second moment.

With an idea of this mechanism of progression in the *Phenomenology*, it is easier to consider the relationship of poetry and philosophy in Hegel's work. We do not now live in a poetic age, though we still have poetry. The two kinds of poetry – that of the first poets, and that which we now have – become clearer as they relate to the work and world of the *Phenomenology*. The first kind of poetic mind is prior to the *Phenomenology*, a mind through which the first poetry comes as the beginning of humanity's attempt to express itself. The made, that expression which is *poiein* as it pertains to humanity, is able to posit spiritual content through thought. This is one sense, Hegel says in his lectures on Greek philosophy, in which we are unlike the animals with their lack of religion resulting from the fact that they only feel.[10] This is said in the context of a discussion of Socrates in whom the determination of the universal, "the infinite subjectivity, the freedom of self-consciousness breaks out."[11]

The second kind of poetic mind resides in a world where prose has developed and become the primary medium of thought and discourse, though its elements were grown from a mind made possible by the rich soil of the first poetry. For the second kind of poetry to stake out its domain and differentiate itself from the prosaic, it must devise formal

[10] G. W. F. Hegel, *Lectures on the History of Philosophy: Greek Philosophy to Plato*, trans. E. S. Haldane (Lincoln: University of Nebraska Press, 1995), 386.
[11] Ibid.

modes of treating the subject as well as a poetic diction. Thus, one fundamental difference between the two poetries is that the second type brings a kind of conscious intent as a force in poetry: "The former is poetic in conception and speech unintentionally, whereas the latter knows the sphere from which it must liberate itself in order to stand on the free ground of art" (*Aesth.*, 974).

The prose sphere from which the poetic mind must distinguish itself in the world of the *Phenomenology* comprises three sorts of thinking. *Ordinary* thought (that kind of thought, as Hegel says, of the man of "sound common sense") takes what is and what happens as accidental and meaningless. This is the type of thought that is not concerned with essence, reason, or connection. The second is *understanding*, which does involve a sense of connection, but which is restricted to that provided by categories such as cause and effect. Both of these kinds of thought lack the totality, unity, and completeness of the subject matter as it was present in the first poetry. Reason has a deeper need than can be satisfied by either of these kinds of prosaic thought. The referent in both cases is always an external life, however vast its range: "For a deeper mind, what is alive in the outside world is dead unless through it there shines something inner and rich in significance as its own proper soul" (*Aesth.*, 975). This deep need is answered by the third kind of prosaic thought, *speculative* thought. It comprises the discursive work of the understanding in which pieces are brought together but not unified by relations or categories. It then "conjoins in a free totality" these elements in a manner akin to the work of the poetic imagination (*Aesth.*, 976). But, unlike poetry, speculative philosophy is capable of grasping abstract universals.

The contrast between this poetry and philosophy has an important coincidence in history. Sophocles portrayed Antigone not as positing truth through thought – the work of speculative philosophy – but rather truth deriving from the eternal law of the gods. Sophocles lived from approximately 496 to 406 B.C. He was the poet who, for Hegel, best showed forth the Greek consciousness capable both of acknowledging fate (*moira*) and of taking responsibility for individual actions. The date has philosophical interest because Socrates lived from 470 to 399 B.C. and is the father of our deeper self-consciousness, this infinite subjectivity that is free. In Sophocles, we see the poetic presentation of a bound subjectivity in whom, nonetheless, self-consciousness has broken forth. In Socrates, we find a free self-consciousness ready for the work of philosophy. Sophocles lies between the mythopoeic poets and the modern poets who have nearly lost their connection to the myth. But Socrates wields the question that makes philosophical irony possible, a new thing on the face of the earth never heard of and never possible in the mythopoeic world.

In this favorite play of Hegel's, *Antigone*, self-consciousness is dramatically presented in the natural and political life as clashing with the world of feeling, which appeals to the gods of Hades. For Hegel, Socrates is the true denouement of Sophoclean tragedy as one displaying unencumbered free self-consciousness. When Sophocles writes poetry, his work is an artifact in the history of consciousness. As such, in *Antigone* we see a fine contrast with the work of speculative thought, a demonstration of the two contrasting modes of attending to the same content – death. This is why Hegel uses the play in the *Phenomenology*.

At one level he uses the play to discuss the ethical life and woman's responsibility for this life and the family. In contrast to Antigone is Creon, a man concerned with human law. The work the play does in the world of the *Phenomenology* is to offer an opportunity to compare Antigone's encounter with death as representative of a type of poetic, mythic feeling and the encounter of the speculative philosopher with the negative, with death. Antigone wants to bury her brother Polyneices. Creon has forbidden this. What is to be gained by burying Polyneices? Here lies a dead body, "a passive being-for-another." The body becomes a sensuous object for "unconscious appetites and abstract entities." About such entities Hegel says in the preface that "they do not just stand idly in front of sensuous things as if these possessed intrinsic being, but, despairing of their reality, and completely assured of their nothingness, they fall to without ceremony and eat them up" (*Phen.*, 19). But the family, by the divine law served up by the theological poets, intervenes and refuses to allow the dead man to satisfy the animals, and so they fulfilled their ethical duty by burying him. "The family thereby makes him a member of a community which prevails over and holds under control the forces of particular material elements and the lower forms of life, which sought to cut loose themselves against him" (*Phen.*, 271).

Antigone, by supporting this, and by being willing to die in order to fulfill this duty, shows the profundity of nothingness externalized. At this point in the *Phenomenology*, the reader is in the stage of spirit, though not that of absolute knowing – far enough along, that is, to recognize more clearly the truth about spirit that has been present from the beginning, namely that "the life of the Spirit is not the life that shrinks from death, but rather the life that endures it and maintains itself in it" (*Phen.*, 19). Allowing Polyneices to become transformed literally into animal excrement is the terror that gives death a peculiar urgency. The move that Antigone makes in burying her brother is an attempt to overcome the gulf between the consciousness that she is and represents and the substance that is her dead brother. We are still not to a level at which consciousness becomes a free self-consciousness. There is no philosophy here, but there is certainly the shadow of the relation finally given to subject and substance in absolute knowledge.

Part of the intensity of the quarrel between poetry and philosophy derives from the similarity of the two. Antigone's goal is not far removed from the goal of philosophy. There can be no tragedy unless it be a tale of the valued pitted against something. Value pitted against nothing provides no progress. Without Creon, Antigone would simply bury her brother, as her family had buried its dead from the beginning.

For Hegel, great characters in tragedy are great precisely because they do not make choices but are simply themselves, so that all they will and do arises from the single fact of who they are. Whether such an interpretation of Antigone is accurate does not matter, for Hegel needs Antigone to represent a stage on the way to absolute knowing. The fact that Hegel's Antigone is tragic in Hegel's peculiar sense – one who does not choose as such, but who rather is her choice – underscores the difference between her mythic posture toward death and the philosopher's manner of tarrying with death. For Antigone, the relation of subject to substance remains external. The meaning of death inheres in the divine law, which prescribes a response to another's death, a remedy. Overcoming the terror of death, of being substance only and no longer subject, can be accomplished once and for all through burial. Maintaining this ethical structure of duty provides assurance that at Antigone's death as well, she will be retained as a member of the community that resists the terror of death, those unconscious appetites and abstract entities.

This portrayal of Antigone enacts the mythopoeic approach as contrasted with the truly philosophical approach to the same things in the *Phenomenology*. What was left as an external for Antigone in an outside arena (where the terror of death could be confronted by reference to the rotting body *over there* and the divine law *up there*, in opposition to the human law embodied in another, Creon) now moves inside where the struggle shall be within us, with both moments maintained as distinct. Antigone faces death, but not as a philosopher, not as one tarrying with death. It is a static conclusion, a resolution of death's terror that collapses the negative and can go no farther in the system as a whole. Such a conclusion in turn becomes a barrier to the free self-conscious subjectivity so important in the person of Socrates and the philosophic system of Hegel. Burial ensures that there are no rotting bodies lying about the yard excluded from the shadowy membership of the prevailing dead. But this is not a solution open to the fullness of the philosophical life: there is no longer "für-das-Bewusstsein-sein des Ansich wird."

Clearly Hegel embraces the power of poetry, but he shows that poetry is not enough. The idea that poetry is adequate to the fullness of self-consciousness is what speculative philosophy resists. He does not exile the poets, far from it. His solution is different. First, he distinguishes a poetry of origins from that poetry which must stake out its claim in a prosaic world. The latter he puts in its place in his great book of wisdom, the *Phenomenology*. But the former, the utterances in the world of the mythmakers – this is the poetry that is not so much a stage preceding the *Phenomenology* as it is a world that the *Phenomenology* is invading. The myth is present in the *Phenomenology*: it is the whole world of the *Phenomenology* now transformed by the fullness of consciousness.

The Greek poets did not take immortality seriously because they could not consider death as does the philosopher: "Only for the later reflection of subjective consciousness on itself, in the case of Socrates, has immortality had a deeper sense and satisfied a more far-reaching need" (*Aesth.*, 523). Until one is fully self-conscious, the meaning of death cannot be fully grasped, for the negative is merely a passing away. The mythopoeic thinkers surrounded death with cheerful images not because of courage or folly, but simply because they had not attained the kind of subjectivity required to see death as a negative of the infinite and so *absolutely* terrifying.

The mythopoeic world is a whole world, finite but all-inclusive for the mind inhabiting such a world. In such a world, meaning relates only to the immediate. But though the mythic mind cannot grasp death as absolutely terrifying, this does not mean they were without terror. Hesiod portrayed the terror of Tartarus, which Hegel identifies with bad infinity, infinity that goes on and on in a linear fashion – Prometheus with his liver insatiably devoured by the Eagle, Tantalus never able to quench his thirst, Sisyphus forever pushing the rock up the mountain only to have it roll down again. "For the Greek, a correct sense of the divine, unlike modern longing, did not regard egress into the boundless and the vague as what was supreme for men; the Greeks regarded it as damnation and relegated to Tartarus" (*Aesth.*, 466).

The notion of an infinite that is a circle, which turns back on itself, which is not an endless line, this infinity is a concept that arises alongside the bursting forth of self-consciousness. The idea of immortality "involves the presupposition that the individual self, the soul, the human spirit is something absolute" (*Aesth.*, 376). Immortality – which to the mythopoeic mind would seem an unbounded linear extension to be dreaded – becomes a postulate that uncovers the infinite value of what is at stake. Death and immortality are, for this reason, central in understanding the difference between the mythopoeic mind and the philosophical mind for Hegel.

The postulate of immortality that is a clue to the burgeoning of self-consciousness does not actually correlate with the content of religious dogmas on the topic. For Hegel, as Charles Taylor has pointed out, our particular death is simply part of the scheme of things, as much a necessity as is the disappearance and falling away of any other part of the external reality. But the impetus behind the postulate of immortality is retained when "we identify with what we essentially are, universal reason. If we really come to see ourselves as vehicles of universal reason, then death is no longer an "other," for it is part of the plan. We are in that sense already beyond death; it is no longer a limit. It is incorporated in the life of reason which goes on beyond it."[12]

For Hegel, insofar as we are universal reason, insofar as we are thus already beyond death, we see that there is nothing that is transcendent to the whole. For the totalizing mythopoeic mind dwelling in the finite, there is always something beyond, however vague – perhaps a bad infinity that is relegated to the domain of Tartarus, perhaps the universal that the poetic mind cannot abstract from the particular, perhaps the gods and their eternal law. In any case, poetic totalizing means finitude, and finitude always implies that there is something beyond. The ultimate expression of finitude for the poetic mind is death, but death merely as a limit.

---

[12] Charles Taylor, *Hegel* (Cambridge: Cambridge University Press, 1975), 123.

The infinite transcends the finite, viewed from a finite perspective, but it also includes it. It must. Again, Taylor points out that if there is some sort of infinite that is "beyond" the finite and other than the finite, then this *finite* becomes a limit, a boundary for the infinite.[13] Because it is finite, not possessing knowledge of the truth as the whole, the poetic sees the infinite as transcendent. Because infinite, insofar as it knows the truth is the whole, the philosophical sees the infinite as immanent. For Hegel, the key that unlocks this distinction is the posture toward death. Thus is the mythic world conquered, and recovered, whole.

[13] Ibid., 240–1.

# 9

# Kierkegaard: A Poet, Alas

"The poetic is glorious, the religious still more glorious, but what lies between is silly talk, no matter how much talent is wasted on it."[1] So says Frater Taciturnus, one important guide to thought about poetry and its relation to life, history, and philosophy. Taciturnus is one guide among many, for in the works of Kierkegaard the relationship of poetry to philosophy not only is a question examined and considered from many angles but is a quarrel and struggle enacted in the works themselves, written under pseudonyms by a writer who, on multiple occasions in his papers and journals claimed, "I'm a poet – alas, just a poet."[2] Kierkegaard did not write formal poems, but he wrote poetry understood in a certain sense: "The subject matter plays a very important role [in]... poetry, this word understood in its widest meaning to denote all artistic production that is based on language and the historical consciousness."[3] In relation to his characters, Kierkegaard explicitly requests his readers to remember, "My wish, my prayer, is that, if it might occur to anyone to quote a particular saying from the books, he would do me the favor to cite the name of the respective pseudonymous author."[4]

[1]  Søren Kierkegaard, *Stages on Life's Way: Studies by Various Persons*, trans. Howard V. Hong and Edna H. Hong (Princeton: Princeton University Press, 1988), 385, hereafter cited in text as *Stages*.
[2]  Søren Kierkegaard, *Papers and Journals: A Selection*, trans. Alastair Hannay (London: Penguin Books, 1996), X, 3, A 660, hereafter cited in text as *Papers*.
[3]  Søren Kierkegaard, *Either/Or Part I*, trans. Howard V. Hong and Edna H. Hong (Princeton: Princeton University Press, 1987), 52, hereafter cited in text as *Either/Or*, I.
[4]  Søren Kierkegaard, *Concluding Unscientific Postscript*, trans. David F. Swenson and Walter Lowrie (Princeton: Princeton University Press, 1968), 552, hereafter cited in text as *Concluding*.

Poetry does a tremendous amount of work in Kierkegaard's presentation of his thought. And yet poetry used as a means of presenting certain perspectives and of bringing us to certain thresholds, fails – and for Kierkegaard fails most miserably – if it becomes something more than a means for realizing that poetry is not sufficient. In some ways, poetry serves best by turning the soul toward a nonpoetic approach to life, but the way out is not philosophy. No, it is religion that meets both poetry and philosophy and claims that neither is sufficient for the needs at hand. Nor is the struggle between the poets and a religious person a struggle to get some answer right: it is a struggle to get a *life* right, and the stakes are not related to the academy, to the completeness of explanation, or to professorial status, but rather the stakes are infinite because concretely attached to the trajectory of the human *soul* as it relates to the eternal.

According to Kierkegaard there are three spheres of existence: the aesthetic, the ethical, and the religious (Kierkegaard does not have a place for the metaphysical – the ontological – in existence as he understands it, for metaphysics is a distraction, and as soon as the "ontological" begins to exist, it does so in one of his three spheres). The aesthetic (which is the realm of the poet) is the sphere of immediacy. The religious is the highest sphere of fulfillment. In between is the ethical, a transition sphere in which the demand is so high (infinite, in fact) that finally one must come to the realization that the infinite debt cannot be paid, so that the only two options are despair or movement toward the highest form of expression in the ethical sphere, that of repentance, which leads to the religious (*Stages*, 476). As there are three spheres of existence, each of which can be authentically lived (though only the religious can be sustained without the despair inherent in persisting to live within the aesthetic or ethical realms), likewise there are three classes of sophistry. For Kierkegaard, sophistry does not mean a false relation to wisdom, as in the works of Plato, but rather a false relation to that highest sphere of human existence, the religious. There are the sophists who try to achieve an immediate relation to the religious from the aesthetic sphere, and so turn religion into poetry and history. Such a one in his poetic enthusiasm can even be mistaken for a prophet. Other sophists enter into an immediate relation to the religious from the ethical sphere and make the highest activity a religious doctrine of obligation rather than repentance, often thereby gaining a considerable following. The third kind of sophist turns religion into a finished history, which can then be transformed into "the system," complete, whole – and unfortunately, as finished, a form (and perhaps *the* form) of perdition (*Stages*, 486). This last temptation is common in the academy, and for Kierkegaard, "There is no one as stupid about Christianity, not even the most stupid among all others, as the 'Professor.' It is a stupidity produced by art and much study" (*Papers*, XI, 2, A 233).

For Kierkegaard, poetry is both a means for presenting ideas and a danger that is at the heart of humanity's most attractive path to perdition. Philosophy's horizon is dominated by the Hegelian system, but as with so many in this history, Kierkegaard begins with Socrates and Plato. In so doing, however, he is careful to observe that Plato was so tied to the mythical in the form of metaphor as an always-present element in any idea's presentation that he never reached the level of speculative thought, never freed himself sufficiently to move from "representation" to "thought" as it existed in the work of Hegel.[5] But Kierkegaard understood what it is to be a poet standing before a reality (Christianity) that will not yield to poetry, and much of his work balances critique of the juggernaut of the Hegelian "system" with the temptation to commit the sin of the poetizer who produces masterpieces of poetic art, while losing his own soul.

The mythical is more clearly distinguished from the poetical in Kierkegaard's work than in that of many others in this history. The primary distinguishing factor is consciousness. The poetic is conscious of itself as such while the mythical is a "state out of which the interests of consciousness have not as yet struggled" (*Concept*, 101n). Indeed, the mythic, though experienced as actuality, is not myth. It becomes myth only when it comes in contact with the reflecting consciousness. There is, however, a period of transition where the reflecting consciousness has not yet destroyed the myth completely: the myth is there, but ready to take its leave, and as it does, it becomes a "mythical presentation" in the imagination of the reflecting consciousness. At such a point, the truth or falsity of the myth is not at issue. The myth has a unity about it that is alluring, and it is viewed with philosophical interest. The myth can be used by a philosopher such as Socrates in this time of transition, but the power of the myth is still considerable, and in this strenuous transition the philosopher can fall prey to the myth. There is almost a sense of being drawn into a dangerous repose by myth when one is so

---

[5] Søren Kierkegaard, *The Concept of Irony, with Continual Reference to Socrates*, trans. Howard V. Hong and Edna H. Hong (Princeton: Princeton University Press, 1989), 103n, hereafter cited in text as *Concept*.

close to the origins. For Plato, "weary of the dialectical work, the imagination begins to dream, and from this comes the mythical.... the mythical is the enthusiasm of imagination in the service of speculation and, to a certain degree, is what Hegel calls pantheism of the imagination" (*Concept*, 101).

The transformative effect of this flicker of awakening witnessed in one such as Socrates cannot be underestimated. It is "a secret, almost inaudible whisper" that is capable of metamorphosing the mythical (*Concept*, 103). What is beckoning through the myth is the idea. To this idea, consciousness awakens. Nonetheless, the imagination still longs for the mythic dreams from which it was pulled by the reflecting consciousness, and this desire is manifested by the imagination's use of metaphor as a means of taking up the mythical into consciousness, mirroring the idea. This is the mythical presentation that emerges in Plato's dialogues, where the myth is no longer pervasively present as preconscious "actuality" or merely in conflict with the dialectic of reflecting consciousness. Rather, the mythical "alternates with the dialectical, and in this way the dialectical and also the mythical are raised to a higher order of things" (*Concept*, 103). This is the dynamism of the quarrel. Everything starts here. This transformation and history will tend toward a new kind of unity that is a conscious unity, Kierkegaard says. But between the unconscious unity of the mythic mind and the conscious unity of the truly religious mind lay many perils.

This is not a once-for-all effort. In the Middle Ages, for example, representation continued to play an important role. This representation of aspects of the totality of what is real in the form of particular individuals was partly conscious and partly unconscious. One individual represents one aspect of reality, and another individual represents another aspect of reality. These two – the knight and the Scholastic, for example, or the clergyman and the layman – are placed side by side, and "dialectic" occurs via these contrasts, which are often comic, as with Don Quixote and Sancho Panza. In the Middle Ages, these representative ideas are not linked to any single poet but rather constitute "one of those powerful, primitive ideas that emerge from the folk consciousness with autochthonic originality" (*Either/Or*, I, 87). How does consciousness find full freedom?

Judge Williams, the pseudonymous author of part II of *Either/Or*, says that philosophy is not the means for freeing the mind. Though history is made by free acts, it is only after the acts have been chosen that philosophy becomes interested because its domains are in the sphere of the necessary – logic, nature, history.[6] Philosophy (and especially Hegelian philosophy) unifies the discursive elements in the world as a totality, and this effort requires not a living contemporary freedom, a lived choice as an individual risking life and choosing even without full knowledge because life *must* be lived; rather, it requires a look back to all that has passed in the world's history, hastening "so fast into the past that, as a poet says of an antiquarian, only his coattails remain present" (*Either/Or*, II, 170). Freedom is tied up with an inner deed, the inward choice of the individual in life, but philosophy is concerned only with the external. This is philosophy as "The System," and it cannot answer the challenges Kierkegaard will embrace.

Philosophy tends to unify discursive elements, and, Kierkegaard says, the ultimate merger is that of God and humanity, a merger toward which the Hegelian systematizers press in their speculative thought. Kierkegaard resists this merger and says the gulf must be maintained in paradox and faith. The only appropriate response philosophy can offer is Socratic ignorance, an ignorance that prevents speculative claims about God and humanity from combining into a unity and sidestepping the tension of faith that is central to Christianity as Kierkegaard presents it. Anti-Climicus in *The Sickness unto Death* says, "Socrates' ignorance was a kind of fear and worship of God…the Greek version of the Jewish saying: the fear of the Lord is the beginning of wisdom."[7] Fear, not unification within a philosophical system. In his ignorance, it was Socrates who was able to stand "on guard duty as a judge on the frontier between God and man, [so] that God and man did not merge in some way, *philosophice, poetice* [philosophically, poetically], etc. into one" (*Sickness*, 99). This interpretation, then, is Kierkegaard's uniquely Christian version of the quarrel, one that will not allow a collapse into the unity of either myth or philosophy, one in which there are only two possible authentic human responses: either the ignorance of Socrates or the Christian's faith in the act of God, bridging the gulf between humanity and God accomplished through the action of God, who becomes a human and walks among us as a living man. Such a response to the quarrel could have come only from God: "No philosophy (for it is only for thought), no

[6] Søren Kierkegaard, *Either/Or Part II*, trans. Howard V. Hong and Edna H. Hong (Princeton: Princeton University Press, 1987), 174, hereafter cited in text as *Either/Or*, II.

[7] Søren Kierkegaard, *The Sickness unto Death: A Christian Psychological Exposition for Upbuilding and Awakening*, trans. Howard V. Hong and Edna H. Hong (Princeton: Princeton University Press, 1980), 99, hereafter cited in text as *Sickness*.

mythology (for it is only for the imagination), no historical knowledge (which is from memory) has ever had this idea – of which in this connection one can say with all multiple meanings that it did not arise in any human heart" (*Sickness*, 109).

The Hegelian perspective comprises a "scientific" movement of thought that travels in history from the lower stages of imagination and feeling to the higher stages, with humanity reaching its highest level in pure thought. But in this course, Johannes Climicus says, "philosophy moves farther and farther away from contrast with primitive existential impressions, and there is nothing left to explore, nothing to express" (*Concluding*, 307). Of course, there are always more puzzles in the material world to unravel. But this is of no interest to Kierkegaard. In his papers and journals, he says that if anything in natural science could aid us in defining and understanding spirit, he would gladly take hold of the microscope and join that labor. "But since I can easily see, through qualitative dialectic, that the world will not have advanced qualitatively a single step more in 100,000 years I will do just the opposite: reserve my soul and not waste a second of my life on curiosity" (*Papers*, VII, I, A 191). Science is a form of "bad infinity" – an endless chain of one thing after another (*Papers*, VII, I, A 189). Elsewhere he records a more visceral sense of frustration with the natural scientists: "The researcher begins right away to distract you with his details: one goes now to Australia, now to the moon, now into an underground cave, now up the arse, for God's sake – after an intestinal worm" (*Papers*, VII, I, A 200).

So Kierkegaard's interest is the realm of spirit. He resists the totalizing effect of mythology and philosophical systematization (including the systemizing world of scientific thought in the natural sciences). The human means of avoiding a collapse into the reassuring but false unity of either is that consciousness engendered by Socratic ignorance, an ignorance that is a kind of active waiting, probing even where the answer will not appear, a living posture that readies the individual for the only answer that is real and true, and which must come not from human activity but from the action of God. That is the ideal. But there are many ways for us to make errors at the cost of our very lives, lives that do not stop or even slow down while we figure out things. Much of Kierkegaard's work addresses these errors, and much of the error results from a different kind of "poetry" – poetizing a life.

Introduced in the *Concept of Irony*, this dangerous sort of poet is made dangerous by the extreme nature of his irony, which keeps him from any real ethical or religious experience. This is the "poetizer." Poetizing is a means of achieving a kind of distance through irony. The possibilities in irony are deeply related to the Socratic gift that facilitated the freeing of the mind from myth, and it is the possibility of Socratic ignorance that allows irony to be used to avoid the collapse back into the mythic world, or the error of claiming knowledge we do not really have. It makes dialectic possible. But the poetizer takes an ironic stance toward everything without regard for whether irony is fitting. It is a stance that is clearly understood from the inside by Kierkegaard, and so he is reliable when he says of such an ironist that "everything in the given actuality has nothing but poetic validity for the ironist, for he, after all, is living poetically.... He himself repents, but he repents aesthetically, not ethically. In the moment of repentance, he is outside and above his repentance, testing to see whether it is poetically appropriate, whether it could do as a line in the mouth of a poetic character" (*Concept*, 283–4). The poetizer experiences one poetized mood after another, and the only continuity such a one has is his boredom – "boredom, this eternity devoid of content, this salvation devoid of joy, this superficial profundity, this hungry glut. But boredom is precisely the negative unity admitted into a personal consciousness, wherein opposites vanish" (*Concept*, 285). Opposites vanish, tension is let go, everything is totalized by irony, the quarrel is nowhere to be found, the mind and soul can go nowhere.

This is an unfortunate state of affairs, but it is not the identity of "living poetically" with the unifying feature of boredom that is most dangerous. The deep danger rests in the fact that a poetic victory over the world provides a *kind* of reconciliation with actuality through poetic transformation of a lived actuality into a "higher" poetic actuality that comes about through negating actuality. The problem is that this kind of reconciliation is not real – I am not reconciled with the actuality in which I am living. The only true reconciliation comes about through religion. Thus, the great danger of living poetically is that we miss true reconciliation, we miss "the highest enjoyment, the true bliss in which the subject is not dreaming, but possesses himself in infinite clarity, is absolutely transparent to himself, which is possible only for the religious individual, who does not have his infinity outside himself but inside himself" (*Concept*, 248).

Living poetically, however, does not mean that one produces poetry, and indeed "what holds for the poet's existence holds also in some measure for every single individual's life" (*Concept*, 325). The world can be poetically experienced, but only rarely does one have "the Divine good fortune to be able to let what is poetically experienced take shape and form itself poetically...the enviable fate of the chosen few" (*Concept*, 326). When the poetizer produces poetry, the poetry stands in stark contrast to the mythic mind living myth, for it makes use of the philosopher's trope, irony, which frees the poet so that he "floats above his artistic work" (*Concept*, 324). Such a poet begins not in the immediacy of myth but in that of genius. And as the use of irony becomes more dominant, the poet is pried away even from the immediacy of genius. "The more a poet has abandoned this [the immediacy of genius], the more necessary it is for him to have a totality-view of the world, and in this way to be master over irony in his individual existence, and the more necessary it becomes for him to be a philosopher to a certain degree" (*Concept*, 325). As the poet takes an ironic stance toward poetry, the relation of the poet to the poem changes. This shifting characterization of the poet was a recurrent theme for Kierkegaard as he worked out his own uneasy status as poet and philosopher.

In *Either/Or I*, edited by the pseudonymous author Victor Eremita, the first chapter opens with a question: "What is a poet?" The answer: "An unhappy person who conceals profound anguish in his heart but whose lips are so formed that as sighs and cries pass over them they sound like beautiful music" (*Either/Or*, I, 19). The poet has many reasons to be unhappy, not least because, being caught in poetizing, the poet cannot return to the immediacy of myth: this option was undone by Socratic dialectic, which ultimately forces humanity forward toward despair at its current situation, which is inauthentic and incomplete, on toward the only answer that remains when all other answers have been tried and found wanting, faith.

The poet cannot be satisfied with poetry. In "The Seducer's Diary," we learn that the poetizer has two forms of enjoyment. The first is the aesthetic enjoyment of poetizing his own living actuality (an encounter with a girl, and another girl, and another girl, or the encounter with each stage of seducing a girl), and the second is poetic reflection in which he enjoys his own poetizing personality that has wrought this poet-existence (*Either/Or*, I, 305). So there are indeed two moments in the poet-existence – poetizing and reflection on poetizing – but these go nowhere and never yield satisfaction. The seducer's diary itself, cast in language, allows the second moment, the poetic recording of the first moment. In *Either/Or II* the character B writes letters to the young man who was the "author" and subject of *Either/Or I*, but now the perspective is ethical rather than aesthetic, the perspective of authentic personhood. B points out that "the poet-existence as such lies in the darkness that is the result of a despair that was not carried through, the result of the soul's continuing to quake in despair and of the spirit's inability to achieve its true transfiguration" (*Either/Or*, II, 210). The poet-existence never reaches the goal, never reaches the infinite, the eternal, which alone answers our true longing. In place of the eternal, the infinite, the poet-existence substitutes an unending series of moods and poetized experiences, the 1,003 lovers of Don Juan. The poetic exploration of erotic love is pagan (*Stages*, 100). The distance necessary for poetizing a human relationship requires that the ethical dimensions of the relationship be falsified, that the relationship become a sort of intellectual pursuit. This poetizing of relationships in actual life is, he says, common among criminals (*Stages*, 154).

What is a poet? The question arises often in Kierkegaard's work, and though poetry will always fall short of the eternal and leave us unsatisfied, the ways in which one can be a poet, the content and actuality the poet poetizes, can vary. In the seducer's diary the content is erotic. This posture is challenged to some extent from the ethical perspective, but it is in *Fear and Trembling* that the poet's inadequacy is made apparent in a philosophically deeper way, as the poet actually comes up against the eternal in the person of Abraham, who experiences a call from God to sacrifice his own son, and who must respond in the gap between his deepest ethical duty and the call of his God to obedience. The author here is Johannes de Silentio, a poet-dialectician. In the opening inscription, he quotes Hamann: "What Tarquinius Superbus said in the garden by means of the poppies, the son understood but the messenger did not." This poet, John of Silence, is not able to comprehend Abraham. He says of himself, "The present author is by no means a philosopher. He is *poetice et eleganter* [in a poetic and refined way] a supplementary clerk who neither writes the system nor gives promise of the system nor binds himself to the system."[8]

Hegel is supposed to be difficult to understand, but Johannes claims to understand him quite well. On the other hand, Abraham, who is "easy" to understand ("to understand Abraham is a small matter," they say) leaves Johannes shattered. Here we come up against the weight of the individual in relation to the eternal, and neither poetry nor philosophy nor theology can find room to fit Abraham into a system. "Love

---

[8] Søren Kierkegaard, *Fear and Trembling*, trans. Howard V. Hong and Edna H. Hong (Princeton: Princeton University Press, 1983), 7, hereafter cited in text as *Fear*.

indeed has its priests in the poets, and occasionally we hear a voice that knows how to honor it, but not a word is heard about faith. Who speaks to the honor of this passion? Philosophy goes farther. Theology sits all rouged and powdered in the window and courts its favor, offers its charms to philosophy" (*Fear*, 32). But none come close to comprehending Abraham. Here, above all, the poetizer in life misses the highest thing and fails to grasp life's point.

Likewise, the one who would turn religion into a finished system cannot comprehend Abraham. The complete system as finished makes it impossible for the individual to approach that stage just before faith, which Johannes de Silentio calls infinite resignation, that step by which we, as individuals, become aware of our eternal validity (*Fear*, 46). This philosophical movement yields our eternal consciousness. It is this eternal consciousness of the individual that, if it goes no farther, will find itself stranded in the ethical sphere. The only way up is faith, and faith is "this paradox that a single individual is higher than the universal," that truth which makes us approach Abraham with a kind of religious horror (*Fear*, 55). Abraham – who apart from faith cannot even be thought of as a tragic hero but rather must be called a murderer – is in faith the single individual set over against the universal, "Thou shalt not kill": "The story of Abraham contains, then, a teleological suspension of the ethical. As the single individual he became higher than the universal" (*Fear*, 66). Though the universal in the ethical is given by God, it is not through duty to the universal that a person comes into relation to God but only through absolute duty to God, even if in abrogation of the universal (*Fear*, 70). This role is inaccessible to poetry or philosophy. That the hero might die for a girl is accessible; that a hero might die for an ethical universal is accessible. But neither the poet nor the Hegelian systematizer can find the way to Abraham.

There is something important to be understood about the value and role of the poetic: "All poetry is life's glorification [*Forklarelse* (i.e. transfiguration)] through its clarification [*Forklarelse* (through being clarified, illuminated, "unfolded," etc.)]. It is really remarkable that language has this ambiguity" (*Papers*, II, A 352). But Christianity with its God-become-man is an offense, and only the leap of faith can carry us across the vast chasm between our actual lives and the reality of this God who is our deepest need. This is made clear by the failure of all alternatives to such faith. Poetry cannot make the leap, and except for Socratic ignorance, philosophy also does not get us far. Kierkegaard says, "Philosophy is life's dry nurse. It can look after us but not give suck" (*Papers*, II, A 59).

As we move in this life toward what matters most, "longing is the umbilical cord of the higher life" (*Papers*, II, A 352). Nonetheless, whatever the dangers of poetizing as an escape from the weight of being fully authentic in our relation to God, poetizing as a glorifying, transfiguring, clarifying, illuminating force must be further explored, for this writer so often taught in philosophy classes says of himself, "I am only a Christian poet and thinker" (*Papers*, X, I, A 281).

The specific poetry Kierkegaard criticizes and counters with the authenticity of the life of faith (and its risk) is romantic poetry. It is this poetry that threatens distraction from the truth in nineteenth-century Denmark (for threats are always in a time and place as with the threat from the poets in Socrates' Athens). Moving between the two poles of actuality as it is given and the vague outlines of what would constitute an ideal actuality, romantic poetry yields an ever higher vision of the ideal, which in turn makes actuality seem ever more mundane and mediocre. And yet this burgeoning ideal, however high it may rise, does not, and never can, well up into an eternal life. Romantic poetry, in moving between these two poles, is not truth: "In no way is the true ideal in the beyond – it is behind in so far as it is the propelling force; it is ahead in so far as it is the inspiring goal, but at the same time it is within us, and this is its truth" (*Concept*, 304).

Romantic poetry is never more than an approximation, never able to achieve adequate expression, "for which reason this poetry is poetry about poetry ad infinitum.... Weary and bored with its old associates, rhyme seeks new and interesting acquaintances. Ultimately the musical element isolates itself entirely, [yielding a kind of poetry] everyone remembers from childhood in the delightful verse: Eeny meeny, hippity dick, dilya dyelya, dominick" (*Concept*, 307). Delightful, yes, but hippity dick is unlikely ever to approach the eternity of the true ideal, and the higher actuality that is supposed to emerge in poetry never shows up but is always out of reach, just over the horizon, "becoming" (*Concept*, 319). If poetry merely serves as the means to inspire longing, bring us to the threshold, and point beyond itself, it works well. But when it claims access to the eternal, it becomes false and, worse, dangerous to the soul. This is why in his own poetic work, the philosopher-poet Kierkegaard is careful in the use of his creations. He makes it clear that the pseudonyms are to be credited with their claims, and he balances the whole with his edifying discourses about which he says, "[As opposed to the pseudonymous works] I am quite literally the author of the *Edifying Discourses*, and of every word in them" (*Concluding*, 551).

Poetry is language connected with immediacy, but it is always in tension with immediacy because it is cast in language, and this is the difference between poetry and music. Poetry and music are nonetheless related. This can be explored by starting with language and "sounding out music." So if prosaic language is least musical, as one moves through the rhythms of oration toward stages of poetry that become ever more metrical, eventually language stops and music begins (*Either/Or*, I, 69). But lest we think this means that music is closer to perfection than language, when we go down the scale from prose we equally lose the concepts carried by language and end up meeting music again in the singsong babbling of an infant. So music is not, as music, higher than language or a more perfect medium than language. Better to say "that language is bounded by music on all sides" (*Either/Or*, I, 69).

Language is bound up with reflection while, for character A, music always expresses the immediate. "Reflection is fatal to the immediate and therefore it is impossible for a language to express the musical, but this apparent poverty in language is precisely its wealth" (*Either/Or*, I, 70). No wonder, then, that myth comes to an end in the quarrel between two language-based human activities – poetry and philosophy – as language itself already contains the seeds for undoing myth expressed in language.

In *Either/Or II*, Judge Williams says that poetry provides "only an imperfect reconciliation with life, [and] when you fix your eye upon poetry and art you are not looking at actuality, and that is really what we should be speaking about" (*Either/Or*, II, 272). Science is unsatisfying because it misses the realm of spirit. But language too, though it is related to the realm of spirit, can become the means by which we are distracted from what is highest. Because poetry requires passion in order to reach the limits of what is accessible to poetry, there is a strong allure to remain enthralled by passion. To relinquish this passion is to relinquish poetry, for there is no room in poetic immediacy for duplexity, as between lovers there cannot be a single doubt about their readiness for love's union. One doubt, and it is over – or least instead of love's union you end up with a sitcom. A passionless poetry is to be disdained. Indeed, it becomes something else entirely, a vapid substitute of no interest to a real poet, nor to one who has, through a higher passion, broken out of that poetic immediacy: "To take passion away from poetry and to compensate for what is lost with embellishments, lovely rural scenery, popular woodland scenes, enchanting theatrical moonshine, is a loss akin to wanting to make up for the badness of the book with the elegance of the binding, something that certainly cannot interest the reader but at most the bookbinder" (*Stages*, 405). When passion, absolute passion, is absent from the consciousness of love, poetry is done with it. And when poetry is done with it, the carcass is turned over to the predatory bird, "here in the shape of novelists, serial story writers, [and] hermaphrodites of tragic-comic writers" (*Stages*, 409). Poetry, meanwhile, must find another passion. If ever passion wanes, leaving us forsaken by poetry, "people will work their way down into finitude until they finally reach politics in the bad sense" (*Stages*, 409). This is why poetry cannot comprehend the death of Socrates. Poetry is passionate about the immediate and so can grasp the tragic in the death of Socrates, or perhaps the comic in his death as he reminds his friends in his final words that he owes a rooster to the god of healing, Asclepius. But it cannot comprehend both. In order for them to be taken together rather than taking the tragic and the comic in succession, the expansive consciousness made possible by Socratic irony is necessary (*Stages*, 418). His friends laugh one minute and cry the next, and so, though they experience both joy and sorrow, they still have not reached Socrates' understanding of his death, a duplexity inaccessible to poetry. In the absence of doubt, the passionate embrace is passionate, indeed. But, Kierkegaard says, there is a higher passion that can lead one to break out of this "rounded-off sphere" of poetic immediacy, and it is not the passion of the poet.

Though the poetic is one kind of reconciliation with the actual, it is a "mediocre reconciliation" and must pick and choose among these things that are appropriate for the aesthetic, the poetic. Love? Certainly. But what about the value of, say, health and illness? No: "Poetry is not supposed to be a hospital" (*Stages*, 458). And yet what an important part of our lives illness is. What the poetic has no room for, a higher passion can accommodate, the passion of religion. Poetry remains lovable, but it also remains poetry, unable and unwilling to deal with suffering, illness, and poverty as they are: whatever joy we take in poetry, it is a mistake to confuse theater with what is real (*Stages*, 461). When reality opens up, and what is seen is not some bounded universe of determined matter and force, but eternity itself, only the religious is capable of a fitting response. This is the place for a person authentically to become joyful: "To be joyful out on 70,000 fathoms of water, many, many miles from all human help – yes, that is something great! To swim in the shallows in the company of waders is not the religious" (*Stages*, 461).

Anti-Climicus in *The Sickness unto Death* says that there are poets who have religious longing and who take up God into their own despair, loving God, but refusing to relinquish their own anguish. Such poets even poetize God and, as poets of the religious, they act the same as the poet of the erotic who became a poet through an unhappy love affair. Such a religious poet has a "God-relationship" and would be lost without it, and yet he never humbles himself, nor does he become himself before God, and cannot do that final act – in faith relinquishing his own despair. But he certainly can speak: "This poet's description of the religious – just like that other poet's description of erotic love – has a charm, a lyrical verve that no married man's and no His Reverence's presentations have" (*Sickness*, 78).

The poet is born in collision with all life, whether in the collision with the immediate, poetizing romantic faith in women as a seducer, or else poetizing the universal with intense passion, "weary of the incessant chatter about the universal and the universal repeated to the point of the most boring insipidity" (*Fear*, 227). Only if the poet collides with something higher in the religious sphere does he discover, not a poem, or a woman, or the status of hero sacrificed for the universal, but something only the individual can have, "a fact of consciousness" established on the basis of a God-relationship (*Fear*, 229). Lurking nearby, however, is the danger of poetic sophistry.

This matter of consciousness, unlike history or systems, can reside only in the living individual, and it is the field in which all the important work is done, in which the quarrel – Kierkegaard's struggle through the spheres of existence – is engaged. "The most concrete content that consciousness can have is consciousness of itself, of the individual himself – not the pure self-consciousness, but self-consciousness that is so concrete that no author, not even one with the greatest power of description, has ever been able to describe a single such consciousness, although every single human being is such a one."[9] And this consciousness, in its struggle from the poetic to the universal to the religious, travels freely. It finds its own freedom revealed through the experience of anxiety, an anxiety that persists throughout the pursuit of finite ends, whether aesthetic or ethical, poetic or philosophical. The anxiety persists until the individual comes to realize the deceptiveness of these finite ends, their

---

[9] Søren Kierkegaard, *The Concept of Anxiety: A Simple Psychologically Orienting Deliberation on the Dogmatic Issue of Hereditary Sin*, trans. Reidar Thomte and Albert B. Anderson (Princeton: Princeton University Press, 1980), 143.

inadequacy. Then, "he who in relation to guilt is educated by anxiety will rest only in atonement."[10]

In atonement there is indeed rest, a living rest. But the religious poet, as poet, cannot arrive at this rest. Such a poet tries to get to the religious through imagination (*Concluding*, 347). The poet as poet can come into only an aesthetic relationship with the religious. For the poet to get to the religious, he must pass through the ethical. And while it may well be true that the poet qua poet can achieve the highest pathos in the aesthetic realm by sacrificing himself for the masterpiece he produces, to the point of selling his soul to the devil, this same poet may well find that the way into the ethical is "to renounce the glittering artistic career without saying a single word" (*Concluding*, 349). That said, in renouncing the glittering career for the sake of the ethical, the poet must not stop there: "Every individual who does not live either poetically or religiously is stupid" (*Concluding*, 408). The error is to lose the poetry of youth for the trek through worldly wisdom, but never to gain a relationship to the eternal.

Nor can philosophy get to the rest of atonement. This is an inward truth, the way of subjectivity, of becoming a subject in truth, subjectivity being the heart of the Christian way as opposed to the way of objectivity taught by philosophy (*Concluding*, 117). There is a very definite reason that the way of philosophical objectivity can never get to its goal: "The existing individual who chooses to pursue the objective way enters upon the entire approximation process by which it is proposed to bring God to light objectively. But this is in all eternity impossible, because God is a subject, and therefore exists only for subjectivity in inwardness" (*Concluding*, 178). This is the key: God is a subject. So, when we look out on the world and see evidence both of wisdom, and of disturbing realities that do not seem consonant with wisdom, goodness, or omnipotence, we are left with an objective uncertainty, and no amount of piecing together bits from the objective world will ever bring us fully before God. Only faith opens up this possibility, faith that is "the contradiction between the infinite passion of the individual's inwardness and the objective uncertainty" (*Concluding*, 182). God is a subject and, as such, cannot be understood or encountered apart from subjectivity, a subjectivity that reaches its highest (and most absurd) form when eternal truth actually enters time and God, as subject, is born, grows up, walks among us "precisely

[10] Ibid., 162.

like any other individual human being, quite indistinguishable from other individuals" (*Concluding*, 188).

What is the value of the poets, then? Their value lies in the act of registering longing, a longing that is itself a compelling clue to the truth of the universe. In *Either/Or* I, character A says that a poet wishes for his subject matter, and while acknowledging that wishing is not an art, he goes on to identify a certain kind of wishing as a gift and great art, the actuality of a mysterious and inexplicable genius, "just as with the divining rod, which never has the notion to wish except in the presence of that for which it wishes" (*Either/Or*, I, 50). Wishing as a divining rod, responding not to what is absent or nonexistent, but rather to what is present – in its many forms, this is at the heart of the mystery of poetry's strange appeal in the quarrel. Character A will not likely be able to draw any mystical conclusions regarding the value and nature of the poetic wish, but Kierkegaard can. And what wish becomes the clue to the deeper reality of being human in this created world? The wish is the desire for the infinite, the longing to become the infinite. The way in which this wish manifests itself can be defined and described by the poet "only by way of its opposite, and if the lines are to have any poetic value, the coloring of the expression must contain the reflection of the dialectical opposite" (*Sickness*, 30). The self feels its finitude, but longs for the infinite, and this is despair. The imagination can carry such a one past finitude, and indeed the imagination "is the medium for the process of infinitizing" (*Sickness*, 30). The imagination is able to move beyond the actuality of the self to the self's possibilities. It is this movement beyond finite actuality that leads one toward the infinite, but the infinite only as possibility: the disjunct between the poet's imaginative foray into the possibility of the infinite and the poet's inability to arrive at fulfillment (apart from faith) leads to despair. This in turn is a divining rod signaling that there is something more, if only the poet can find a way across the chasm. So this despair is an important clue and prompt, and it appears in several forms.

Fantasy can overtake the self so that the self becomes consumed with the fantastic as possibility, but without moving beyond fantasy. In the fantasized religious sphere, this sort of despair is particularly consuming: "That a sparrow can live is comprehensible; it does not know that it exists before God. But to know that one exists before God, and then not instantly go mad or sink into nothingness!" (*Sickness*, 32). While this kind of despair risks annihilation because of a consciousness of God, another kind of distraction can occur in despair that leads an individual consciousness to relinquish the infinite, narrowing and truncating the self, "emasculating oneself in a spiritual sense" (*Sickness*, 33). When this occurs, it is largely unnoticed (*Sickness*, 34). These are the people who go about their business, perform their functions, follow the health of their retirement funds, but they do not exist in any deep sense, and, "spiritually speaking, they have no self, no self for whose sake they could venture everything, no self before God – however self-seeking they are otherwise" (*Sickness*, 35).

For such a one, prayer is impossible, because prayer requires three elements – God, a self, and possibility. "That God's will is possible makes me able to pray; if there is nothing but necessity, man is essentially as inarticulate as the animals." In the absence of imagination that can carry us toward such possibility (with poetry and prayer now moving toward a fitting relationship to one another), life becomes "a certain trivial compendium of experiences as to how things go, what is possible, what usually happens" (*Sickness*, 41). This is a pathetic life bereft of God and of the authentic self. Here is a sinister type of immediacy that reduces the human to the level of lower animals, and it is imagination that can resist this by ripping such a one out of his trivial string of experiences and by teaching both fear and hope, rendering him aware of his self and God. This is the poetic imagination at its best, and it is ignored at the peril of the soul. For those who do not move up to this awareness, time merely passes: "This form of despair is: in despair not to will to be oneself, or even lower: in despair not to will to be a self, or lowest of all: in despair to will to be someone else, to wish for a new self" (*Sickness*, 52).

Here is the threshold that can lead to unconditional repentance in the face of the inadequacy of all ways but one: "Sin is: before God, or with the conception of God, in despair not to will to be oneself, or in despair to will to be one self" (*Sickness*, 77). And the most "dialectical frontier" between despair and sin is that of the poet-existence in which sin verges on the religious (making it most dangerous) and which consists in "poetizing instead of being, relating to the good and the true through the imagination instead of being that – that is, existentially striving to be that" (*Sickness*, 77). In its dialectical nature with its obscurely conscious awareness of being sin, it is impenetrable. At least in the midst of despair there is the possibility of repentance. But the poetizing of everything prevents this possibility for the one living a poet-existence. This dynamic within a consciousness is impervious to the ignorance of Socrates in countering the certainty of the mythic mind and, likewise, impervious to the experience of traveler in the aesthetic or ethical sphere, either of which can escape by reaching the point of despair and breaking through, ultimately via faith, into the true religious: the poet-existence would poetize even God, at which point there is no resalting the salt that has lost its flavor.

There may be a limit, however. A person might poetize himself as a god, or God as himself, but no poet could "poetize that the god poetized himself in the likeness of his being, for if the god gave no indication, how could it occur to a man that the blessed god could need him?"[11] The idea that God, the eternal, becomes a historical event among us in time and space, so that our own point of departure for our conscious-ness of eternity (which is the foundation of our happiness) is a histor-ical event – this no poet has ever dreamed. This, so different from any human poem, is finally no poem at all, but what Johannes in *Philosophical Fragments* calls "The Wonder."

Wonder, for Johannes Climicus, is an immediate category, as opposed to doubt, which is a reflective category, and together they form the two ways in which philosophy begins. When it begins in wonder, as with the Greeks, there is a kind of continuity between the philosopher and the Greeks. When it begins in doubt, as with Descartes, it is always the case that continuity is broken, for by its very nature, "doubt is precisely a polemic against what went before."[12] When philosophy begins with doubt, however much it tries, the remedy for doubt will not come from philosophy itself. In his *Papers and Journals*, Kierkegaard writes that "doubt is conquered not by the system but by faith, just as it is faith that has brought doubt into the world" (*Papers*, IV, B 13:18). Faith, which does not trade in the currency of certainty, makes doubt possible, and it is a long road from the doubt made possible by faith to the faith that answers doubt.[13]

---

[11] Søren Kierkegaard, *Philosophical Fragments / Johnannes Climacus*, trans. Howard V. Hong and Edna H. Hong (Princeton: Princeton University Press, 1985), 35.

[12] Ibid., 145.

[13] Cartesian doubt has a slightly different flavor than the doubt engendered and answered by faith, because of the Cartesian posture toward existence (which is the sole interest of speculative thought). In *Concluding Unscientific Postscript*, Johannes Climicus men-tions Aristotle's remark that poetry is higher than history because history only tells us what has happened, whereas poetry addresses the realm of the possible by telling us what might have happened and what should have happened. So from the poetic per-spective, possibility is higher than reality, and its only interest is the possible – about the remainder of "reality" it is indifferent. What bothers Johannes Climicus about Descartes is, namely, "This indifference is forgotten in the Cartesian *cogito ergo sum*, which injects a disturbing element into the disinterestedness of the intellectual and affronts speculative thought, as if it were instrumental to something else" (*Concluding*,

When the poet does encounter reality as a poet, it should be an occasion only, "a point of departure from which he goes in search of the identity of the possible" (*Concluding*, 347). The poet will never reach the end qua poet, but the poet, in pointing beyond actuality as it is encountered at face value, draws close to the threshold where the end, the *telos*, might be reached. Philosophy can aid in this by responding to actuality in its own way; however, as it approaches "absolute knowledge" in the system, it too will necessarily fail to reach the end, although there is hope at the end of either failure if the failure is acknowledged and not made itself an idol and point of existence. Most important, though, is to avoid being lulled into that workaday world, that form of despair in which a life is merely lived doing one thing after another, accumulating the things one accumulates, never being hooked or grabbed, whether from inside poetry or inside philosophy, by a passion that starts one toward the inevitable failure of both poetry and philosophy, a failure that becomes the very threshold to the authentic existence of the individual in relationship to God: "What unites all human beings is passion. So religious passion, faith, hope and love are everything – the great thing is to live one's life in what is essential for all human beings, and in that to have a difference of degree. Being a philosopher is just about as good a difference as being a poet" (*Papers*, IV, C 96).

So, to ask again, what is it to be a poet or a philosopher? This question is at the heart of Kierkegaard's work, and he asks it often. He says that if it were not for the fact that he was raised as a Christian, and if he had not suffered inwardly as a child, and yet knew what he had learned as an adult, he would have been a poet. "I can't think that there has lived a poet before me with a deeper knowledge of existence and especially of the religious" (*Papers*, X, I, A 11). But he says also that he would not want to be the kind of poet presented in the person of A and approved of by B in *Either/Or*. He does not want to be a poet of the sort that has a vision in the imagination but who refutes the vision in his personal life,

282). This instrumental approach to speculative thought and poetry lures them both into deserting "the lofty disinterestedness of the possible in order to reach out for reality" (*Concluding*, 283). Poetry becomes unpoetical in reaching out for reality, and speculative thought in its reach for the real disastrously assures us "that whatever is thought is real, that thought is not only capable of thinking reality, but of bestowing it, while the truth is the direct opposite" (*Concluding*, 283). And so we forget what it is to exist, and in abandoning the authentic existence of the individual for a poeticized version of the "real" or else a wayward historical consciousness such as that which we find in the Hegelian system and other systems that followed, we live unethically.

as did many of the thinkers in Kierkegaard's time (so he judges). Nor does this criticism stop at thinkers. Priests also come under critique. "Priests are poets in this respect and, because they are priests, are in a far profounder sense 'tricksters,' as Socrates himself called the poets" (*Papers*, X, I, A 11). None of these relate personally to their vision, allowing the imagined possibility to break out into life, existence. He says that priests, poets, and professors of philosophy "have taken over as servants of the truth, by which no doubt they themselves are well served, but not truth" (*Papers*, X, I, A 11).

Kierkegaard struggles from inside this understanding of what poetry and philosophy are, and how poetry and philosophy relate in his own work, with a sense of wanting to move past the thresholds either is capable of reaching. Eight years after writing *The Concept of Irony*, Kierkegaard said of himself, "I have up until now been a poet, definitely nothing more, and it is a despairing struggle to want to go beyond my boundary" (*Papers*, X, I, A 510). But he does claim to have gone beyond poetry and philosophy in one sense at least, by daring to expose himself to ridicule and holding out (which was, he acknowledges, helped by the fact that he was financially independent) (*Papers*, X, I, A 558). He finds the title that fits him best to be "poet of the religious" but not in the sense that he poetizes Christianity, or in the sense that his personal life is something different and set apart from poetic creation. His very striving is part of the means by which he explores and discovers. He is a poet struggling toward the ideal and living the struggle, but not in a way that makes the struggle more important to him than the ideal: he is a poet but not an idolater. Regarding Christianity, his task as a "poet of the religious" has been always "with poetic fervor to present the whole ideality according to the most ideal standard – always ending with: I'm not it, but I strive" (*Papers*, X, 2, A 106).

He is only on the way, but he is on the way indeed, as a single individual. This existential category cannot be approached or expressed by science, which is why he finds it odd that people deify the scientific. Such efforts are nonsense. Nor can "the system" of the Hegelians portray it. There are only two ways the existential can be portrayed, and these are through either "realization in life or poetic presentations, *loquere ut videam* [speak so that I may see]" (*Papers*, X, 2, A 414). And the category of a single individual can be introduced only poetically (*Papers*, X, 3, A 660). It is imagination that forces people toward actuality, toward existence, imagination that helps "to get them far enough out, or in, or down into existence. And when imagination has helped them get as far out as they should be – that is when actuality generally begins" (*Papers*, XI, I, A 288). This is what is meant by the idea of "poetic openings."

Likewise, Kierkegaard says (as Augustine did in his own theodicy) that God is like a poet, and this is why, in relating to creation, "God puts up with evil and with all the rubbish and misery of triviality, and mediocrity, etc." (*Papers*, XI, 2, A 98). God is present everywhere poetically and poetically lets everything come out, including the shades and shadows of good and evil. But what leads to God's decision to act as a poet is not the pagan notion of God wiling away the time, an image of eternal boredom of a sort, but rather the fact that God's passion, an infinite passion, is to love and be loved. It is this that Kierkegaard ultimately contrasts with "the Hegelian rubbish about the actual being the truth." No, in our truest existence toward which we are ushered by the poetic imagination, we meet not the Hegelian Absolute but a God who is bound to us by the power of love's passion, "bound fast as if it were a weakness, whereas the extent to which his love is not subject to change is indeed his strength, his almighty strength" (*Papers*, XI, 2, A 98).

Such passion toward which the poetic imagination ushers us ends in the light of infinite love, which is our hope for being preserved rather than annihilated in the face of the infinite. Poetic passion plays as deep a role, but with a very different ending point, for the next philosopher in this brief history, William Dilthey.

# 10

# Dilthey: Poetry and the Escape from Metaphysics

In Plato's *Republic*, it was clear that establishing the relationship of poetry and philosophy was important. William Dilthey agrees. But Dilthey's conclusions differ considerably, and he embraces a near inversion of the Platonic view. Whereas for Plato the transcendent was most real, for Dilthey the transcendent in principle can play no role in philosophy; and in Dilthey's work, unlike in the *Republic*, poetry takes a preeminent place among the arts and, along with the other arts, is of critical importance to the work of philosophy: "It is one of the most vital tasks of contemporary philosophy to reestablish, through the further development of aesthetics, the natural relationship among art, criticism, and an engaged public."[1]

The content of both poetry and philosophy ranges across all of human experience. When one asks about the relationship of the two, no answer that does not attend to this common content will finally be satisfying. This may be especially true for Dilthey, for whom, some have argued, the entire conception of the human sciences is rooted in the conception of aesthetics.[2] The efforts of poetry and, more broadly, of art in general aim at the understanding of human life. Indeed, Dilthey goes so far as to say, "None of us would possess more than a meager part of our present understanding of human conditions, if we had not become used to seeing through the poet's eyes."[3] If he is right, the notion of a poetics becomes much more than a critical tool for literary specialists: poetics becomes an arena for philosophical inquiry in which questions

[1] Wilhelm Dilthey, *Poetry and Experience*, ed. Rudolf A. Makkreel and Frithjof Rodi (Princeton: Princeton University Press, 1985), 175, hereafter cited in text as *Poet.*

[2] Michael Lessnoff, "Dilthey," *Routledge History of Philosophy*, vol. 7: *The Nineteenth Century* (New York: Routledge, 1994), 213.

[3] H. A. Hodges, *The Philosophy of Wilhelm Dilthey* (London: Routledge, 1952), 233.

of value, meaning, and knowledge are central. As such questions are asked, and the history of answers reviewed, a second area of philosophy that commonly arises in the discussion of philosophy's relationship to poetry – metaphysics – becomes important, but in a new way.

For Dilthey, the fundamental aim of philosophy is to grasp reality methodically and then to analyze it "within the limits prescribed by the critique of knowledge."[4] His project is not unlike Hegel's insofar as his philosophy invades and takes over a domain. But in this case the domain is less that of myth than that of metaphysics. One difference between Dilthey and Hegel lies in their analysis of the subject matter. Dilthey says, "The scientific outlook was preceded by a conceptual world that held that reality proceeds from divine knowledge. I will show how this conceptual world is the product of the totality of our mental powers" (*Intro.*, 281). For him, the failure to see this is one of the great errors in philosophy, an error that has run from Plato through the history of European thought, an error that must be corrected by understanding it historically if philosophy is no longer to be held under its power.

When critically evaluating ideas such as those of metaphysics in which one sees a great error, but which nonetheless have great power, it is reasonable to ask *why* the idea has such power and, in turn, to consider whether the force of the idea can be made to better serve the inquiry when purged of its error. In considering this question, an important corollary question is this: where did the idea come from in the first place? Dilthey's approach is to explore the origins of metaphysics in order to understand the tenacious hold it has had on the minds and imaginations of thinkers.

Metaphysics functions for Dilthey the way that the myths seemed to function for Socrates, as something to be overcome. "Man will completely overcome metaphysics – like any other great spiritual phenomenon that he has outlived, but whose tradition drags on – only by comprehending it" (*Intro.*, 175). The result of such comprehension will be to dissolve the false dichotomy between the empirical and the rational domains that inhere in the positing of metaphysical knowledge and, thus, to make room for Dilthey's project of understanding how the human sciences are interconnected (*Intro.*, 176).

---

[1] Wilhelm Dilthey, *Introduction to the Human Sciences*, ed. Rudolph A. Makkreel and Frithjof Rodi (Princeton: Princeton University Press, 1989), 173, hereafter cited in text as *Intro.*

In *Metaphysics as Foundation of the Human Sciences: Its Dominance and Decline,* Dilthey opposes both empiricism and speculative philosophy from the same vantage point: the real sociohistorical world (*Intro.,* 174). The history he offers to support this opposition is quite detailed, but briefly metaphysics falls under the weight of two things. The first is the content of its own statements. The requisite comprehension of metaphysics, which has as its yield the overcoming of metaphysics, requires familiarity with the various metaphysical systems proposed by Schelling, Hegel, Schopenhauer, and others. Each philosopher offers his reasons for embracing his particular system. But the systems are mutually exclusive, each offering a truth content that is relative to the system itself. The outcome, to the ear of an honest thinker attending to each system with equal vigilance, is what Dilthey calls "metaphysical anarchy" (*Intro.,* 192). Equally tenable systems that can be supported only from within, cannot all be true, and are unable to defeat each other cannot possibly form the foundation for reasonable inquiry.

The second cause Dilthey offers for the collapse of metaphysics is the development of intentional autonomy, a capacity that is needed to break free from the shackles of a single metaphysical system and to move to a vantage point from which the various systems can be weighed and their definitions better understood. Beginning with Aristotle's efforts to establish knowledge of the primary causes that ground reality as a whole, Dilthey traces the relationship of metaphysics to the intellectual development of the human race and so is able to demonstrate the *historical* limits of metaphysics. This constitutes part of the proof against such speculative philosophy, for metaphysics has as its referent that which underlies the fluid variations of history. If metaphysics itself can be interpreted as a phenomenon contingent on sociohistorical circumstances, its claims to veracity are brought into question.

On one side of metaphysics was a theological posture toward the world holding that reality proceeds from divine knowledge. On the other side was the development of the positive sciences that broke with medieval schemes and gave rise to "a new attitude of the knowing subject toward reality" (*Intro.,* 189). Such individual freedom and autonomy marked the end of metaphysics' historical role. Though people continued to ask about the truth that lies behind appearances, the particular sciences developed independently of religion, and people "had had enough of abstract inferences about transcendent objects and of the metaphysical cobwebs which had been spun from the immanent to the transcendent" (*Intro.,* 190). When Kant and Laplace offered mechanistic theories that finally replaced divinity as the explanation of planetary systems, metaphysical thinking was destroyed (*Intro.*, 197). It is important that metaphysics for Dilthey came to an end when the *planetary* systems were explained mechanistically – when, that is, the night sky became a different *kind* of thing.

What remained after this destruction of metaphysics? The answer is "the *metaphysical mood or state of mind*, a basic metaphysical feeling in man which had accompanied him through the long period of his history" (*Intro.*, 197). Here, Dilthey says, belief in God finds its psychological origin. Where does the mood come from? Dilthey says it comes from such things as "the immensity of space," "the pure radiance of the stars," and "the intelligible order." These are the philosopher's night thoughts born at a time when a thinker could read the sky as filled with meaning, read it like a poem in which the stars are placed in such a way that they might delight our minds with their intended meaning, with their unaccidental mystery bearing the weight of human longing. In a remarkable passage, Dilthey says, "Metaphysics is silenced – but in the quiet of the night there still rings from the stars, even for us, a harmony of the spheres that the noise of the world merely drowns out, as the Pythagoreans said. This produces an indissoluble metaphysical mood that undergirds every demonstration and will outlive them all" (*Intro.*, 198). One concern that is raised by this passage is whether such a mood truly will outlive them all if neither metaphysics nor theology as disciplines referring to a transcendent entity or truth is possible.

In this passage, we find the point in Dilthey's thought where the disposition, the impulse toward metaphysics (and toward a certain kind of theology) is distilled and transferred into his own thought, most dramatically in his work on poetry and aesthetics. This feeling, which is the only remnant that survives Dilthey's analysis of metaphysics, becomes the centerpiece of his aesthetics, which in turn is the centerpiece of his philosophy. Precisely because of the importance of this feeling to Dilthey, he is very concerned to ensure that it is neither engulfed by the anarchy of metaphysics nor dismissed with the critique of metaphysics.

The thorn in metaphysics that sticks in Dilthey's side and prompts this dismissal is thus not the fundamental wonder that starts the whole enterprise of philosophy but rather the character of the claims being made. The metaphysicians are serious about their speculations: on what basis is the positive content of metaphysical systems rejected? At the very least, he suggests, one can and should maintain an alert agnosticism toward the systems and their claims. If it is in principle impossible to prove the veracity of one metaphysical claim versus another, it is also hard to disprove any such claim beyond pointing to the fact that the systems are mutually exclusive and cannot all be true. Dilthey's solution is to explore further the underlying impetus leading thinkers to engage in metaphysics.

Why does the immensity of space, star light, and so forth prompt the beginning of metaphysics in the first place? This question prompts the further question whether this "metaphysical mind," this yearning for such explanation, this thing that Kant calls the natural disposition for metaphysics, might itself point to the possibility of a peculiar kind of truth accessed only through such exploration. If an amnesiac finds himself in the desert feeling great thirst, the fact that there is no water and that he cannot recollect what water is does not diminish the connection between his thirst and the existence of something that satisfies his thirst. To expand the analogy, if every pool of water he chases is a mirage, the *possibility* that such will quench his thirst is founded on the fact that water *might* be there. Finally, not to stretch this too far, if, on the basis of the fact that every pursuit turns out to be a mirage, he stops pursuing what looks like an answer to his thirst and instead turns to what is "real" – the sand under his feet, the sun in the sky, the lizard on a hill – he will certainly die. Mirage or no, pursuing what looks like water is the only way to sustain his spirit and leave open the possibility for his survival. Dilthey appreciates this, but because he cannot embrace the possibility of a transcendent reality such as God, he must resort to other explanations. This is where poetry looms large in Dilthey's philosophy.

With the introduction of mechanistic explanation and with the demise of metaphysical thought, the expression of the totality of our life – of the whole from which metaphysicians always start, motivated by the sense that there is always an "unexplained remainder" at the end of any description or explanation – began to find its place in poetry "with the power of an irresistible natural phenomenon" (*Intro.*, 204–5). This did not involve beautiful semblance of form but rather was a *consciousness* of "a powerful feeling of life" (*Intro.*, 205). Dilthey calls this the *joyous truth* of the poet, a truth that simply cannot exist for science. It is qualitatively different (*Intro.*, 206). The problem with metaphysics as a science is that it tries to project this element into the domain of the natural world. As soon as it does this in the form of a metaphysical system, the vitality of human nature outstrips the content of the system. Expressing what might be thought of as his own version of Plato's *Seventh Epistle*, Dilthey says, "What is given in the totality of our being can never be entirely reduced to ideas" (*Intro.*, 229). In our thinking, we find only a *logical nexus*. When we try to represent in a system this feeling of totality, this feeling of life, we project our inner being onto nature. This becomes "a poetic play of analogies," and the only yield we get from it is "the insight that the world contains more and different things than logical order" (*Intro.*, 230). Dilthey concludes that "*the conceivable* in metaphysics is only an abstract expression for *the imaginable*" (*Intro.*, 237).

Here Dilthey has given his judgment of metaphysics. The stopping point of his analysis of metaphysics is, as I have suggested, the starting point of his poetics. Now that he has isolated this metaphysical mood that refers to something beyond experience, which gives a sense of the whole and which functions poetically even if its systematic conclusions are in error, he can go on to ask as a philosopher about the proper nature and function of poetry. We do not yet know why a philosopher's thought at night yields metaphysics. But for now the attention shifts from speculative philosophy to poetry as the repository of this metaphysical mood and impulse. The poets return triumphantly from exile, and the philosophers see to it that transcendence is dispatched. We are certainly far from where we started.

In his discussion of Goethe, Dilthey returns to a similar formula for the origin of the metaphysical mood as presented nearly two decades before in *Introduction to the Human Sciences*: "The finitude of existence, bounded by birth and death and restricted by the pressure of reality, awakens in me the longing for something enduring, changeless, and withdrawn from the pressure of things, *and when I look up to the stars, they become for me the symbol of such an eternal untouchable world*" (*Poet.*, 237; emphasis added). Now this is expressed in poetry not as an intellectual object or as a testable claim about reality, but as "the most vivid experience of the interconnectedness of our existential relations in the meaning of life" (*Poet.*, 238). One difference between a metaphysical statement and a poetic statement is that only the former claims to be knowledge of reality. It is this claim to being such knowledge that Dilthey wants to exorcise. And when the claim is dissolved, the domain of metaphysics is shifted into that of poetry.

When he turns to poetics, Dilthey encounters yet another anarchy – the anarchy of taste (*Poet.*, 31). This sort of anarchy emerges when new forms of art are unfolding, and he seems to think that the urgency and power of aesthetics involves comprehending and subduing the anarchy. When he establishes as his fundamental question the way in which we relate the uniformity and sameness of human nature to its variations in the particulars of history, he is asking something very interesting indeed. For Dilthey's work, the motives behind expressions of totality and of the feeling of life are rooted in the same sort of wonder that generated much of the history of philosophy. Accounting for how this impulse plays out now in poetry is, for the philosopher, a way of connecting contemporary issues of meaning and value in the philosophic domain with the origins of philosophy. The particulars of Dilthey's study of poetic technique are perhaps less likely to succeed in combating this anarchy than is the gesture toward the common feeling that was teased out of the history of metaphysics. This is in part because the study of poetic technique is largely based on the poets' own accounts of how their poetry developed, accounts that themselves may be fiction, or outright lies.

Not surprisingly, Dilthey begins with history. And he notes that, as poetry developed in eighteenth-century Germany, the poets began to become aware of their power to generate a world (*Poet.*, 176). The meaning that inheres in poetry does not imitate some prior reality, nor can it be expressed by nonpoetic means. This is precisely the insight that was taught us by metaphysics, namely, that there is more to the world than physical objects and a logical order. He notes that such a view is always in danger of lapsing into speculative thought, as it does with Schelling. Having worked hard to lift the metaphysical consciousness from the shackles of metaphysics as a science, Dilthey will not let it slide back into error at the hands of the romantics. This is in part the importance of the philosopher to poetry – to act as a kind of guardian.

He approaches this issue in a manner similar to his analysis of metaphysics. That is, he tries to get at "a core content of poetry which is common to all literature beginning with its simplest forms" (*Poet.*, 59). This core turns out to sound remarkably similar to the core extracted from metaphysics: It is "lived experience... related to the totality of human existence through reflection... [and thus] understood in its essence, that is, its meaning" (*Poet.*, 59). The intuitions of the poets are shaped by this sort of lived experience as related to the whole. When the poet expresses this sort of vitality, our own sense of life is awakened (*Poet.*, 60). The same was true for the metaphysicians. However, the poet is different because now the connections and images that the poet offers transcend reality but not in the sense of referring to a *transcendent reality* (*Poet.*, 76). Rather, the unity that results is an articulation of the unity of an individual's psychic life. Jacob Owensby has put the matter this way: "An image acts as a focal point around which acquired experiences are gathered as it were and through which their internal relations are made determinate."[5] This approach is altered by Dilthey later in his *Fragments for a Poetics* where he emphasizes that, while these images and connections transcend reality, they nonetheless also serve to help us understand experience more deeply (*Poet.*, 115). The fact that the poet's images and connections deepen our own experiences, that "every heart with feelings can recreate and appreciate the work in question," constitutes the universal validity of the poem. Here in the structure of images the meaning of our experiences is made intelligible (*Poet.*, 116).

Several aspects of Dilthey's discussion of poetic technique underscore the difference between the feeling as expressed in metaphysics and the feeling as expressed in poetry. First, the whole that is produced by the poetic transformation of lived experience is illusory (*Poet.*, 129). It neither corresponds to nor is limited by reality. The gift of poetry is the preservation of this fleeting meaning, this transitory moment, the elements of which are offered by reality, but the cohesion of which is fixed by the poetic mind (*Poet.*, 131). It is the imagination that "strives to give unity, inwardness and meaning to this reality" (*Poet.*, 139).

Because the poetic world has its existence in the imagination, it must submit to the laws of the psyche. If it is not in accord with the acquired psychic nexus, the illusion will not seem plausible, and so will not serve the purpose of intensifying our feeling of life (*Poet.*, 153). This accounts for the fact that past poets may not enliven us the way they did their contemporaries. Because we are historical creatures, a poetic world that once seemed plausible may no longer be in accord with a contemporary acquired psychic nexus. When this is the case, the aim of poetry falls flat. So the eternal metaphysical consciousness remains constant as a kind of need or potential, but because we are historical, no poetry retains any essential core of *meaning* that is itself eternal (*Poet.*, 173). This, at least, is the conclusion of *The Imagination of the Poet* published in 1887. It is not Dilthey's final word.

In *Fragments for a Poetics*, which comes twenty years later, we find Dilthey moving away from the psychological explanation of the poet in which poetry is an expression of the poet's individual acquired psychic nexus and toward the notion that the poetry itself is an expression of lived experience.[6] Here, the art of words displays something that is

---

[5] Jacob Owensby, "Dilthey and the Historicity of Poetic Expression," *Journal of Aesthetics and Art Criticism* 46 (1988): 502.

[6] Ibid., 503.

communal.[7] In the *Fragments* he says, "The liberation of the imaginative process from contingency is also its liberation from the personal"
(*Poet.*, 227). This does not mean that any particular work could come
about without the peculiarity of the artist's psyche. Rather, as Rudolf
Makkreel has put the matter, "The work creates its own framework of
meaning which transcends the personal. Nevertheless, the personal is
always presupposed. Without personal suffering Beethoven could not
have composed his moving adagios, but in hearing this music we do not
feel sorrow for Beethoven."[8]

On the side of the artist, psychology is still an important consideration in the production of the work. But the aim is less to display his own
emotions than it is to exhibit a world of value. This is attested to both
by the *Fragments* and by *Other Persons and Their Expressions of Life*. In the
former, Dilthey speaks of meaning as a category of life, as something on
which art is based, but which is not restricted to the domain of aesthetics. When our attention is not distracted by the chores of daily life, we
can apprehend this meaning. Dilthey goes so far as to say that "this is
the natural view of life. In the poet this manifests itself more intensely"
(*Poet.*, 230). The poet's articulation gives a meaning that stands apart
from the poet: "Since...in a great work, something spiritual is set free
from its creator (the poet, artist, or author), we here enter a realm in
which deception ends.... *Truthful in itself*, it stands fixed, visible, perma-
nent." There is something common among people in these objectified
expressions, and such expressions are not limited to art but include such
things as the way we landscape, the way we arrange our rooms, the way
we set our life goals. Precisely this renders possible a reexperiencing of
a nexus of lived experience in a poem. But now, Dilthey says explicitly,
"We are here interested only in what the process yields; a psychological
explanation of it is unnecessary."[9]

How powerful is this process that yields the possibility of "re-experience" otherwise inaccessible within the bounds of an individual's actual
life? Dilthey gives a striking demonstration: when he reads the writings
of Luther or wanders about a cloister, even he gains access to "a religious
process of such eruptive power and of such an energy (a matter of life

---

7  Rudolf A Makkreel, "Toward a Concept of Style: An Interpretation of Wilhelm Dilthey's
   Psycho-Historical Account of the Imagination," *Journal of Aesthetics and Art Criticism* 27
   (1968): 179.
8  Ibid.
9  Wilhelm Dilthey, *Descriptive Psychology and Historical Understanding*, trans. R. M. Zaner
   and K. L. Heiges (The Hague: Martinus Nijhoff), 133.

and death!) that it lies beyond anything that a present-day man could possibly experience. I can however re-experience it" (*Descriptive*, 134). Thus, art and history free us from the bonds of what is possible in our daily life. What is given here is a kind of inner awareness of a psychic reality that exceeds the power of logic to represent it. This points to the fact that "there is something irrational in all understanding, just as life itself is irrational" (*Descriptive*, 132). This is what Morris Philipson has called the "dark" side of Dilthey's two most important concepts, "life" and "understanding."[10] The irrationality of these elements is simply an acknowledgment that neither life nor understanding is fully describable or explainable in rational terms. The task set for the philosopher is, as far as possible, to grasp and articulate the structural elements of both. Such moments can be evaluated only in terms of their circumstances, moving from the individual parts to the whole structure and back again, the task of hermeneutics.

There is a chronological development of a common thread connecting the distillation of the metaphysical mood (1883); the relevance of this mood to the poet's feeling of life (1887); the experience of the meaning of life, manifested most intensely in the poet, as the natural view of life (1907); and, finally, the capacity to reexperience something that lies outside the boundary of our daily life (1910). Throughout, Dilthey has remained uncompromising in his posture toward metaphysics. Even the problem of the relation of God to the world reflects nothing more than the relation between higher and lower worlds within ourselves.[11] We need look no farther than our own experience to find the elements of both the metaphysical problems and solutions to those problems.

When Dilthey resists metaphysics and when he attacks speculative thought about the transcendent, he has an immediate pragmatic purpose for doing so: it is an inadequate basis for the foundation of the sciences. Dilthey's attack on metaphysics is not unlike Socrates' attack on the poets, at least in flavor and aim. They are both attacking something that, to their respective minds, makes a false claim to veracity, a claim that nonetheless convinces people of its truth-value. For both thinkers, such false claims are a positive hindrance to knowledge. The problem with metaphysical formulations is that they contradict one another and that no single formulation can be borne out in experience; such formulations are in principle alien to life experience. Makkreel summarizes

---

[10] Morris Philipson, "Dilthey on Art," *Journal of Aesthetics and Art Criticism* 17 (1958): 72.
[11] Hodges, *The Philosophy of Wilhelm Dilthey*, 348.

the objection this way: "The metaphysician above all seeks to prove that his systematized *Weltanschauung* [world view] is universally valid. This is a purely abstract ideal common to all metaphysics and there is no *Erlebnis* [lived experience] that can provide a concrete core or context for such a system, since no experience can justify claims for absolute necessity."[12]

Metaphysical formulations cannot be justified – no metaphysical formulation can. This is true even for the religious point of view, which, nonetheless, is an important kind of experience able to change fundamentally how we view life, how we direct the particulars of our lives. Again, Makkreel points out that "the interdependence of functions that Dilthey had already established for the psychic system can also exist in a *Weltanschauung* when it is related to our actual *Erlebnis* of life. This, however, is demonstrable only for religious and poetic forms of *Weltanschauung*, not for their metaphysical formulations" (*Philosopher*, 354). Two problems remain. First, how can one account for the fact that *these* formulations developed? Second, if the claims made from inside these metaphysical systems are not justifiable within Dilthey's system, might they nonetheless be justified in a different way?

Dilthey discusses in great detail the origin of the metaphysical mood. What about the religious *Weltanschauung* with its references to the transcendent and the invisible? The religious originates in and refers to the invisible. Clearly, when speaking of religious lived experience, Dilthey's account cannot incorporate an actual transcendent or supernatural referent. Any reference must be to this life, which is the root and source of everything. As with Hegel, for whom the posture toward death was an important mark of distinction between the philosopher and the poet, now for Dilthey it becomes one test of the transformative power of his philosophy – the ability of his philosophy, that is, to retain meaning and significance without requiring a reference to the transcendent, to God. According to Makkreel, "For Dilthey, the religious *Erlebnis* of death, which has traditionally been understood to involve a reference to a beyond, is to be interpreted as an awareness of the dark depths within. Death is not to be viewed as transcending life, but as a way of estimating its value" (*Philosopher*, 353). Hegel suggested that for a philosopher such as Socrates death and immortality burgeon out from this new appreciation of the infinite value of what is at stake. So religious *Erlebnis* has as

---

[12] Rudolf A. Makkreel, *Dilthey: Philosopher of the Human Studies* (Princeton: Princeton University Press, 1975), 354, hereafter cited in text as *Philosopher*.

its primary notion the idea of infinite value, and for a religious person "the great *Erlebnis* of an unconditional, infinite objective value, to which all others are subordinated... determines his entire objective apprehension [of reality] and his overall projected ends" (*Philosopher*, 368). But this religious *Erlebnis* is brought back into the realm of the immanent.

For a religious person the peculiar form of the longing for something eternal and unchanging *essentially* refers to infinite value in a *particular* form. But if this form is removed, we no longer have *religious Erlebnis*. Rather, we have a crisis. The feeling may remain, but a new account must be given, and perhaps more important, a new expression. This new expression is poetry, which begins in feeling, is penetrated by thought, and is connected to religion and philosophy through the *inner* bond of the meaning of life, meaning that in turn simply *is* the comprehension of life as a unity in memory and the relation of this memory "to other lived experiences in the totality of life" (*Poet.*, 231).

Here arises a question that has been present in some form throughout the history of the quarrel between poetry and philosophy: might the *manner* in which these various things have been expressed in history – speculative thought, religious dogma, longing for the eternal, the metaphysical mood – itself be a clue to something more than Dilthey is willing to acknowledge, but which need not, in fact, be alien to his system? That is, might there be a remainder for which Dilthey does not account but which presents an important challenge to his fundamental thesis?

For Dilthey, of all forms of expression poetry is best suited to deliver the vividness of our experience of "the interconnectedness of our existential relations in the meaning of life" (*Poet.*, 238). This exhibition of the world of value is an exhibition of something that transcends the personal. But if one could show the possibility of the transcendent as a referent, the character of religious experience, philosophy, and poetry might be quite different. There are many ways to test whether Dilthey's analysis of the metaphysical mood, poetic feeling, and the transcendent actually eliminate the possibility that there might be a legitimate *transcendent referent* of feeling, but one interesting approach to this challenge is found in the work of Dilthey's contemporary, Rudolph Otto.

In his book *The Idea of the Holy*, Otto states as his purpose to make "a serious attempt to analyze all the more exactly the *feeling* which remains where the *concept* fails" (*Philosopher*, 324). To be sure, he approaches this endeavor from a starting point very different from Dilthey's, and this fact is important. But they also have a number of things in common. Otto says that, having spent years examining the rational aspects of his field of inquiry, he finds that there are parts that are nonrational. He is careful to separate belief from experience: "It is one thing merely to believe in a reality beyond the senses and another to have experience of it also; it is one thing to have ideas of 'the holy' and another to become consciously aware of it as an operative reality, intervening actively in the phenomenal world."[13] His primary concern is with an experience, not with a system of thought. He calls the capacity to genuinely realize the holy in its appearances the faculty of *divination* (*Idea*, 143). He says explicitly that this feeling does not depend on rational criticism, fluctuations in exegesis, historical apologetics, or any of the metaphysical systems that, compared to each other, appeared anarchic to Dilthey (*Idea*, 144).

At the same time, he is aware that his account of and witness to this particular category of human feeling will not be received by everyone. From the start he says that if one can recollect no moment of deeply felt encounter with the holy, that person may as well not read the book (*Idea*, 174). Further, "There can naturally be no defense of the worth and validity of such religious intuitions of pure feeling that will convince a person who is not prepared to take the religious consciousness itself for granted. Mere general argument, even moral demonstrations, are in this case useless, are indeed for obvious reasons impossible from the outset" (*Idea*, 8).

Dilthey supports Otto's point in many ways. The elements that Otto requires for his experience are all present in Dilthey's work. The recognition of the metaphysical mood, the *feeling* that generates metaphysics and poetry, the capacity even to *reexperience* religious meaning upon reading Luther's works or walking through a cloister – all of these aspects of Dilthey's thought would fit quite comfortably in Otto's world. Otto wrote his book twelve years after Dilthey's death. Yet Dilthey asserted that the actual experience to which Otto claims access (an experience of the holy as extant, as a referent that is objective in a sense not allowed by Dilthey, an experience that for Dilthey can only in some sense be "reexperienced") is one that "lies beyond anything which a present-day man could possibly experience" (*Idea*, 173). Why?

Dilthey largely appeals to historical circumstance, as when he contrasts Luther's world with his own, those of the "present-day man." If this

---

[13] Rudolph Otto, *The Idea of the Holy: An Inquiry into the Non-rational Factor in the Idea of the Divine and Its Relation to the Rational*, trans. John Harvey (Oxford: Oxford University Press, 1958), foreword, 1, hereafter cited in text as *Idea*.

is so, Dilthey's judgment is also conditioned by historical circumstance. This is an old point. Between Dilthey and Luther, we have two mutually exclusive conclusions regarding reality and our possible knowledge of it. But insofar as both conclusions are conditioned by historical circumstance, historical circumstance is not a *sufficient* court of appeal to determine which of the two might reasonably be judged as true. In one sense Dilthey agrees. Had he been Aristotle's pupil, he likely would not have written the books he did in fact write. In another sense, he would offer a qualified disagreement. In the same way in which Dilthey produced a meta-aesthetic that can provide the basis for any aesthetic system, here he seems to offer an approach that can account for any philosophical system. Indeed, through our capacity to reexperience, we can approach any work – metaphysical, religious, poetic, botanical – and experience circumstances that are otherwise inaccessible to us. In this sense, his philosophy is capacious.

The problem is that a system that makes room for religion (as long as it does not bring along notions of a God who actually exists), for the metaphysical mood (as long as there is no metaphysical formulation), and for poetry (as long as it is understood that "what is expressed in this universal content of the literary work is not knowledge of reality") is, for thinkers like Otto, a system in which the price outweighs the appeal. The objection for which Otto can be marshaled as an example is that explaining certain things, such as one's own capacity to reexperience religious feeling, may rather be explaining away one's experiences without adequate justification. Indeed, if Otto is right that in some cases one must simply begin with a certain posture, a willingness to grant certain possibilities (be this God, the transcendent, eternal verities, the Good, or anything else), then such cases are in principle impenetrable by Dilthey's sort of analysis. The lingering question, of course, is how one decides between a willingness to grant such things (Otto) and an unwillingness to do so (Dilthey).

This question is important. At the very least, it should be pressed far enough so that it is clear that if we take up, for example, religious experience into our system but deny the existence of God, we are not really taking up religious experience but rather a translation of the experience. This is similar to the point that arose in the work of Vico, the distinction between the experience of Jove as *Jove* and that of Jove as the *myth* of Jove. The translation is qualitatively different from the original experience. Nor is it evidence against the possibility of such original experience. At most it is simply a different sort of thing, perhaps even irrelevant to the original experience, taken as such by the likes of Luther or Otto.

Otto claims to have an actual experience of the holy, an experience he finds expressed in every culture. He claims that this peculiar feeling has as its referent something objective. Either it does have this referent, or it does not. The question is whether the categories of "reality" to which Dilthey contrasts our freedom can include such a referent. Dilthey cannot appeal only to a historical circumstance to resolve the question, because before he can explain Otto's experience in terms of historical circumstance, he must already have decided that such an experience is not possible. And *that* decision cannot itself be based on experience, because one cannot experience such a negative, except, perhaps, as that type of religious experience noted in the laments of the mystics as one contrasting with a prior taste of the joy of a positive experience (e.g., Saint Ignatius of Loyola or Saint John of the Cross); one cannot point to an experience of the *absence* of the holy as an objective referent to justify a categorical elimination of such from the domain of experienceable reality.

Part of Dilthey's professed motivation in his writing was to rid the world of false transcendental entities and cobwebs. But Otto has offered something that is based in experience, which is a feeling, which takes stock of the fact that some of our legitimate experiences are nonrational, and which also claims to refer to something that is objective, but which is not contained in "reality" as Dilthey presents it. The feeling of the holy is a category explained by nothing more, less, or other than the holiness of its referent. In every aspect except the last, Otto's position is consistent with Dilthey's. Precisely because so much of Dilthey's system is based on experience, it may well be that an outright rejection of Otto is inconsistent with the principles of the system: such rejection leaves the realm of experience and begins to spin out hypotheses about why the holy cannot be an objective referent of a certain kind of feeling.

This is not to say that something like "the holy" cannot exist for Dilthey. Indeed, Dilthey's own posture toward the metaphysical mood, the poet's sense of life, and the reexperiencing of religious feeling in a cloister or in Luther's works strongly suggests a category of feeling that might be intimately akin to Otto's category of feeling. While it may be no more than coincidence, it is at least interesting that both Dilthey and Otto extensively studied Schleiermacher, the former choosing to address his hermeneutics, the latter seeing him as a rediscoverer of the *sensus numinis*.

If the referent of this feeling is transcendent, if this feeling is the category of experience through which the transcendent is known, then precisely because the objective referent is transcendent, no immanent expression – communal, poetical, or historical – will completely express it. The transcendent, because remaining transcendent, will not be found among the immanent artifacts falling in the wake of such an experience. At best, such things will provide hints or clues. If one limits the field of inquiry a priori to an arena that in principle cannot contain the transcendent, one should not wonder when the transcendent is not found. This is what happens when one limits the field to experience and then defines experience such that, even *if* the transcendent were somehow truly felt, that experience also would, mistakenly, be interpreted as something other than what it is – something more appropriate for "the present-day man." If there is such a thing as the holy that is accessible to experience, our notion of reality must be expanded to include the objective referent of this feeling. When this is done, we might well ask the following question: are there hints toward such a referent in the metaphysical mood and the poetic feeling of life that might have been missed in an analysis that assumed from the start that such a referent is impossible? We can acknowledge with Dilthey *that* we need the feeling of eternity. This new sort of question asks rather *why* we need it. Why should space, vastness, and the like *ever* yield such a result, and so widely, in human experience? The poets, in short, may be revealing even more than Dilthey allows, and in the metaphysical mood there is room for such a discussion related to the work of Dilthey. There is no such sentiment, no friendly openness to the cloister or the works of Luther in the next figure in this history, Friedrich Nietzsche.

# 11

# Nietzsche, Heidegger, and the Saving Power
of Poetry

More than two millennia after the start of the quarrel, Friedrich
Nietzsche revisited the idea that the deity speaking to a poet – in this
case, Euripides – might in fact be a demon, but a demon of a particular sort who was responsible for wrecking Greek tragedy, with cata-
strophic consequences for those who followed. "Dionysius had already
been scared from the tragic stage by a demonic power speaking through
Euripides," he says in *The Birth of Tragedy*. "Even Euripides was, in a
sense, only a mask: the deity that spoke to him was neither Dionysius
nor Apollo, but an altogether newborn demon, called *Socrates*."[1]

Whenever something is apparently gained, it is fair to ask the cost,
and this is what Nietzsche does. To achieve the gains made through dialectic, through the addition of the philosophical question to the tools
available to the human mind, what was the loss? For Nietzsche what
is lost is a kind of metaphysical comfort that tragedy reveals to us and
reminds us of, the comfort that, whatever may happen with appearance,
life finally remains a powerful presence that outlives all individuals, all
nations (*Birth*, 59). Nietzsche is vehement in his criticism of the forces
that resulted in this loss. When we assert that our temporary states of
pleasure and pain and our own existences somehow rightly lay claim
to eternal importance, we disfigure the very pleasure and pain experienced, twisting the experiences into a mangle of misplaced heights and
valleys. In the arrogance of what our immediate culture serves up to
us, we think we have access to the truth of things. We do not: the "man
of culture" is lost. Far closer to reality's truth is the satyr chorus in the
tragedy, rejecting finery and leading us to the hard, living heart of what

---

[1] Friedrich Nietzsche, *The Birth of Tragedy* and *The Case of Wagner*, trans. Walter Kaufman
(New York: Vintage, 1967), 82, hereafter cited in text as *Birth*.

is real (*Birth*, 61). The tragic poet did not live outside the bounds of reality, but rather brought people into the heart of it. Unlike philosophers who latch on to concepts, the poet grasps metaphors as images beheld, characters as living people. Philosophy should learn from such poets rather than retreating from or taming such visions. "The philosophy of wild and naked nature beholds with the frank, un-dissembling gaze of truth the myths of the Homeric world as they dance past: they turn pale, they tremble under the piercing glance of this goddess [truth] – until the powerful fist of the Dionysian artist forces them into the service of the new deity" (*Birth*, 74). This Dionysian art, this Dionysian truth, took hold of myth and transformed it into a vehicle for its own kind of wisdom struggling to prevent it from becoming hedged in by the exigencies of the narrow demand that myth correspond to historical reality. Systematization of myth leads to its inevitable death, a withering collapse. The force of Dionysius answers this wrinkling retreat by infusing life, strength, power. It was precisely this power, Nietzsche says, that Euripides plundered (*Birth*, 75).

The mere spectator should stay out in the audience observing, watching. Euripides brings the spectator on stage through the degenerate form of theater known as "the new comedy." Tragedy is gutted and civil mediocrity is given a voice (*Birth*, 77). As Euripides brings the mass of spectators onto the stage, he looks around for other spectators who are his equal. He is very observant, not as a poet living life to its fierce depths, but as a thinker. As such, he is aware of the only other superior spectator, Socrates. But Socrates does not comprehend tragedy. Though this odd man does not esteem tragedy for lack of comprehension, Euripides the artist comprehends the greatness of Socrates, who opens up a new world for the poet, now free of the shackles of working in the shadows of Sophocles and the others who created out of the Dionysian spirit. And so the new opponents in the quarrel are "the Dionysian and the Socratic – and the art of Greek tragedy was wrecked on this" (*Birth*, 82).

Art is driven by two impulses: the Apollonian, with its simplicity, precision, lucidity, and calm contemplation; and the Dionysian, with its ecstasies embracing nature in its most forceful form. Euripides is neither. "Euripides is the actor whose heart beats, whose hair stands on end; as Socratic thinker he designs the plan, as passionate actor he executes it. Neither in the designing nor in the execution is he a pure artist" (*Birth*, 83). Any effectiveness he has comes from replacing the Apollonian contemplation with "cool, paradoxical thoughts" and the Dionysian ecstasies with "fiery *affects*." This state of affairs reveals the nature of what Nietzsche calls *aesthetic Socratism*, whose supreme law is this: "To be beautiful everything must be intelligible" (*Birth*, 84). This dictum, along with the Socratic counterpart "Knowledge is virtue," led Euripides to an all too reasonable approach to poetry, using rationality to measure and correct the elements of drama. Beauty and pathos were lost in reason's effort to solve "the problem of the background history," an effort contrasting with that of the other type of poet berated by Plato as "incapable of composing until he has become unconscious and bereft of understanding." Euripides as the poet of aesthetic Socratism "is essentially an echo of his own conscious knowledge" (*Birth*, 85–6). The priority given to the reasonable, the rational, the conscious killed especially the Dionysian elements in tragedy, and so effectively killed tragedy. The quarrel is now revealed as a quarrel between Socrates and Dionysius.

Among the statesmen, poets, and artists of Athens were many people producing tragedy, art, and the rule of cities. But these were exposed by the one who knew nothing, the one who wields the question as his primary tool and thereby discovers that all of these people worked "only by instinct" rather than with the conscious insight valued in Socratism. What do we lose by abandoning instinct for the conscious knowledge of the sort Socrates valued?

Plato was a poet, and he could not escape poetry merely by throwing away his own youthful poems when he turned to follow Socrates. Rather, Nietzsche says, poetry found a new channel in Plato, forcing its way through. Plato pushed back under the influence of Socrates and bent poetry into the form of the dialogue, where art was left to cling weakly to the powerful presence of philosophic thought. "Indeed, Plato has given to all posterity the model of a new art form, the model of the *novel* – which may be described as an infinitely enhanced Aesopian fable in which poetry holds the same rank in relation to dialectical philosophy as this same philosophy held for many centuries in relation to theology: namely, the rank of *ancilla*" (*Birth*, 91). In this transformation, Plato claimed that the supreme music was no longer poetry but philosophy.

Nietzsche disagrees. It is precisely music that is lost when we so overwhelmingly favor the conscious advance of the philosophical question against "instinct" in dialectic. "Optimistic dialectic drives *music* out of tragedy with the scourge of all its syllogisms; that is, it destroys the essence of tragedy" (*Birth*, 92). Art resisted this, and continues to resist this. "Art in the metaphysical, broadest and profoundest sense" will always push the lingering doubt that the limits of logic are not the limits of wisdom, the limit of the intellect is not defined by what is intelligible to *me* (*Birth*, 93). And in this struggle the quarrel continues, now between art and that distilled version of critical inquiry, science.

The artist stops at the surface and marvels. The "theoretical man" uncovers and "enjoys and finds satisfaction in the discarded covering and finds the highest object of his pleasure in the process of an ever happy uncovering that succeeds through his own efforts" (*Birth*, 94). The illusion is that we can dig down to the deepest parts of being and not only know it but even correct it. The perversity, Nietzsche says, is that such a venture itself must move on faith and is itself an instinct that drives science. This illusion "leads science again and again to its limits at which it must turn into *art – which is really the aim of this mechanism*" (*Birth*, 95–6). Ultimately, then, science and its optimistic pursuit within the limits of logic finds itself wrecked at these limits where it encounters that which will not be subsumed by logic and "suddenly the new form of insight breaks through, *tragic insight* which, merely to be endured, needs art as a protection and remedy" (*Birth*, 98).

Nietzsche is not out to find a system, or to find the truth. His life, all life, is flux – it does not go past that. Books have order, but it is the order of art, what we make in joy. He paid no attention to those who wrote criticism of his work – so he said. And why should he, if there is no truth to approach in the process of statement and critical response? But sixteen years after writing *The Birth of Tragedy*, he revisits it briefly and restates its two innovations – its understanding of the Dionysian as one root of all Greek art, and its understanding of Socratism, its recognition of Socrates "for the first time as an instrument of Greek disintegration, as a typical decadent."[2] The yield of this decadence is a lie that works against life and fails to recognize that "nothing in existence may be subtracted, nothing is dispensable" (*Ecce*, 272). Say yes to life, to all of life – this is Dionysian. When reading Plato, we asked whether there can be a poet of the Forms. Nietzsche, who "smelled the decay" in Plato, embraced a different formulation, drawing on this power undergirding art, calling himself the first *tragic philosopher*. He transposes the Dionysian into philosophical pathos and creates *tragic wisdom*. This is the highest art. The tragic philosopher is the one who lives in a world made decadent by the conscious rationality of Socrates, the one who shows the way to reach

---

[2]  Friedrich Nietzsche, *Ecce Homo*, trans. Walter Kaufman (New York: Vintage, 1989), 271, hereafter cited in text as *Ecce*.

back toward the poetry that flourished before the onslaught of Socratic dialectic, the birth of the quarrel.

Such a philosopher must begin by avoiding the failures of past philosophers, who lack a historic sense, who strive for some version of timeless Platonic Forms, and who fail to see that "everything *essential* in the development of mankind took place in primeval times, long before the four thousand years we more or less know about.... there are *no eternal facts*, just as there are no absolute truths."[3] The illusion that there is some second real world that can be approached through metaphysics arose, Nietzsche says, when barbarous peoples had dreams and believed this world encountered in the dream was another world (*Human*, 5). And even if there were such a metaphysical world that we could come to know, such knowledge would be the most useless knowledge. We do not come to understand any second metaphysical world through the dream, but we can come to understand something of the mind of primeval humanity as "in sleep and dreams we repeat once again the curriculum of earlier mankind" (*Human*, 12). Recognizing this takes the thinker a step closer to overcoming metaphysics.

So what, then, are all the visions, raptures, and results of *theia mania* that have occupied this history from the start? They are basically misinterpreted pathological conditions, illnesses that, because of religious and psychological errors, come to be understood as oracles, prophecies, and wisdom. "Thus the daemon of Socrates too was perhaps an ear infection which, in accordance with the moralizing manner of thinking that dominated him, he only *interpreted* differently from how it would be interpreted now" (*Human*, 126). That said, the artists know that the fantastic, the mythical, the symbolical, the extremes are all useful for art, and so they will not relinquish interpretations that contribute to their art (*Human*, 146). Poets borrow light from the past and shine that beam on the toilsome present of humans and, in doing so, "can be employed as bridges to quite distant ages and conceptions, to dead or dying religions and cultures" (*Human*, 148). This can be soothing for a time, but it can also distract people from the work of actually improving their conditions. The Enlightenment undermined much of religion, but religious feeling continued and found a home in art, a point close to the perspective of Dilthey, though Nietzsche is not as welcoming of

---

3 Friedrich Nietzsche, *Human, All Too Human: A Book for Free Spirits*, trans. R. J. Hollingdale (Cambridge: Cambridge University Press, 1986), sec. 1 (all references are to sections and numbered paragraphs), hereafter cited in text as *Human*.

the cloister. "Wherever we perceive human endeavors to be tinted with a higher, gloomier coloring, we can assume that dread of spirits, the odor of incense and the shadows of churches are still adhering to them" (*Human*, 150). The metaphysical need is powerful, and even after a person has done the hard work of achieving freedom from the metaphysical, one passage in Beethoven's Ninth Symphony can cause the dream of immortality to well up. "If he becomes aware of being in this condition he feels a profound stab in the heart and sighs for the man who will lead him back to his lost home, whether she be called religion or metaphysics" (*Human*, 153).

Such art does not come easily. There are certainly great improvisers, but despite the artist's interest in "the existence of a belief in the sudden occurrence of ideas, in so-called inspirations, as though the idea of a work of art, a claim, the basic proposition of a philosophy flashed down from heaven like a ray of divine grace," in fact high art is shaped by the artist's power of judgment – by the ability not only to invent but also to complete the work of "rejecting, sifting, transforming, ordering" (*Human*, 155). Poetry is labor, and the poets know what they are doing.

Art is a dangerous business, however, because in this whirl of creation an artist can regress to ideas from ages in which art had a grander kind of flourishing. When this happens, "the artist acquires increasing reverence for sudden excitations, believes in gods and demons, instills a soul into nature, hates the sciences, becomes changeable of mood as were the men of antiquity, and longs for an overthrowing of everything unfavorable to art, and he does this with all the vehemence and unreasonableness of a child" (*Human*, 159). This is a cause for sorrow, this recognition that the highest works of art elevate false conceptions, and religious and philosophical errors, apart from which the greatest art could never have then produced. It is grievous to think that such art – Dante's *Divine Comedy*, Michelangelo's frescoes, Raphael's paintings, the Gothic cathedrals – can never again flourish because it "presupposes not only a cosmic but also a metaphysical significance in the objects of art" (*Human*, 220).

This leaves us with the question, Where do we go next with poetry? The modern spirit is restless. It is immoderate and does not want to be bound. In the context of this freedom, the modern is qualitatively different from the spirit of those people who could enjoy the poetry only grown up within their own single and singular language. Rather, "for a time this unfettering enables us to enjoy the poetry of all peoples, all that has grown up in hidden places, the primitive, wild-blooming, strangely beautiful and gigantically irregular, from the folk songs up to the 'great barbarian' Shakespeare" (*Human*, 221). But as these many voices enter, no longer rooted in the original ground from which they grew, poets necessarily become "experimenting imitators and foolhardy copiers," leading ever more toward the tendency to "value artistic power for its own sake…no longer [enjoying] the elements in terms of the work of art if not in *isolation*" (*Human*, 221). Eventually the people will *demand* this sort of artistic isolation, and this, Nietzsche says, constitutes art's dissolution. Soon the artist may well be a relic in the absence of the metaphysical, which gave such value to art as touching upon something eternal. "The best in us has perhaps been inherited from the sensibilities of earlier ages to which we hardly any longer have access by direct paths; the sun has already set, but the sky of our life still glows with its light, even though we no longer see it" (*Human*, 223). One wonders how long even the glow will last, if Nietzsche is correct.

So what direction should poetry go? What are the poets to do? Nietzsche does offer an answer. Rather than depicting the contemporary world or imaginatively reconstructing the past, poetry should be devoted to "signposting the future," and this will involve following the example of earlier poets who imaginatively developed images of the gods, but rather than attending to gods, the poet working in the modern world should spy out, right in the middle of reality, possibilities for the great and beautiful soul who will chart out and embody "the ever increasing elevation of man" (*Human*, 99). But to do this, the poet must be in love with reality (*Human*, 135). Nietzsche, who will later make his own attempt at such an endeavor in *Thus Spoke Zarathustra*, says emphatically, "To the representation of the *ultimate* man, *that is to say the simplest and at the same time the most whole*, no artist has so far been equal" (*Human*, 177). So far. Nietzsche's task is now identified.

How is the task to be accomplished? The Greeks came closest. "What is required…is to stop courageously at the surface, the fold, the skin, to adore appearance, to believe in forms, tone, words, and the whole Olympus of appearance. Those Greeks were superficial – *out of profundity*."[4] The surface is what lives. It is not something we "get behind" to approach objective reality, to get to the thing-in-itself. There is only appearance and, further, appearance as it appears to my consciousness.

---

[4] Friedrich Nietzsche, *The Gay Science: With a Prelude in Rhymes and an Appendix of Songs* (New York: Vintage, 1974), sec. 4 (all references are to sections), hereafter cited in text as *Gay*.

"Consciousness is the last and latest development of the organic and hence also what is most unfinished and unstrong." Therefore, it is susceptible to error. Far from being what is "eternal, ultimate and most original" in humanity, "consciousness relates to errors." It is shaped by what lies in humanity's preconscious past, again, with consciousness being awakened to the reality that we are only dreaming, never getting past the floating flux of appearance to some internal "essence" (*Gay*, 54). How we name things and give shape to experience eventually becomes part of the thing, and this perspective can be passed on, often mistakenly represented as "reality." Nietzsche admits, "This has given me the greatest trouble and still does: to realize that what things are called is incomparably more important than what they are" (*Gay*, 58). Even as lovers, we love the surface, not what lies under the skin. He claims, "The magic and the most powerful effect of women is, in philosophical language, action at a distance, *actio in distans*; but this requires first of all and above all – *distance*" (*Gay*, 60). From a distance, gazing upon the surface, passion arises, and this is the magic.

In many ways, magic accounts for the origins of poetry. The rhythmic force of poetry was meant to impress the gods and garner their attention for our petitions. "Thus one tried to *compel* the gods by using rhythm and to force their hand: poetry was thrown at them like a magical snare.... Every action provides an occasion for song: *every* action depends on the assistance of spirits, and the magical songs in the spell seem to be the primeval form of poetry." Poetry offered one the force of a God. It is a power that continues to be marshaled in surprising ways, Nietzsche observes: "Isn't it rather amusing that to this day the most serious philosophers, however strict they may be in questions of certainty, still call on what poets have said in order to lend their ideas force and credibility?" And, as with many in this history, though with his own perspective, Nietzsche goes on to point out the irony that if the poet agrees with your truth rather than contradicting it, so much the worse for your truth, since, as we have heard repeatedly, "The poets tell many lies" (*Gay*, 84).

Nietzsche is another of the philosophers in this history who wrote poetry. He observes that most prose masters are also poets. "Good prose," for Nietzsche, "is written only face-to-face with poetry. For it is an uninterrupted, well-mannered war with poetry.... Everything abstract wants to be read as a prank against poetry and as with a mocking voice; everything dry and cool is meant to drive the lovely goddess into lovely despair" (*Gay*, 92). Following Heraclitus (frag. 53), who said that "war is the father of all," Nietzsche affirms that "war is also the father of good prose" (*Gay*, 92). There is a kind of playful humor in this. The war allows the play to continue, to keep us, despite our weight and seriousness, from taking ourselves too seriously as philosophers or as poets. We don the fool's cap, and this does us good: "We need it in relation to ourselves – we need all exuberant, floating, dancing, mocking, childish, and blissful art lest we lose the *freedom above things* that our ideal demands of us" (*Gay*, 107). This laughter toward ourselves prepares us to bear what is coming. But what is coming is far from easy to bear.

"God is dead; but given the way of men, there may still be caves for thousands of years in which his shadow will be shown. – And we – we still have to vanquish his shadow too" (*Gay*, 108). The world is for all eternity chaos. There is no purpose. There is no accident. There are no eternal substances. It is a mistake to say that death is opposed to life. "The living is merely a type of what is dead, and a very rare type" (*Gay*, 109). All of these things are residua, shadows of God in our minds. The attempt to vanquish God is awesome and terrifying. The madman in the marketplace asks, "Whither is God?" and then cries "I will tell you. *We have killed him* – you and I. All of us are his murderers. But how did we do this? How could we drink up the sea? Who gave us the sponge to wipe away the entire horizon?" (*Gay*, 125). The conditions of belief have changed. The ancients lived the world differently because in everything there was a god shining, the oracles and the prophets spoke secrets, and the madman could be the voice of a god – that same *theia mania* that has followed through the whole history of the quarrel (*Gay*, 152).

This leaves the poets in a lurch. The five-act tragedy is being written, and in act 4 the gods are slain for the sake of morality. How should the tragedy end? "From where am I to take the tragic solution?" he asks. "Should I begin to think about a comic solution?" (*Gay*, 153). The world of the poets that made the gods possible was broken open by Socrates standing on the temple of the god of poetry. Who could have known how long and drawn out the quarrel would be, how profound its consequences? In the labor of this battle, much sickness and decay has occurred in philosophy, as diagnosed by Nietzsche. But the bridges are burned. And now the only way forward, he says, is a "gay science."

One thing is needful. This is his advice for how we continue on in the absence of God. The one needful thing is "that a human being should *attain* satisfaction with himself, whether it be by means of this or that poetry and art, only then is a human being at all tolerable to behold. Whoever is dissatisfied with himself is continually ready for revenge, and we others will be his victims, if only by having to endure his ugly sight. For the sight of what is ugly makes one bad and gloomy" (*Gay,* 290). It is art that shows us how to do this, not some philosophical or religious system. It is art, he says, that is concerned with the surface of things rather than what is supposedly behind the surface. We must be wiser than the artists, but we must learn from them. "We want to be the poets of our life – first of all in the smallest, most everyday matters" (*Gay,* 299). As we make our lives thus, however, there is always the temptation to hang on to the delusion that one is seeing some stable thing he calls his life, while overlooking the fact that "he himself is really the poet who keeps creating this life" (*Gay,* 101). Such is the danger chiefly of the contemplative.

In any case, once we embrace the one needful thing, life ceases to have the character of duty, calamity, or trickery and instead becomes a means to knowledge: "With this principle in one's heart one can live not only boldly but even gaily, and laugh gaily too" (*Gay,* 324). This boldness opens up whole worlds. "Philosophy, as I have so far understood and lived it, means living voluntarily among ice and high mountains – seeking out everything strange and questionable in existence, everything so far placed under a ban by morality" (*Ecce,* preface, sec. 3). He most clearly expressed this in his book *Thus Spoke Zarathustra,* a book that he says is the greatest present ever given to humanity: "This book, with a voice bridging centuries, is not only the highest book there is...it is also the *deepest,* born out of the innermost wealth of truth, an inexhaustible well to which no pail descends without coming up again filled with gold and goodness" (*Ecce,* preface, sec. 4).

What, then, does he say about the quarrel in this special book of his? As in the works of Kierkegaard, the philosophers do not fare well at Nietzsche's hand: "You have served the people and the people's superstitions, all you famous philosophers – you have not served the truth!"[5] They are tepid and cowardly, neither hot nor cold, unable to endure the spirit's pride and even less the spirit's modesty. He says that spirit "is the life that itself strikes into life," but despite philosophy's claim to spirit as its domain, at most philosophers have understood "the sparks of the

---

[5] Friedrich Nietzsche, "Of the Famous Philosophers," in *Thus Spoke Zarathustra: A Book for Everyone and No One,* trans. R. J. Hollingdale (New York: Penguin, 1961), hereafter cited in text as *Thus Spoke.*

spirit" rather than the anvil and the hammer that are the spirit. This anemic grasp and response to the ferocity of spirit lead the speaker to say of the philosophers, "You behave in all things in a too familiar way with the spirit; and you have often made of wisdom a poorhouse and a hospital for bad poets" (*Thus Spoke*, "Of the Famous Philosophers," 128).

And what about the poets? The preface to the question is as old as the quarrel: a disciple reminds Zarathustra that he once said that the poets lie too much. Here is the perpetual conundrum: "Yet what did Zarathustra once say to you? That the poets lie too much? – but Zarathustra too is a poet" (*Thus Spoke*, "Of Poets," 149). And indeed, he affirms, poets do lie too much. They must because they know so little and are such bad learners. As such, the poets have listened to all manner of things – to old women chatting in the evening, to nature whispering through tender emotions, to things between heaven and earth and even above heaven, for all gods are the poets' images. And from these images come longings to move upward toward "cloudland," to move among the gods beyond, glimpsed through the poets' art: "Alas, how weary I am of all the unattainable that is supposed to be reality. Alas, how weary I am of the poets!" (*Thus Spoke*, "Of Poets," 150).

The poets are shallow. They have never plumbed the depths. They are tedious. "All their harp-jangling is to me so much coughing and puffing of phantoms" (*Thus Spoke*, "Of Poets,"151). He is weary of the poets. But he sees that the poets may also be weary of themselves. And this can be transformative. It is from such transformed poets that repentance for mediocrity in relation to spirit will come. Indeed, Nietzsche might say it has already come: again, "Zarathustra is a poet."

Here is the true poet, acting as corrective to the new poetry introduced by Plato. Nietzsche returns again and again throughout his writings to Socrates and Plato as "symptoms of decay, as agents of the dissolution of Greece, as pseudo-Greek, as anti-Greek."[6] Socrates substituted dialectic for nobler taste (*Twilight*, 41). Dialectic, so praised and loved by thinkers throughout its history, is for Nietzsche an option of last resort. The Socratic embrace of rationality at any cost against instinct is a form of sickness, and far from leading to happiness, it merely leaves us in conflict with that powerful part of our life that is instinct (*Twilight*, 44). When we turn to reason as the only source of what is true, we falsify what is apparent to the senses – the flux and change, the coming to be and

---

[6] Friedrich Nietzsche, *Twilight of the Idols*, trans R. J. Hollingdale (London: Penguin, 1990), 39, hereafter cited in text as *Twilight*.

passing away of life – and fall prey to the lie of unity, essence, substance, and duration as the "real world" (*Twilight*, 46). In this way, the philosophers have led us to think of the emptiest concepts as the highest concepts: "That mankind should have taken seriously the brainsick fancies of morbid cobweb spinners! – And it has paid dearly for doing so!" (*Twilight*, 47). That "other reality" is completely indemonstrable, and the characteristics of so-called real being contradict the actual world. All talk about this other "better" life constitutes revenge upon the life we actually have. This is where the tragic artist is so vital, for such a one values appearance and reinstates appearance as the only reality: "The tragic artist is *not* a pessimist – it is precisely he who *affirms* all that is questionable and terrible in existence, he is *Dionysian*" (*Twilight*, 49).

This is the source of value, life as it appears, a matter of perspective rather than something that is an absolute truth, a form, a "thing-in-itself" – "that *horrendum pudendum* of the metaphysicians" (*Twilight*, 55, 60). The philosophers sever us from the world and make us grieve in the middle of the abundance that is the world as it appears. Nietzsche labors to correct this and to restore us to the world – as belonging to the world, but liberated from any sense of accountability that weighs us down through some false ideal of morality: "*Nothing exists apart from the whole!*" (*Twilight*, 54).

The antidote is art – tragic art. And there is one indispensable precondition for this art: intoxication (*Twilight*, 81). There are many kinds of intoxication – sex, feasting, cruelty, destruction, meteorological influences such as spring, narcotics, will. Apollonian intoxication allows one to gain the power of vision – so, the painter, the sculptor, the epic poet (*Twilight*, 83). Dionysian intoxication intensifies the emotions and is realized in music, though music today is a mere vestige of the original histrionic outpouring. This passion struggles against any imposed sense of moral purpose in art. Moral purpose is false, as there are no moral facts for Nietzsche. But this does not mean art is without purpose: "Art is the great stimulus to life: how could it be thought purposeless, aimless, *l'art pour l'art!*" (*Twilight*, 91). Even as art embraces what is ugly and hard and questionable in life, the tragic poet is fearless, victorious – "Whoever is accustomed to suffering, whoever seeks out suffering, the *heroic* man extols his existence by means of tragedy – for him alone does the tragic poet pour this draught of sweetest cruelty" (*Twilight*, 92). In *The Will to Power*, he affirms the difference in tempo between the two – Dionysian intoxication, involving sexuality and voluptuousness, and the Apollonian, in which these are not absent but in which there is also a calmness – "*The highest feeling of power* is concentrated in the classical type. To react slowly; a great consciousness; no feeling of struggle."[7]

The philosopher working out of the tradition that has grown from the time of Socrates' early quarrel with the poets has now become king of a fanciful domain, with only play soldiers to fight the battle. The philosophers, Nietzsche says, do not attend to what has been or to what is coming, but driven by the metaphysical need to find a thing behind the thing, the thing-in-itself, the philosopher attends only to what *is*. "But since nothing *is*, all that was left to the philosopher as his 'world' was the imaginary" (*Will*, 307). It is a brittle world with none of the festal joys, animal excitation, and bodily invigoration that Nietzsche associates with the "aesthetic state" of which art reminds us. "The sober, the weary, the exhausted, the dried up (e.g. scholars) can receive absolutely nothing from art, as they do not possess the primary artistic force, the pressure of abundance: whoever cannot give, also receives nothing" (*Will*, 422).

We gain a certain faith in our life through that gift of the poet – the capacity to lie. Our past shows a substantial gift for such artistic lying in the face of the terror of existence, the suffering – such are metaphysics, morality, religion, and science. The philosophers tried to conquer the world of the poet through the question, rationality, dialectic. But, Nietzsche says, such a one turns out to be just another poet, just another artist, just another liar (*Will*, 451). But once this is known and affirmed – revealed, as it were, by Nietzsche – art becomes the great stimulant of life and an antidote to anything that would deny life. Art becomes the point; it becomes "life's *metaphysical* activity" where the deep need is met in a healthy way, embracing all life, including that part that involves suffering. "A highest state of affirmation of existence is conceived from which the highest degree of pain cannot be excluded: the *tragic-Dionysian* state" (*Will*, 453).

And this is where the quarrel finds itself at the end of Nietzsche's work, with a thorough reversal of the vision of philosophy as somehow redemptive of the poets' occasional accidental hits upon the truth in their nonconscious mania: now it is the poet who redeems from decay the lost and unhealthy philosopher. Affirmation of life in all its forms, including those that bring suffering, affirmation that frees us to rejoice in the world absent the cobwebs of the metaphysicians that, for a time, seemed to shield us from terror – this is the bridge, he says, to the tragic

---

[7] Friedrich Nietzsche, *The Will to Power*, trans. Walter Kaufman (New York: Vintage, 1968), 420, hereafter cited in text as *Will*.

poet. Nor is the aim some sort of Aristotelian catharsis that helps us to rid ourselves of pity and terror, "but, beyond pity and terror, *to realize in oneself* the eternal joy of becoming – that joy which also encompasses *joy in destruction*. . . . And with that I again return to the place from which I set out – *The Birth of Tragedy* was my first revaluation of all values: with that I again plant myself in the soil out of which I draw all that I will and *can* – I, the last disciple of the philosopher Dionysius – I, the teacher of the eternal recurrence."

Heidegger, like Nietzsche, does not have at hand the prophets of God. And, like Nietzsche, he feels the lack. But far from being tired of the poets, Heidegger finds there the closest thing to the prophet of God he can embrace, the poet using most purely the medium of language, which he calls "the house of Being." Heidegger is listening in on something in the language of the poets that is deeply important for the philosopher.

A theme that has arisen repeatedly in this history is the effort of seekers to respond ever anew to that dictum at the front end of philosophy sculpted into the temple to the god of poetry, "Know thyself." Returning to this question, Heidegger says of our fundamental character, "Man speaks. We speak when we are awake and speak in our dreams. . . . We speak because speaking is natural to us. It does not first arise out of some special volition. Man is said to have language by nature." Heidegger points back to Hamann, who also returned to language when he was trying to get at what reason actually is: "If I were as eloquent as Demosthenes I would yet have to do nothing more than repeat a single word three times: reason is language, *logos*. I gnaw at this marrow-bone and will gnaw myself to death over it." Getting to this relationship between who we are, how we know, and the speaking that is our very nature is at the heart of the quarrel.

Heidegger was a great reader of Nietzsche, one who was aware that Nietzsche had been dismissed as a "poet-philosopher," dismissed as an unrigorous thinker who silenced abstract thought. Heidegger disagreed with this assessment, pointing out that it makes no sense to say this of one who can write in *The Will to Power*. "For many, abstract thinking is toil; for me, on good days, it is feast and frenzy."[8] Feasts, Heidegger points out, "require long and painstaking preparation." It is in such preparative efforts that he approaches Nietzsche, for whom

---

[8] Friedrich Nietzsche, *Will to Power*, XIV, 24, quoted in Martin Heidegger, *Nietzsche*, vol. 1: *The Will to Power as Art*, trans. David Farrell Krell (New York: HarperCollins, 1991), 5.

being an artist is a way of life.[9] For him, art is properly grasped in terms of the creator, not the consumer, and it is always the experience of the beautiful had by the creator that is the standard for art. Art runs counter to nihilism in the act of creation and the bestowal of form (Heidegger, I, 73). It is more valuable than so-called truth (Heidegger, I, 75). That single indispensible physiological precondition necessary for art, namely intoxication, is better rendered in the context of Heidegger as "rapture," the basic aesthetic state (Heidegger, I, 97). It is better rendered as "rapture" because, Heidegger says, it is not "mere chaos that churns and foams, the drunken bravado of sheer riotousness and tumult....For Nietzsche rapture means the most glorious victory of form" (Heidegger, I, 119).

Art, which must be grasped in terms of the artist's own creative behavior, is worth more than truth. What is truth? This, Heidegger says, "is the primal question of philosophy" (Heidegger, I, 141). Between these two – art and truth – is a "discordance that arouses dread" (Heidegger, I, 142). These basic words, art and truth, along with others such as Being, knowledge, beauty, history, and freedom, must be approached with a mindfulness that the essence of what is named by these words is concealed even as whatever is named is inextricably caught up with our act of being as humans (Heidegger, I, 143–4). As we approach the most thoughtful utterances of such basic words, there will be a kind of "telling silence" that accompanies the truest saying. This is an echo of Socratic ignorance, an echo of the way of unknowing. "Such utterance corresponds to the most profound essence of language, which has its origin in silence. As one in touch with telling silence, the thinker, in a way peculiar to him, rises to the rank of poet; yet he remains eternally distinct from the poet, just as the poet in turn remains eternally distinct from the thinker" (Heidegger, II, 208). Art and truth, the poet and the thinker. The quarrel goes on, but now with a renewed flavor of curiosity about these poets, how they differ from philosophers, and how the philosopher is to respond in fullness to what is found in the poets. Heidegger says that this fullness of response, new in its reclaimed receptivity, has the work of Nietzsche as preface.

"The highest decision that can be made and that becomes the ground of all history is that between the predominance of beings and the rule of Being" (Heidegger, III, 5). Nietzsche stands within this decision

---

[9] Martin Heidegger, *Nietzsche*, vol. 1: *The Will to Power as Art*, trans. David Farrell Krell (New York: HarperCollins, 1991), 69, hereafter cited in text as Heidegger.

between beings (including gods, men, the world, and the earth) and Being, "whose dominion first enables or denies every being whatsoever to be *the* being it can be." Nietzsche, more than any thinker before him, brings about and affirms the predominance of *beings* over Being, an important step toward what Heidegger calls "the consummation of metaphysics," meaning, "the unimpeded development of all the essential powers of beings, powers that have been reserved for a long time, to what they demand as a whole" (Heidegger, III, 7). This is new. This grounds the modern age. "Nietzsche, the thinker of the thought of will to power, is the *last metaphysician* of the West" (Heidegger, III, 8).

His is a metaphysics of subjectivity. This subjectivity "is absolute as subjectivity of the body; that is, of drives and affects; that is to say, of will to power" (Heidegger, III, 147). If a human is a rational animal, for Nietzsche (unlike Hegel, for whom subjectivity was determined by the *rationalitas*) the dominant aspect is that of *animalitas* so that "at the end of metaphysics stands the statement *Homo est brutum bestiale* – the possibilities that once seemed to exist for metaphysics are exhausted, and if there is to be any future metaphysics after Nietzsche, it will have to be built anew, at most using the history of metaphysics for raw materials that might be transformed and used" (Heidegger, III, 148). So does Heidegger's own project begin as he turns his attention to Being.

Central to his own question regarding Being is that entity – which each of us is – which is capable of inquiry into Being, an entity he refers to as Dasein (*Da*, meaning "there" or perhaps better "here" in the immediate environment, and *Sein*, meaning "to be": Dasein, then, means a "Being-there" or a "Being-here," which is capable of inquiring into its own Being). This art of understanding what it means to be is itself an important and defining characteristic of Dasein's Being. Our disposition toward such inquiry is itself interesting, important, and integral to our character as Dasein. Indeed, this questioning of existence is the foundation for other inquiry. This entity, Dasein, is unique because we are not merely close to it as with all other beings: "We *are* it, each of us, we ourselves."[10] This is a singularly unique kind of immediacy. At the same time, it always tends to understand itself in terms of the world in which it finds itself. This means that even though we are this entity Dasein, we cannot come at it directly, but rather "it is to be shown as it is *proximally and for the most part* – in its average *everydayness*," that uncritical

---

[10] Martin Heidegger, *Being and Time*, trans. John Macquarrie and Edward Robinson (San Francisco: Harper Collins, 1962), 36.

mode of daily life lived everyday by everyone, Heidegger included (*Being*, 37). But this everydayness should be contemplated alongside the fullness of the philosophical act that leads to an understanding of this Dasein, of ourselves. Two aspects of this philosophic act are joined in the word *ekstasis*, two aspects described by Hans Urs von Balthasar as "the dread (*Ent-Setzen*) and fear of the finite spirit that, by thinking, discovers in itself the opening up of infinity, and the rapture (*Ent-zücken*) at sighting the fullness of this fountain which bestows itself and gathers men into itself."[11]

Dasein is in the world. Statements such as this in the work of Heidegger, though central to his thought, can be difficult to unpack. This so-called Being-in-the-world is disclosed through two fundamental realities, namely, states-of-mind and understanding. States-of-mind that disclose Dasein are expressed in discourse, which Heidegger identifies as the "existential-ontological" foundation of language (*Being*, 203–4). Discourse is the expression of the state-of-mind, which is itself the disclosure of Dasein, and this discourse is expressed in language. But because Dasein is in the world, shown in its average everydayness, the state-of-mind that is expressed through discourse in language should not be considered as something internal finding its way out through language. Rather, it is the very fact that it is already out there in the world that makes Dasein known in the first place. When we talk, this is what finds its way into the talk, through our talking – this "Being-outside." That said, "poetical" discourse goes a step farther: such discourse is "the communication of the existential possibilities of one's state-of-mind [which] can become an aim in itself, and this amounts to a disclosing of existence" (*Being*, 205). Dasein is Being "there." The quality of being "there" is made of states-of-mind and understanding. Discourse is constitutive for the Being of the "there," and this is why language has the enormous role it does in Heidegger's work. The relationship between language and the discovery of the Being of Dasein is the foundation for the peculiar relationship he uncovers between poetry and philosophy as thought. This Being of Dasein includes such things as our encounter with tools, our mundane exchanges, the way in which we hear the tapping on wood of a woodpecker not as mere tapping but precisely as the tapping of a woodpecker. This is how we learn about Being.

---

[11] Hans Urs von Balthasar, *The Glory of the Lord: A Theological Aesthetics*, vol. 1, trans. Erasmo Leiva-Merikakis (San Francisco: Ignatius Press, 1982), 158.

"Being able to learn presupposes being able to question."[12] Asking the question is the activity of philosophical thinking. Philosophical thinking is of a different order from scientific thinking with its questions about the beings it encounters (Heidegger says, "All scientific thinking is just a derivative and rigidified form of philosophical thinking") (*Intro.*, 28). Philosophy is of a higher order, an order shared only by poetry: "In the poetry of the poet and in the thinking of the thinker, there is always so much world-space to spare that each and every thing – a tree, a mountain, a house, the call of a bird – completely loses its indifference and familiarity" (*Intro.*, 28).

Having identified the fundamental question of philosophy as "Why are there beings at all instead of nothing?" Heidegger points out that this question cannot be approached directly until we have grasped Being itself, meaning that we must ask a prior question: "How does it stand with Being?" (*Intro.*, 35). Immediately we realize what a challenge we are up against in asking this. We say that a house *is*, the thunderstorm gathering in a distant mountain range *is*, the portal to a cathedral *is*, a country or state *is*, a painting *is*, the content of the painting *is*, a mathematical formula *is*. "Where does Being lie and in what does it consist?" (*Intro.*, 36). In asking such a question, Heidegger is not returning to the scrapheap of metaphysics in order to rehearse all the other attempts to get at the answers. Nor, indeed, is a philosophical question the sort that one answers and is done with, so that one can move on to the next question: "Philosophical questions are in principle never settled as if some day one could set them aside" (*Intro.*, 44). Heidegger's aim is to restore something to human beings, to restore humans' Dasein, that power of Being. Nietzsche, as the last victim of that misguided and bungled chasing after beings that is the failed history of philosophy, pronounces that concepts such as Being are no more than a vapor, "the final wisp of evaporating reality."[13] As Kant confessed to Mendelssohn that he thought the fate of mankind rests upon metaphysics done well, Heidegger asks, in response to Nietzsche's assessment, "Is Being a mere word and its meaning a vapor, or does what is named with the word 'Being' hold within it the spiritual fate of the West?" (*Intro.*, 45).

Asking such fundamental questions brings the thinker to consider human Dasein's relation to beings and its relation to the whole, Dasein's

---

[12] Martin Heidegger, *Introduction to Metaphysics*, trans. Gregory Fried and Richard Polt (New Haven: Yale University Press, 2000), 23, hereafter cited in the text as *Intro.*

[13] Nietzsche, *Twilight of the Idols*, VIII, 78, "'Reason' in Philosophy."

inception and its future. This is why such questioning is characterized as historical. In particular, it leads to the topic of how such fundamental questioning of Being relates to and belongs to the world history of the earth, understanding "world" as the *spiritual* world. This world is changing. "On the earth, all over it, a darkening of the world is happening. The essential happenings in this darkening are: the flight of the gods, the destruction of the earth, the reduction of human beings to a mass, the preeminence of the mediocre" (*Intro.*, 47). Within this darkening, the spirit is diminished, disempowered, and misinterpreted.

The misinterpretation has at least four aspects. Spirit can be misinterpreted as mere ingenuity, mere intelligence capable of calculation, observation, and modification of these observed things. This in turn reduces spirit to a tool that can be used to achieve some goal, such as improved productivity or the thorough classification of things that we encounter in science. Such an instrumental interpretation of spirit then impacts the powers of the spirit expressed in poetry, fine art, statecraft, and religion, shifting these into areas of culture "where they can be *consciously* cultivated and planned." And finally, once spirit is misinterpreted as intelligence, intelligence made a tool to serve goals, and the tool and resulting products demarcated as realms of culture that have meaning for themselves only through limiting themselves to self-validation based on their "standards" they have set for themselves ("poetry for poetry's sake, art for art's sake, science for science's sake"), spirit as intelligence and spirit as culture "finally become showpieces and spectacles that one takes into account along with many others, that one publically trots out and exhibits as proof that one does *not* want to deny culture in favor of barbarism" (*Intro.*, 49–52).

This darkening of the world and thinning out of spirit are uncovered by the questioning of Being that sets us on the road to an awakening of the spirit in response to this dangerous state of affairs. For this reason, Heidegger affirms that it is no exaggeration to ask whether Being will remain "a mere vapor" or become the fate of the West. One of the most important places where this thinning has occurred is in language, where not only Being has been made an empty word, but where much of language "is used up and abused," something that has become "an indispensible but masterless, arbitrarily applicable means of communication, as indifferent as a means of public transportation, such as the streetcar, which everyone gets on and off" (*Intro.*, 53). We no longer know what language is about. The fate of language, he says, "is grounded in the particular *relation* of a people to Being, [and so] the question about *Being* will be most intimately intertwined with the question about *language* for us" (*Intro.*, 54). It is in this connection between philosophy's questioning of Being and the relation of Being to the fate of language (and of the West) that philosophy and poetry will yet again meet on new terms.

Poets, thinkers, and statesmen are the creators (*Intro.*, 65). These are the ones who struggle and, in struggling, bring about the hitherto unheard, unthought, unsaid. "When the creators have disappeared from the people, when they are barely tolerated as irrelevant curiosities, as ornaments, as eccentrics alien to life, when authentic struggle ceases and shifts into the merely polemical, into the intrigues and machinations of human beings within the present-at-hand, then the decline has already begun" (*Intro.*, 67). The warning to us of our state of decline is the emptiness of language and, in particular, the emptiness of the word Being (*Intro.*, 73).

Heidegger is not entirely certain that "emptiness" is the right word: "There is no such thing as an empty word – only one that is worn out, yet remains full" (*Intro.*, 83). The work of philosophy is, in part, to find the way back into that fullness. One way back in is to begin with some other universal representation – he uses the example of "tree." As we start to get to the essence of a tree, we might look first at various species with their various examples. But how is it that we are able to find examples of trees unless we have already found our way into the universal representation "tree"? No matter how many trees we encounter, unless the way is lit up by knowledge of *the tree as such*, "then all this will remain an idle enterprise in which we cannot see the tree for the trees" (*Intro.*, 84). We encounter trees in the light of the representation of what a tree is in general. When we know the tree as such, we see trees.

Questioning Being is the highest task of philosophy, and indeed, the highest task. Without the questioning of Being, we cannot understand Being, and without understanding Being, without "opening up Being," we could not be "human" in the first place. The aim is not to arrive at some answer the way science does, an answer that, once reached, is finished. Rather, this kind of questioning is an activity, and in the activity philosophical truth opens up. If the activity stops, the opening stops, and we are diminished. "Philosophy is a happening that must at all times work out Being for itself anew" (*Intro.*, 90).

At the starting point, at every start of this questioning, there will stand a division between Being and Becoming (*Intro.*, 100). This contrast was set forth by the poetic thinker Parmenides (fifth century B.C.). "Being essentially unfolds as *phusis*" (*Intro.*, 107). It appears, steps forth, and thus there come to be beings. As we regard beings, as they appear to us, they *seem*, and as they seem, what is revealed is glory. Such glory is, for the Greeks, the highest manner of Being – it is revelatory: "If for Pindar glorifying constitutes the essence of poetry and *is* poetizing, and to poetize is to place in the light, then this by no means indicates that for him the concept of light plays a special role but simply that he thinks and poetizes as a Greek – that is, he stands in the allotted essence of being" (*Intro.*, 108). This takes us a step closer to the goal of understanding the quarrel in Heidegger's work as dividing and binding. The essence of poetry is *placing in the light the glory of Being.*

There is a peculiar aspect of experience uncovered in poetry – this aspect of seeming – that must be understood as part of sorting out what poetry is and does. To get at this, Heidegger uses the example of the sun. Everyone knows that the earth goes around the sun. And yet for the vast majority of people, the *experience* is one of seeing the sun rise and seeing the sun set. The fact that things seem thus is neither untrue, nor nothing, nor merely an appearance of relations that are otherwise in nature. Rather, it is "an essential domain of our world" grounded in poetry with its historical character (*Intro.*, 110). It was by engaging in a struggle between this seeming (grounded in poetry) and Being (elevated by Plato to the supersensory realm as idea) that the chasm appears – ripped open – between apparent beings (down here) and real Being (up there) (*Intro.*, 111). This is the deep impact of the quarrel. This antagonism between Being and seeming were portrayed in Greek tragedy even before Plato teased out the abstraction of Being and the Forms (*Intro.*, 112).

Seeming is an aspect of Being. The way in which seeming belongs to Being is as "Being appearing," but we must keep in mind that appearances can be deceiving (*Intro.*, 114). The quarrel between poetry and philosophy has to do not with a contrast between Being and non-Being, but rather between Being and what seems to be. Seeming does not correspond with non-Being. Though seeming is a distortion, it is nonetheless an appearance of Being, and so it is that human beings, in their encounters with both poetry and the work of philosophy, do well to experience seeming as belonging to Being but also exposed as seeming rather than as exhausting the truth of Being. Experiencing the swirl of appearances on the way to grasping both Being and the terror of Nothingness is the way to superior knowledge: "To this knowing belongs what the Greeks in their great age called *tolma*: to dare everything with Being, not-Being, and seeming all at once.... What is an inexhaustible source of wonder is not only the mature sureness of this fundamental orientation to Being, but also the richness of its formation in word and stone" (*Intro.*, 120).

Being and seeming stand in a relationship to each other that is very different from the next division, that between Being and thinking, for in thinking, Being is re-presented, and so it stands against thinking as an object (*Intro.*, 123). In this distinction between Being and thinking, Heidegger says, we find a fundamental orientation of the spirit of the West that is so much a part of us that we find it difficult to test or question. This opposition is important for understanding Being and our relation to Being, and so Heidegger asks the question, What does it mean to think? "Thinking brings something before us, *represents it*" (*Intro.*, 125). When this occurs with a particular thing, we do not stop with the particular but, in thought, try to get at the thing in general, the concept, the universal. The encounter with universals leads us to logic, which is the science of thinking. So, Heidegger goes on to ask: What does "logic" mean? Logic is the science of *logos*, which in turn means "assertion." But why assertion? Why is logic about saying and discourse? Heidegger wants to take us back to an originary meaning of *logos*, "the relation of one thing to another," which he calls "gathering" (*Intro.*, 132).

At the inception of philosophy, then, there is Being, which is *phusis*, and there is *logos*, which is "gathering." How do these relate? "*Logos* is constant gathering, the gatheredness of beings that stands in itself, that is, Being" (*Intro.*, 138). As with many philosophers, such as Plotinus and Vico, sorting through the language Heidegger uses requires returning to it from different angles until the meaning comes clear. He says, "*Phusis* and *logos* are the same." Now comes an important move in relation to *logos*. Vocabulary is empty, is not fully "word" unless it is directed toward Being, toward *logos*, and vocabulary becomes "word" only where *logos* opens up (*Intro.*, 140). Those who cannot grasp *logos*, in the words of Heraclitus, "are able neither to hear nor to say" (frag. 19). Such people are like dogs who "bark at everyone they do not know" (frag. 97) or like donkeys who "like chaff better than gold" (frag. 9). They constantly encounter beings but never encounter Being. "Only those who are capable of this [have any] rule over the word – the poets and thinkers" (*Intro.*, 141). In the domain of the quarrel, Being is apprehended along with the grasping of beings as *belonging* together, even as they contend and strive, an image of gathering contrasted with mere "driving together and piling up" (*Intro.*, 142).

This belonging together of what contends and confronts is the Oneness referred to by Parmenides. Likewise, the struggle and confrontation of that which belongs together is the flux of Heraclitus. For Heidegger, Parmenides, and Heraclitus, though often presented as saying the opposite, are in fact saying the same thing. Humanity gets to this only when it "sets beings into limits and forms, projects something new (not yet present), originally poetizes, grounds poetically." The thinking of Parmenides and Heraclitus is "poetizing thinking," a thinking poetry, tragic poetry, "in which Greek Being and Dasein [a Dasein belonging to Being] were authentically founded" (*Intro.*, 154). This is Heidegger's formulation of the poetic starting point that has repeatedly emerged in this history of the quarrel. Parmenides says that thinking and Being are the same. In this, he provides the guiding principle of Western philosophy, but it became such "only after it was no longer understood, because its originary truth could not be held fast" (*Intro.*, 154). Heidegger wants to return to the original truth of the saying, and his starting point is to seek help from the poets, beginning with the poet and tragic poem that has appeared several times in this history, Sophocles' *Antigone*.

"Manifold is the uncanny, yet nothing / uncannier than man bestirs itself, rising beyond him."[14] Among the uncanny, humanity is the uncanniest, and this very feature reveals an abyss, an ultimacy, the terrible, awe, and indeed the violent in Being. "Such Being opens itself up only to poetic-thoughtful projection" (*Intro.*, 159). The uncanny throws us out of the homey, the accustomed, the usual, the unendangered. Humanity, in history, builds the *polis*, assembling the elements of home. The uncanny is violent in that it throws us out of what is homey and homely, and this is calamitous, overwhelming (*Intro.*, 162).

In the growth of human presence, the entrance into the living earth and sea, "humans cast their snares and nets; they tear this life away from its own order, enclose it in their paddocks and pens, and force it beneath their yoke" (*Intro.*, 165). But the inception of this history is not, Heidegger insists, some incremental progress from primitives who are "backward, clumsy and weak." Such a view is a false transfer of natural science to the human. The inception itself is what is most uncanny, the inexplicable and mysterious inception that is never approachable with the tools of science, "ferreting out the primitive and collecting bones," but is rather mythology (*Intro.*, 166). Those unique elements of

---

[14] *Antigone*, lines 332–3, apparently read in Greek by Heidegger in the original delivery of the lectures that became *Introduction to Metaphysics*, and quoted here from the Fried and Polt translation, 156.

human existence – language, understanding, building, poetry – are not invented bit by bit but rather *break forth* at this inception as a kind of violence that humanity must then discipline and surmount (*Intro.*, 167). And as humanity lays down its paths and applies its skills, it eventually cuts itself off from Being and gets enmeshed in the tangle of its own world, caught up in "seeming." The only thing that is not susceptible to this subjugation is death, and so it is that at the limit of this "no-exit of death" uncanniness happens: "With the naming of *this* violent and uncanny thing, the poetic projection of Being and of human essence sets its own limits for itself" (*Intro.*, 169).

It is through the happening of uncanniness that "beings as a whole open themselves up" – when human beings become homeless, the home is disclosed as home (*Intro.*, 178). In the uncanny, in the overwhelming, in "the breaking away of humanity into being" lies the origin of language, and this is at the very center of Heidegger's understanding of poetry and what is discovered in philosophy. Language is the primal poetry in which people poetize Being. In turn, the great poetry by which a people steps into history begins through the formation of its language (*Intro.*, 183). The Greeks experienced this through Homer.

Language, once developed, can also be used to tame the overwhelming, at which point it becomes undisciplined chatter and covers up Being instead of opening it (*Intro.*, 184). This is the dulling multiplication of throwaway words, the circle of the world and paths of language that become ruts, indeed, cliché, catching humanity in its web. "The opening up of beings happens in *logos* as gathering," and this opening up of beings is preserved in language, which is in turn passed on and repeated. As language is passed on, the constant danger is that it becomes "mere hearsay" and no longer opens up beings (*Intro.*, 198). Where truth originally meant this unconcealment, the detachment of *logos* from *phusis*, of truth from beings, changes the essence of truth into a matter of "correctness," where only remnants remain in the form of the "idea" and the "assertion" (*Intro.*, 203). This results in a philosophy occupied with ideas and categories, but never able to arrive at the relation between its own thinking and Being (*Intro.*, 204). This is the collapse of truth.

The originary division is the distinction between Being and beings: the question is how philosophy can reaccomplish the thinking of this distinction. The perspective from which this questioning can be started is that of our own Being, "Being-here," Dasein (*Intro.*, 219). But it is not a task simply to be accomplished once and for all. It is always *questioning*: "Being able to question means being able to wait, even for a lifetime" (*Intro.*, 221). This thinking will have a poetic character. Here is the crux of the relationship of poetry and philosophy for Heidegger: "Poetry that thinks is in truth the topology of Being."[15] Once the task is clearly set forth in the way Heidegger has presented it, including marking the ways in which thinking has gone astray, the relationship of poetry, language, and thought comes to the center of the thinker's work – getting to the truth requires both philosophy and poetry, the thinker and the poet.

We are in a rut, enmeshed in such a way that we are hindered from getting to truth. Both philosophy (as it is done by Heidegger) and poetry (as understood by Heidegger) can help us out of this tangle and into the light:

1. "Beauty is one way in which truth occurs as unconcealedness."
2. "Art...is the becoming and happening of truth."
3. "*All art*, as the letting happen of the advent of the truth of what is, is, as such, *essentially poetry*." (*Poetry*, 72)

Poetry illuminates, unfolds, unconceals. And because language names beings, bringing them to word and appearance, among the arts whose essence is poetry (i.e., that which lights projection of the truth), Heidegger says the poem, in the more narrow sense, holds a unique and privileged place among the arts. Poetry will have an important role in accomplishing what the philosopher sees as needed. "The nature of art is poetry. The nature of poetry, in turn, is the founding of truth" (*Poetry*, 75).

Philosophy yet again returns to poetry for starting places. Poetry grounds truth through striving against the familiar and the ordinary, containing "the undisclosed abundance of the unfamiliar and extraordinary" (*Poetry*, 76). Like Kierkegaard, Heidegger asks, in the words of Hölderlin, "and what are the poets for in a destitute time?" (*Poetry*, 91).

Again drawing on the image of darkness in the world, he says, "Ever since the united three – Herakles, Dionysius, and Christ – have left the world, the evening of the world's age has been declining toward its night. The world's night is spreading its darkness" (*Poetry*, 91). This darkness is forged by God's failure to show up and gather together things and humanity. What is even worse than God's default is that the world is now

---

[15] Martin Heidegger, *Poetry, Language, Thought*, trans. Albert Hofstadter (New York: Harper and Row, 1971), 12, hereafter cited in text as *Poetry*.

so dark it is no longer capable of discerning God's default as a default. Now we have no ground for the world: the world hangs in an abyss. In such a darkness arises the question, "...and what are the poets for in a destitute time?" (*Poetry*, 91).

The answer is this: the poets utter the holy in the middle of darkness, sensing and singing clues about that which eludes a benighted age. "Poets are the mortals who, singing earnestly of the wine-god, sense the trace of the fugitive gods, stay on the gods' tracks, and so trace for their kindred mortals the way toward the turning" (*Poetry*, 94). Where humanity cannot even find hints to return to the lost tracks that lead to the gods, the poets think their way into the lightening of Being and enter into a dialogue with thinking, "a dialogue that is of the history of being....Philosophers consider the dialogue to be a helpless aberration into fantasy. But destiny pursues its course untroubled by all that" (*Poetry*, 96). The poet follows the habits of the language of metaphysics, designating beings as a whole with the names, "nature," "life," and "the open" and calling the whole "Being." "Being, as itself, spans its own province, which is marked off by Being's being present in the word. Language is the precinct, that is, the house of Being. The nature of language does not exhaust itself in signifying, nor is it merely something that has the character of sign or cipher. It is because language is the house of Being, that we reach what it is by constantly going through this house" (*Poetry*, 132). Thus, his example of the tapping of the woodpecker that we hear not as a rapid thud but rather as a woodpecker tapping. If we walk through the woods to get to a well, he says, we are going through the words "well" and "woods." The only place where objects such as woodpeckers and wells *are* as woodpeckers and wells is in this precinct, this house of Being, language.

"Song is existence," Rilke writes in *Sonnets to Orpheus* (part 1, sonnet 3).[16] The word for existence here is Dasein, "a synonym of Being." Of this phrase Heidegger says, "To sing, truly to say worldly existence, to say out of the haleness of the whole pure draft and to say only this, means: to belong to the precinct of beings themselves. This precinct, as the very nature of language, is Being itself. To sing the song means to be present in what is present itself. It means: *Dasein*, existence" (*Poetry*, 138). It is the song of the poets that calls us into "the healing whole in the midst of the unholy" (*Poetry*, 140).

---

[16] Quoted in ibid., 138.

Science never brings us to the reality of a thing but can only encounter objects as represented by the standards of science accessible to the kinds of investigations carried out by science. Many facts can be stated about an object viewed from the perspective of science. But the thing as a thing is lost in scientific description, annihilated: "The nature of the thing never comes to light, that is, it never gets a hearing" (*Poetry*, 170).

The way science handles a thing and the way into a thing through a poet's language, the way we meet a thing in a peculiar light, is expressed by John Steinbeck in *Sea of Cortez*:

> The Mexican Sierra has "XVII-15-IX" spines in the dorsal fin. Those can easily be counted. But if the sierra strikes hard on the line so that your hands are burned, if the fish sounds and nearly escapes and finally comes in over the rails, his colors pulsing and his tail beating in the air, a whole new relational externality has come into being – an entity which is more than the sum of fish plus the fisherman. The only way to count the spines of the sierra unaffected by this second relational entity is to sit in a laboratory, open an evil-smelling jar, remove a stiff colorless fish from formalin solution, count the spines, and write the truth "XVII-15-IX." There you have recorded a reality which cannot be assailed – probably the least important reality concerning either the fish or yourself.[17]

In the darkness of the world, what is spoken is often nothing more than a remnant or residue of true speaking. Because our nature is to speak, when our speech is so diminished, we are diminished. In true speech, language speaks, and if we want to get to that speech that reveals language as the stuff of our human nature, we must go to language that is spoken most purely: "What is spoken purely is the poem" (*Poetry*, 194).

That said, a poem is an invention, an imaginative and fictive art composed by a poet who uses images to evoke our own imagination. Is this in conflict with the idea that in speaking, and particularly in the pure speaking that is poetry, language speaks? In the poem, does the poet speak or does language? The answer, Heidegger says, is that language speaks. But the way to reconcile this with the fact that a poem is a poet's utterance is to ask more deeply what it is that happens when a person speaks. Once we move past "language" as that residue we live within our current darkness, we see that language, naming of things, calls the things *as* things into their "thinking." Through naming, through language, things arrive on the scene as bidden, invited, a character of things abiding in the world that is inaccessible to mere scientific description: "The

---

[17] John Steinbeck, *The Log from the Sea of Cortez* (London: Penguin Books, 1977), 2.

snowfall brings men under the sky that is darkening into night. The tolling of the evening bell brings them, as mortals, before the divine. House and tables join mortals to the earth. The things that were named, thus called, gather to themselves sky and earth, mortals and divinities" (*Poetry*, 199).

Once we understand the depth of what it is for mortals to speak in their own way in sounds, bidding the world to come, we can understand that when we speak most truly, it is at the same time language speaking. True language opens the world in this way, and the opening of the world is our evidence that we are speaking truly. Language speaks, Heidegger says, and in speaking truly, the poet speaks as one listening to and responding to language: "What is purely bidden in mortal speech is what is spoken in the poem. Poetry proper is never merely a higher mode of everyday language. It is rather the reverse: everyday language is a forgotten and therefore used up poem, from which there hardly resounds a call any longer" (*Poetry*, 208).

We do not shape true language: true language shapes us. Because of this, if we are going to move toward a true philosophical response to the command, "Know thyself," we will have to return to language, most purely spoken in poetry. Poetry, then, becomes a measure of humanity, and so the centerpiece of our response to the command, "Know thyself" is that, in speaking, the poet is always seeking to uncover the god who is, but who, as the one who is, is unknown. The poet is always after the mystery that god who is unknown can be revealed only as the one who is unknown. Humans are measured not by God, not by the sky, but by that which the poet in longing tries to say over and over again: "The measure consists in the way in which the god who remains unknown is revealed *as* such by the sky" (*Poetry*, 223). Poetry takes this mysterious measure, the measure of the invisible that discloses itself *as* that which is concealed, unknown, spoken in images that are not "mere fancies and illusions but imaginings that are visible inclusions of the alien in the sight of the familiar" (*Poetry*, 226). Humanity measures itself against the godhead and thereby becomes more fully human, and thus capable of knowing itself as philosophy spurs it on. This is the crux: philosophy returns again and again to poetry because philosophy needs the gods.

# 12

# Mikhail Bakhtin and Novelistic Consciousness

This history has concentrated on the quarrel as it is portrayed and expressed in writing. Throughout, poetry and the poets show up in philosophy as a source of language, a source of ideas, or source of inspiration, or else an obstacle to ideas, a foil, a source of lunacy, a punching bag. It is a persistent relationship, so far looked at from the perspective primarily of the philosophers, though the same quarrel might be addressed from the perspective of the poets with a very different tale resulting. In this history, despite the recurrent appearance of the poets, the importance of the idea of poetry, and the background and foundation provided by poetry for the work of philosophy, it is rare to see what it might look like for various poetic voices – singular voices singing, as did Homer and Hesiod, through the Greek rhapsodes – to be forced into the arena of consciousness created by the philosophical impulse to question and made to stay in the cauldron. All too often in the writings of the philosophers, the poets are made use of, their methods critiqued, some of their claims mocked, and their resources pillaged (often with respect, of course, as with Hegel, Dilthey, and Heidegger), while they are made to serve the singular narrative of the singular philosopher who has seen what is of value and found its place in the world – thus retaining for philosophy legislative authority.

There is a place, another kind of writing, where the voices remain themselves even in the cauldron, where they come up against other voices without being reduced or canceled or synthesized or otherwise taken out, and this is what Mikhail Bakhtin calls *novelistic consciousness*. In this arena the quarrel finds new form, but a new form that has its deepest roots in Socratic dialogue. In novelistic consciousness, something occurs that is of great importance for understanding the multi-voiced character of the quarrel between poetry and philosophy since

Plato – the quarrel comes alive precisely *as* the relation to something larger than either poetry or philosophy as generally conceived.

Put in a way that has recurred in the work of thinkers throughout this history, poetry arises within a single language. Philosophy introduces the critical question that destabilizes the monolith of this poetry (at least as conceived in hypothetical, ahistorical, terms). This new kind of consciousness moves among languages. This consciousness is activity that is bound by neither a static unitary language nor the unified reality of a god already complete in the fullness of wisdom. It is a living act.

This chapter considers novelistic consciousness as a peculiar manifestation of the quarrel with the power for exploration that is inexhaustible and unique, a power of great importance to the tasks of philosophy and theology, especially in their resistance to monologic discourse. The force that resists single-voiced "monologism" is one of the central concepts in Bakhtin's work, which he calls "dialogism." Dialogism is a concept that trades on the irreducibility of one consciousness to another, and the way in which these two consciousnesses seeking the truth of things and of themselves encounter each other and express themselves in language, but language that will always be incomplete so that the conversation must continue. We need it to continue. This multivoiced conversation rising in the marketplace, the tavern, the university is the act that most deeply characterizes who we are as seeking human beings, and this living act erupts in language.

Language will never be a transparent window on the world as it really is. Of course, this point was granted thousands of years ago. Language is an image and artifact of the activity of consciousness making inroads into the truth of the world as all that is the case. But language and the consciousness that grows in the atmosphere of language is always on the way, allowing an approximation, always a made thing. Through poetry, the first moment of consciousness advances in its own monologic way, with a single voice, a single language. When two such voices meet, something new happens, if not in the minds of the poets, at least in the mind of the one listening and trying to comprehend two voices. This is dialogism, the fundamental force in novelistic consciousness, a force that emerges as the defining characteristic of the quarrel, never silencing individual voices as seekers find their way, but never calling one expression the whole story either. It is this meeting of voices that the novelist portrays. Bakhtin says that novelistic consciousness does not speak *in* a language but *through* a language, language that has materialized and become objective. The novelist merely ventriloquates.[1] And again a bit later, "novelistic consciousness can register every shade of discourse with all the opposites present *as* opposites, while still registering the entire discourse as a whole" (*Dia.*, 300). This is contrasted with the poet who "[is unable] to oppose his own poetic consciousness, his own intention, to the language that he uses for he is completely within it and therefore cannot turn it into an object to be perceived, reflected upon or related to" (*Dia.*, 286).

Socrates was the occasion of the birth of this strain of exploration and expression that grew into the form of the dialogic novels most fully explored by Dostoevsky. In his writing, Dostoevsky uncovered a new life form of the quarrel, one that opens an entire world at the boundaries of literature, philosophy, and theology as the disciplines that carry us to the threshold of what transcends our own closed world that we experience as a life, creating a literary space in which closed worlds encounter each other. There are other kinds of events, literary or otherwise, in which the various sorts of particular worlds encounter each other – religious, cognitive, ethical, and aesthetic. The type of event is deeply dependent on the number and type of consciousnesses of participants. So, for example, when an author's view coincides with that of the hero, or when the author is the antagonist of the hero, an ethical event results, and its expression is the polemical tract, the manifesto, and so forth. If there is no hero, the result is the cognitive event expressed, for example, as a treatise or lecture. If the other consciousness is that of God, the event (e.g., prayer, worship, ritual) is religious. But in the *aesthetic* event that will become the dialogic novel, there is no absolute consciousness, but rather "two non-coinciding consciousnesses," which remain "non-coinciding" even as they encounter each other – resisting the encompassing religious event, the single voiced expression of the cognitive event, or the relation of consciousness to a value rather than to another consciousness seen in the manifesto.[2]

The consciousnesses do not merge into each other, but neither are they alone. "A single voice ends nothing and resolves nothing. Two voices is the minimum for life, the minimum for existence."[3] This insight is

---

[1] Mikhail Bakhtin, *The Dialogic Imagination*, trans. Michael J. Holquist (Austin: University of Texas Press, 1981), 299, hereafter cited in text as *Dia.*

[2] Mikhail Bakhtin, *Art and Answerability*, trans. Vadim Liapunov (Austin: University of Texas Press, 1990), 22.

[3] Mikhail Bakhtin, *Problems of Dostoevsky's Poetics*, trans. Caryl Emerson (Minneapolis: University of Minnesota Press, 1984), 252, hereafter cited in text as *Dost.*

the opening that lets light illuminate the role of other activities that have been important as places for encounters, the festival and the feast, bringing the hitherto cognitive endeavor back into the marketplace, the living room, the church. Such a theme, which includes laughter, eating, drinking, and all the aspects of our bodily lives, is fundamental in Bakhtin's review of the history and development of novelistic consciousness. His favorite example of this as portrayed in literature on the way from Socrates to Dostoevsky is Rabelais.

Medieval laughter was as universal as seriousness and was directed at the same objects, with its own whole world mirroring the official world.[4] The comic is what tests the official monologic world. Laughter overcomes fear, whether it is the fear of God, nature, or guilt in relation to that which is taboo. This is important for the change of consciousness as the medieval world moved toward the Renaissance: "Through this victory laughter clarified man's consciousness and gave him a new outlook on life" (*Rab.*, 91). People in the Middle Ages participated in official life and in carnival life, two aspects of the world coexisting in consciousness (*Rab.*, 96). This humor found its way into literature, the highest expression of which was Rabelais's novel *Gargantua and Pantagruel*.

Such folk humor is not opposed to all seriousness – only to the form of seriousness that is intolerant and dogmatic (the sort dominant in the Middle Ages, according to Bakhtin). One form of nondogmatic seriousness is tragic seriousness expressed most fully in Greek tragedy, making possible the notion of tragic philosophy. Such seriousness exists alongside laughter and embraces it as a welcome corrective (*Rab.*, 121). The critical philosophy founded by Socrates and linked to antiquity's carnival forms is another form of seriousness. This form is not separate from laughter but rather grows insofar as it is free from one-sided rhetorical seriousness: "True open seriousness fears neither parody, nor irony, nor any other form of reduced laughter, for it is aware of being part of an uncompleted whole" (*Rab.*, 122). The mistake is to think one has the whole story, complete and finished. Laughter completes seriousness in a way by keeping it from becoming petrified. This is the function of laughter in the development of culture and literature: "Laughter does not permit seriousness to atrophy.... It resists this ambivalent wholeness" (*Rab.*, 123).

A similar force uncovering incompleteness was at work as different cultures and languages encountered each other, as medieval Latin

---

[4] Mikhail Bakhtin, *Rabelais and His World*, trans. Helene Iswolsky (Bloomington: Indiana University Press, 1984), 88, hereafter cited in text as *Rab*.

came up against national popular languages, high speech encountering low speech and so revealing in the encounter how much of the old was actually dead, and it was this that Rabelais captured, "the gay death of a language with senile lapses, wheezing and coughing," portrayed, for example, in Master Janotus de Bragmardo's speech. Dialect encountered dialect, and as this happened, "the modern time became conscious of itself. It too could reflect its face in the 'mirror of comedy'" (*Rab.*, 468). This role was tremendously important in Rabelais's novel. All of philosophy was transferred to the vernacular, with dialects clarifying each other in the process. As the naive coexistence of languages came to an end, "the new consciousness was born not in a perfected and fixed linguistic system but at the intersection of many languages and at the point of their most intense inter-orientation and struggle. Languages are philosophies – not abstract but concrete, social philosophies, penetrated by a system of values inseparable from living practice and class struggle" (*Rab.*, 471). This confrontation between languages is the only way to place oneself outside one's own language, to overcome one's own linguistic consciousness, and it is just such an event that allowed Rabelais's novel. Here the quarrel is portrayed not as a question directed at an idea fixed in myth and poetry, but rather as whole languages encountering each other and, in this clash, prying one out of the singular consciousness engendered by one's linguistic dogmatism. This is the drama revealed in Rabelais's novel, freed by laughter. "Linguistic life enacted that same drama: simultaneous death and birth, the aging and renewal of separate forms and meanings as well as of entire philosophies" (*Rab.*, 473). Laughter undoes the totalizing effect of both poetry and philosophy. Laughter is at the heart of the quarrel. "Every act of world history was accompanied by a laughing chorus" (*Rab.*, 474).

The artistic portrayal of voices and consciousnesses reaches a new level in the novels of Dostoevsky. Here the quarrel is revealed as fundamentally an artistic entity (rather than an abstract and concept-oriented entity) because it allows the meeting of contraries and opposites, and it resists the finalizing, totalizing tendency of dogmatic thought by remaining fallible in relationship to reality. The quarrel is best displayed and enacted in art because, in the pursuit of what is true, it insists that no one has the whole truth and that one who is struggling after truth is actually closer to the goal when the finality of dogma is disrupted than when a partial version of the whole is claimed as infallible, official, authoritarian, final. This artistic characteristic of the quarrel is what is so fully expressed in Dostoevsky. "A plurality of independent and unmerged voices and consciousnesses, a genuine polyphony of fully valid voices is in fact the chief characteristic of Dostoevsky's novels" (*Dost.*, 6). What emerges is a plurality of consciousnesses with equal rights and each with its own world. This is not a portrayal of a world with no truth but rather as one in which we are fallible in our grasp of truth and always on the way. Such a polyphonic novel is "dialogic," because it does not merely contain the conversation but actually juxtaposes whole worlds and sets them in relation to one another without having one eliminate the other, and without having the author's consciousness unify them. These dialogic relationships, Bakhtin says, "are an almost universal phenomenon, permeating all human speech and all relationships and manifestations of human life – in general, everything that has meaning and significance" (*Dost.*, 40). If, again, we are to respond to the dictum "Know thyself," we are served by attending to what is revealed through dialogism, a concept that is trying to move beyond encounters with consciousness – our own or others' – as objectivized, and trying rather to attain to the authentic presence of consciousness that occurs only when consciousness is related to another consciousness dialogically. And this is what Dostoevsky has portrayed in his novels, this broadening approach to consciousness in the sense of "a special dialogic mode of communication with the autonomous consciousness of others, something never before experienced, an active dialogic penetration into the *unfinalizable depths of man*" (*Dost.*, 68; emphasis added).

In the novel, what are presented are idea-images, but these are not "made up" any more than a painter "makes up" the horizon or portrait being painted. This is a distinguishing factor about the novelist. "As an artist, Dostoevsky did not create his ideas in the same way philosophers or scholars create theirs – he created images of ideas found, heard, sometimes divined by him *in reality itself*, that is ideas already living or entering life as idea-forces" (*Dost.*, 90). These living idea-images are brought artistically to the novelistic plane. In this arena "Dostoevsky placed the idea on the borderline of dialogically intersecting consciousnesses. He brought together ideas and world views, which in real life were absolutely estranged and deaf to one another, and forced them to quarrel" (*Dost.*, 91).

Dostoevsky's aim was not to assemble thoughts, determine their truth or falsity in relation to the world, and organize them into a system – a project that has been repeated from the first time utterance met question or, in the parlance of this work, the poet met the philosopher. Rather, Dostoevsky is interested in the way consciousness encounters the world – the physical world, the intellectual world, the spiritual world. Thought is expressed in and through persons, and it is persons who meet in his artistic world: "In Dostoevsky, two thoughts are already two people, for there are no thoughts belonging to no one and every thought represents an entire person" (*Dost.*, 93). Listening and questioning are the actions that constitute thinking, and these actions cannot be abstracted from the person, the personal, the one who is conscious, experiencing an orientation of one sort or another. For Dostoevsky, "even *agreement* retains its *dialogic* character, that is, it never leads to a *merging* of voices and truths in a single *impersonal* truth, as occurs in the monologic world" (*Dost.*, 95).

Dostoevsky's novels arise from two sources already encountered in this history – the Socratic dialogue (which Nietzsche identified as the forerunner of the novel) and Menippean satire (which reached its medieval culmination in Boethius). The Socratic dialogue itself, Bakhtin argues, grew out of a carnivalistic base and "is thoroughly saturated with a carnival sense of the world" (*Dost.*, 109).

In Socratic dialogue, truth is not an abstraction that occurs in an individual's mind but is rather something that occurs among people as they reach for the truth together. This involves juxtaposing different views and probing the view expressed by participants in order to have the views fully expressed in the conversation (*Dost.*, 110). Extraordinary situations are used as a cauldron in which the deepest parts of an idea are forced to the surface. In the *Apology*, for example, the trial and looming death sentence are the context for Socrates' discourse, "the summing up and confession of a man standing *on the threshold*" (*Dost.*, 111). Bakhtin points out that in contrast to Dostoevsky's presentation of the "image of an idea," in the Socratic dialogue the philosophical concept had not yet been fully differentiated from the artistic image so that the Socratic dialogue functions as a "philosophical-artistic genre" (*Dost.*, 112).

Menippean satire was introduced as a genre by another thinker important to both Augustine and Vico, namely, Varro, who wrote satires he called *saturae menippeae*. This genre combined literary forms, juxtaposed genre, and "became one of the main carriers and channels for the carnival sense of the world in literature and remains so to the present day" (*Dost.*, 103). Part of the importance of this genre to the quarrel is its combination of philosophical invention and freedom of plot (*Dost.*, 114). It makes use of extraordinary situations to test philosophical ideas. Heroes go up to heaven, down to the Netherlands, and into the as-yet unexplored and unknown, putting such fantastic events at the service of the testing of truth, of the philosophical idea. It is the test of the wise man, the seeker of wisdom, so that "the content of the menippeae is the adventure of an *idea* or a *truth* in the world: either on earth in the nether regions, or on Olympus" (*Dost.*, 115). These philosophical adventures occur anywhere, with no inclination to avoid the slum, the brothel, the marketplace. Philosophical dialogue is brought into the thieves' den, probed in the tavern, tested in the prison – always with an eye toward ultimate questions and philosophical positions.

Most importantly, we find yet again, at the heart of human search for truth, the necessary risk of losing one's mind, of "being beside oneself" in the sense of no longer coinciding with oneself – something explored in Varro's *menippeae*, *The Double Marcus*, an artistic discovery that impacted Augustine's own *Soliloquia* (*Dost.*, 116). "In the menippeae there appears for the first time what might be called moral-psychological experimentation: a representation of the unusual, abnormal moral and psychic states of man – insanity of all sorts (the theme of the maniac), split passions bordering on madness, suicides and so forth" (*Dost.* 115). Through all of this, however, there remains an organic unity, an integrity, and an inner logic to the genre of the *menippeae* that linked apparently disparate elements and so was immensely important in the history of the novel (*Dost.*, 119).

This dialogic character of the *menippeae* reaches its peak and is renewed in the work of Dostoevsky. It is indeed transformed by the emergence of *polyphony*, something for which the *menippeae* along with the Socratic dialogue provided the generic conditions (*Dost.*, 122). His innovation is the polyphonic novel, which continues the dialogic line from the Menippean and the Socratic dialogue. This is more than a genre innovation, however. It is an innovation in humanity's artistic thinking, what Bakhtin calls *polyphonic artistic thinking*, a mode of thought that "makes available the sides of a human being, and above all the *thinking human consciousness and the dialogic sphere of its existence*, which are not subject to artistic assimilation from monologic positions" (*Dost.*, 270).

Thinking human consciousness cannot be captured through a monologic artistic approach but is visualized through the polyphonic novel first developed by Dostoevsky, following in the history of the back-and-forth between voices sounding the truth and voices sounding dissent, the battle, the marketplace squabble, the quarrel. Philosophy continues to be something that occurs in the activity of living people. But in writing – in all writing – the activity is only portrayed. It is worthwhile here to recall one of our earliest observations about Plato's curious approach to writing and his equally curious assertion that he had never written down his philosophy. Rather, he produced an image of philosophy, at the heart of which was the destabilizing reality of the quarrel, always moving back and forth between single voices, pronouncements of the gods or the wise, and the testing in dialogue of ideas and truth. This is what Dostoevsky portrays so powerfully in his novels. "We must renounce our monologic habits so that we might come to feel at home in the new artistic sphere which Dostoevsky discovered, so that we might orient ourselves in that incomparably more complex *artistic model of the world* which he created" (*Dost.*, 272).

The gift, the faculty exercised in this novelistic approach, is the *dialogic imagination*. If something unique has occurred in the artistic way in which Dostoevsky handles ideas, if this emerging approach arises from the very history in which we find many of the people who have populated the story – Socrates, Plato, Varro, Augustine, Boethius, Vico, Hegel, and so forth – exploring the features of this approach will be the final task of this book. We began with Platonic dialogues representing Socrates as he comes up against ideas often rooted in the mythic past expressed by the theological poets. The history itself grows as a back-and-forth between poets, prophets, and philosophers, with never a final resting place, resolution, or system. We end with an artistic model that brings many voices together without reducing one to another, without finalizing the dialogue, and without blunting the force of contrary ideas, while retaining an integrity that is both the new image of the quarrel as relation between the poetic a priori and the living impetus to continue in the search that is the activity of living, human consciousness.

Central to this last effort to come at the quarrel between poetry and philosophy will be the effort to keep in mind the poetic wisdom that has been repeatedly discussed and the contrasting features of *prose wisdom*, which is what we find rising through the dialogic imagination and artistically presented most fully in the novel. The novel is distinguished from other genres by three characteristics that were deeply impacted by the encounters of various languages and cultures, forcing parts of European civilization out of linguistic and cultural isolation. These three characteristics are "(1) its stylistic three dimensionality, which is linked with the multilanguaged consciousness realized in the novel; (2) the radical change it effects in the temporal coordinates of the literary image; (3) the new zone opened by the novel for structuring literary images, namely, the zone of maximal contact with the present (with contemporary reality) in all its open-endedness" (*Dia.*, 11).

Creative consciousness grows as artistic cultures, once closed within their own language, encounter other languages, and the experience of the world becomes polyglot. This is not to say that the world itself was not already full of languages – it was. But creative consciousness initially grew up within closed languages, or at least the myth of closed languages (*Dia.*, 12). The cultural stories are tales of history remembered, national identities grounded in the absolute past where language was pure and the culture untouched. "In the past, everything is good: all the really good things (i.e., the first things) occur *only* in this past. The epic absolute past is the single source and beginning of everything good for all later times as well" (*Dia.*, 15). In contrast with the epic – which has been encountered throughout this history – the novel looks toward the future and is grounded in experience and knowledge. Contemporary reality is the subject of the genres that eventually lead to the novel – Socratic dialogue and Menippean satire (*Dia.*, 22). Within such genres, unlike the epic, laughter is possible. "Laughter demolishes fear and piety before an object, before a world, making of an object a familiar contact and thus clearing the ground for an absolutely free investigation of it" (*Dia.*, 23). Socrates is a great model for this, coming up against the "absolute past" as it was contained in the poetry of Homer and Hesiod and in the Greek mind as he encountered it through the rhapsodes or else in those who claimed to be wise or those who merely manipulated for the sake of gain. Combining his own vision of what is lofty and serious with laughter and irony, he allowed a newly free investigation of the world. And such investigation begins among the people, in contemporary reality with many kinds of speech. "Socratic laughter (reduced to irony) and Socratic degradations (an entire system of metaphors and comparisons borrowed from the lower spheres of life – from trades-people, from everyday life, etc.) bring the world closer and familiarize it in order to investigate it fearlessly and freely" (*Dia.*, 25).

The myths about a perfect golden age, a paradise, an ancient truth, Bakhtin says, involve a *historical inversion* in which something that could be realized only in the future is portrayed as something out of the past (*Dia.*, 147). This point is at the center of Plato's own struggle against the myths of the theological poets, for, as he constructs his own philosophy, myth is always at hand in one form or another, a point noted by Kierkegaard in his analysis of Socratic irony. When "the mythic past" is transposed into the otherworldly, translated, that is, and taken over by the philosophers (which we have seen repeatedly), "the historical inversion in philosophical structures is characterized by a corresponding assumption of 'beginnings' as the crystal-clear, pure sources of all being, of eternal values and modes of existence that are ideal and outside time" (*Dia.*, 148). But language by its very nature assimilates time and makes it palpable in the course of a narration (*Dia.*, 251). It is, perhaps, the very link of language with time that contrasts most fully with the eternal and leads Plato to assert that he never wrote down his philosophy. But given that this is the state of things, it is not surprising that when Plato made use of language, he did so in the form of the Socratic dialogue. It is not too much of a stretch to speculate that if Plato were alive today, he would write not treatises but rather novels.

The image Bakhtin uses is that of the living organism, an image that brings to mind Hegel's reflections on tarrying with death, and the fate of the dead who are eaten up. An organism lives in an environment, draws life from the environment, and is enriched. If it is removed from the environment, it dies. And yet its very life requires it to resist fusion with the environment (*Dia.*, 254). Such is the relation between the "real" world and the "represented" world. They are bound up with each other, interacting, refusing the absolute sequestering of the eternal verities (of the Platonic "real world") from our speaking of the world. Poetry speaks forth, and then along comes another speaker and another until the question arises which of the contradictory representations of the world is closest to the truth, and that is a question of philosophy as an act of consciousness. This living act of consciousness resists fusion with its environment, and insofar as philosophy is spoken, its environment is language born in and through poetic utterance. This is why quarrelsome philosophical responses to the mythopoeic world expressed in the language of now one culture, now another, are so close to novelistic consciousness, in which "the language of the novel is the system of its 'languages'" (*Dia.*, 262). Even aside from the monologic nature of whole myths told within a language, within a culture, kept whole through lack of questioning or testing of the ideas, most poetic genres require "the unity of the language system and the unity (and uniqueness) of the poet's individuality as reflected in his language and speech, which is directly realized in this unity" (*Dia.*, 264). Novelistic prose, by contrast, stratifies languages and uses novelistic discourse that is still poetic discourse, "but one that does not fit within the frame provided by the concept of poetic discourse as it now exists" (*Dia.*, 269).

The poetics that have extended from Aristotle to Augustine, through the medieval church to the "Cartesian poetics of neoclassicism" and the "abstract grammatical universalism of Leibniz" all express a force in language that Bakhtin calls "centripetal" – that is a force that unifies and centralizes the verbal-ideological world leading to a unitary language (*Dia.*, 270–1). But this force operates in the middle of a multilanguaged world where "centrifugal" forces disrupt, decenter, and resist unification. Our living speech in which we sing, prophesy, pronounce, promise, and philosophize is always in tension between the centripetal forces and the centrifugal forces, and this is the distilled image of the living back-and-forth that is a recapitulation of the quarrel as a reality right at the heart of human meaning and speaking. "Every utterance participates in the 'unitary language' (in its centripetal forces and tendencies) and at the same time partakes of social and historical heteroglossia (the centrifugal, stratifying forces)" (*Dia.*, 272). In the language of this history, the centrifugal force of the philosophical question keeps our consciousnesses from being fused within the environment of the poetic, and yet ripped away from poetry it dies because all languages are poetic. This is what is captured in the contrast of poetic and novelistic art: "At the time when major divisions of poetic genres were developing under the unifying, centralizing, centripetal forces of verbal-ideological life, the novel – and those artistic-prose genres (such as Socratic dialogue) that gravitate toward it – was being historically shaped by the current of decentralizing, centrifugal forces" (*Dia.*, 272–3).

The poetic image reaches for pure play between the word and its object, ignoring the fact that any object in a poetic image "has its own history of contradictory acts of verbal recognition." Prose, on the other hand, witnesses both the internal contradictions in an object and "the Tower-of-Babel mixing of languages that goes on around any object" (*Dia.*, 278). The same object, the same world, and world of objects has been encountered, explored, probed, wondered at, and named in many languages and from many perspectives by the time any poet speaks of it, and it is in the encounter with the alien words that discourse becomes a living discourse. "Only the mythical Adam who approached a virginal and as-yet verbally unqualified world with the first word, could really have escaped from start to finish this dialogic inter-orientation with the alien word that occurs in the object" (*Dia.*, 279).

Socrates introduced centrifugal force into the world dominated by Homer and Hesiod. The centripetal forces, once sustained by poetry, had to be located elsewhere once the quarrel had begun. Plato locates them in the Forms. And so, however much in our searching ignorance we disrupt and dismantle false claims to complete ideas of justice, beauty, and the good, discourses and consciousnesses encountering each other are held together by the eternal unity of the goal – the form of justice, the form of beauty, the form of the good. There the myth is located, and these forms precisely give the power that distinguishes the mess of philosophical inquiry in the marketplace from complete relativism, intellectual anarchy. The centripetal forces of the Forms, taking over from poetry, indeed provide hope and make the living activity of philosophy, as it moves along its way, a journey that might yet be a journey toward something, rather than mere meandering on the way to death. The Forms are themselves an image of that toward which we move, though, to recall Socrates' words, we do not have wings that will take us to that height. Yet. Philosophy is a hopeful activity.

We do not live in the world of pure Forms, and the moment we began making utterances about the pure Forms, we are not speaking pure truth about them. But we are speakers. What is given to us is poetry, poetry encountering other poetry with ensuing questions about the real nature of the world. Though we may always be fallible in our knowledge of the truth, our conversation is our active striving after that which we cannot but long for, that which we strive to say. In this striving, there will always be a tension between the one "speaking the truth" and the one questioning the speaker. "The poet is not able to oppose his own poetic consciousness, his own intentions to the language that he uses, for he is completely within it and therefore cannot turn it into an object to be perceived, reflected upon or related to" (*Dia.*, 286). Idealized, the poetic genre becomes a priestly language (*Dia.*, 287).

Each of these unitary languages is unique, each comprises points of view on the world, each finds its way of conceptualizing the world and language, including the objects in the world, the meaning, the value. "As such [these languages as world views] may be juxtaposed to one another, mutually supplement one another, contradict one another and be interrelated dialogically. As such they encounter one another and coexist in the consciousness of real people – first and foremost, in the creative consciousness of people who write novels" (*Dia.*, 292).

It is not a novelist only who lives among languages, but the novelist can represent the interrelation of languages, ideas, and consciousnesses. Even the illiterate peasant, Bakhtin says, who is immersed unshakably in a rural world, lives among languages, praying to God in one, speaking to his wife in another, negotiating with authorities in yet another (*Dia.*,

295). Each of these languages is the language of the world. This hetero-glossia is the grain of consciousness as we live it, and awakening to this is part of what occurs in philosophy (What is the structure of justice? Why do we speak to authorities in this way rather than that? Why do we see x as beautiful and y as ugly? Why do we embrace z as good?). It is also what is portrayed through novelistic consciousness.

It contrasts with the poet who, as a poet, embraces the idea of a uni-tary monologic language in which every word expresses not a swirl of influence and intention from others but rather directly expresses the poet's meaning. "Everything that enters the work must immerse itself in Lethe, and forget its previous life in any other contexts: language may remember only its life in poetic contexts (in such contexts, how-ever, even concrete reminiscences are possible)" (*Dia.*, 297). But every concrete context comes under the aspect of a single language, a single "conceptual horizon," a unity and wholeness strengthened and solid-ified even by the rhythm of the poetic language that, "by creating an unmediated involvement between every aspect of the accentual system of the whole...destroys in embryo those social worlds of speech and of persons that are potentially embedded in the word" (*Dia.*, 298). Rhythm literally beats the ideas, voices, and languages in the poem into a uni-fied whole.

Novelistic prose is entirely different. Other voices are invited in, set against one another and thereby intensified and revealed. This is the power of dialogue, drawing in everything and testing idea against idea, consciousness against consciousness, person against person until "[fewer] and fewer neutral, hard elements ('rock bottom truths') remain that are not drawn into dialogue" (*Dia.*, 300). This is where we began, in Athens with Socrates surrounded by conflict, other minds, many of whom spoke from within a unified world and with certainty until, forced into dia-logue, their myths were exposed as fallible, susceptible to revision.

Such a task is not without risk – witness Socrates on his deathbed. And yet even death did not disrupt Socrates' peace, rooted in whatever it was rooted in. And that is a marvelous question – what was it that allowed Socrates to be at peace even in the face of death, and was this source of peace the same source of his wonder and his courage in asking ques-tions? All is well, he says to his friends. We need not be afraid to speak as we respond to longing and question the world trusting that only what is false will finally fall away, and to plunge into life headlong, knowing there is only one way for it to end – and, even then, trusting that all is well.

This peace allows the task to become play, with room for the comic – room for laughter, and laughter making room. Laughing and quarreling are two ways in which minds meet without reducing to one another. This is by no means introduces relativism. On the contrary, individual consciousnesses can be unconditional in their intentions. But the novel allows the room for such consciousnesses to be tried with conflict or laughter. This sort of novelistic prose is a fair portrayal of human discourse, the active engagement of others in other worlds. "If the art of poetry, as a utopian philosophy of genres, gives rise to the conception of a purely poetic, extra historical language, a language far removed from the petty rounds of everyday life, a language of the gods – it must be said that the art of prose is close to a conception of languages as historically concrete and living things" (*Dia.*, 331). No language is unitary or sacrosanct for the novelist (*Dia.*, 332).

At the beginning of the story, in response to Plato's claim that he had never written down his philosophy, I suggested that what was written down was an image of philosophy, an image of poetry, and above all an image of the quarrel between the two. Bakhtin makes a similar point when he locates this quarrelsome tension within language meeting language, those artifacts of living consciousness. "If the subject making the novels specifically a novel is defined as a speaking person in his discourse, striving for social significance and a wider general application as one distinctive language in a heteroglot world – then the central problem for a stylistics of the novel may be formulated as the problem of artistically representing language, the problem of representing the image of a language" (*Dia.*, 336). This is our effort to show forth our thinking, our consciousness, our being in the world. Heidegger identifies the human as one who speaks. Bakhtin goes farther and adds a dimension of listening, responding. "The transmission and assessment of the speech of others, the discourse of another, is one of the most widespread and fundamental topics of human speech. In all areas of life and ideological activity, our speech is filled to overflowing with other people's words" (*Dia.*, 337).

This story has, in one sense, been about books, primarily books of philosophy, and more specifically the way the books of philosophy have responded to use of another kind of speaking that also finds itself recorded in books – that of poetry and, related to some kinds of poetic utterance, prophecy. Because it has been about books, I have chosen to end the inquiry with attention to the peculiar kind of book that has its roots in the starting point I used, Socratic dialogue – that is, to end with the novel.

Another reason for this choice is the affinity of novelistic consciousness and the philosophic consciousness in response to poetry as myth.
Repeatedly, whatever the character and role of poetry in the prosaic
world, the first poets have been identified as mythmakers, the first language as poetry often about the gods, and the connection between
poetry of all sorts and revelation – mythic or otherwise – as important
to the fostering of the human search for wisdom. The quarrel between
poetry and philosophy, while drastically impacting the status of mythic
statement, is also a deep acknowledgment of the power of poetry. Poetry
as myth reveals a whole world, a world unified, in which everything has
its place and its name – including Jove, who accounts for thunder in the
world. Like philosophy, "the novel begins by presuming a verbal seman-
tic decentering of the ideological world, a certain linguistic homeless-
ness of literary consciousness, which no longer possesses a sacrosanct
and unitary linguistic medium for containing ideological thought.... [It
involves] loss of feeling for language as myth, that is, as an absolute
form of thought" (*Dia.*, 367). This is possible only when consciousness
participates in multiple mutually illuminating languages. This is consciousness in the marketplace, at the port, at the Piraeus.

Repeatedly the absolute power of myth over language (first language
as poetry) and of language (poetry) over human perception of what is
real has been located in what Bakhtin calls the prehistorical (and therefore necessarily hypothetical) past of language consciousness (*Dia.*,
369). Once a culture becomes aware of itself as one among many, there
is a new relationship between consciousness and language, and it is this
that is made possible by the force of which the quarrel is an image, and
this that makes possible novelistic consciousness that wanders among
languages, "easily detaching any material from any language (that is,
from among the languages available) and assimilating it into 'its own'
language and world" (*Dia.*, 378).[5]

In this process, heteroglossia emerges in *literary* works that express
the heteroglossia that is a *reality* in the world. What the novel contributes to this growth is a new kind of understanding of consciousness and
dialogue between languages (meaning, again, not merely languages
of nations, but the languages of the priest meeting the merchant, the
lawyer meeting the shoemaker). Bakhtin puts the point in Hegelian
terms, reminiscent of the two moments of the *Ansich* when he says that

---

[5] In a footnote Bakhtin says that such assimilation of alien material is accomplished in
the literary-language consciousness of an epoch rather than in the consciousness of
individual novelists; the individual consciousnesses are part of the process (*Dia.*, 378).

"heteroglossia-in-itself becomes, in the novel and thanks to the novel, heteroglossia-for-itself" (*Dia.*, 400). Here too – as with the encounters of the great questioner Socrates with those in Athens who "knew" certain truths – the languages of the people who have power (priests, kings, scholars) are opposed by the languages of the rogue and the fool, and in the process our consciousness of language and its uses grows. The rogue and the fool make use of "gay deception," that is, they tell lies that are justified because they are told to liars (bringing to mind Vico's idea that philosophy was born through deception allowed by divine providence) (*Dia.*, 401). In this mocking deceit, Bakhtin says, "falsehood is illuminated by ironic consciousness and in the mouth of the happy rogue parodies itself" (*Dia.*, 402). The fool serves to make the conventional world strange. "By representing stupidity, the novel teaches prose intelligence, prose wisdom" (*Dia.*, 404).

How very close this is to the starting point of this whole journey, namely, Socrates on the steps of the temple of Apollo at Delphi identified as the wisest of men because he knows that he does not know – a posture that allows him to move about Athens asking questions of those who "know." This image with which we began is rightly the image with which we end. Both poetry and philosophy begin in wonder, say Aristotle and Aquinas, finding within the world at hand mystery, and within the ordinary the extraordinary. It is certainly a kind of ignorance, but a hopeful ignorance, that derives not from the absence of anything true, but rather from the inexhaustibility of what is most true, and this is why the seeker who does not know but who continues in wonder finds something else: "Along with not-knowing, and not-giving-up, wonder is also...joy, as Aristotle said, and the Middle Ages agreed with him: *omnia admirabilia sunt detectabilia* – the source of joy and the source of wonder are the same thing."[6]

Why this is the case is at the heart of human mystery. That this is the case is at the heart of human meaning. In conversation that is fallible but hopeful, set against the backdrop of this strange universe in which we find ourselves, poets and philosophers, all of us, seek and search, aware that of the handful of certainties allotted us, death looms the largest, reminding us that this is no trial run. But as we list what matters to us as mortals – love, beauty, wisdom, goodness, longing, curiosity, creating, the capacity for grief and anxiety that accompany the risk of love

---

[6] Joseph Pieper, *Leisure, the Basis of Culture* (South Bend: St. Augustine's Press, 1998), 107; Aristotle, *Rhetoric*, 1.2; Aquinas, *Summa Theologica*, I-II, q32, a8.

and care, and the joy that erupts with no obvious explanation for itself but compels many of us toward gratefulness, and toward the search for the One to whom we might rightly be grateful – as we list these, neither the poets nor the philosophers are likely to scratch any of these off their list of proper concerns. We will not gain infallible answers, but we are compelled to search. Engaging in this joyous folly is at the heart of human flourishing.

# Index

CPSIA information can be obtained
at www.ICGtesting.com
Printed in the USA
LVOW11s0013051217
558601LV00003B/264/P